Changing Britain 1850-1979

(Second Edition)

Donald Morrison
(Principal Teacher of History)

Elliot Morrison
(Assistant Head Teacher)

Tom Monaghan
(Principal Teacher of History)

Pulse Publications

Contents

Published and typeset by
Pulse Publications
45 Raith Road, Fenwick, Ayrshire KA3 6DB

Printed and bound by
J Thomson Colour Printers, Glasgow

British Library Cataloguing-in-Publication Data
A Catalogue record for this book is available from the British Library

ISBN 0 948 766 64 6
© Morrison, Morrison & Monaghan 2000

Acknowledgements

The authors and publishers would like to thank the following for permission to reproduce copyright material.

Punch Cartoon Library 11; Popperfoto 13, 26, 33, 38, 40, 47, 58, 85, 88, 89; Illustrated London News 15, 19; Hulton Getty 22, 34, 41, 60, 62, 65, 70, 71, 72, 74, 76, 87; Mary Evans Picture Library 48, 49, 51, 53, 66, 81; Scots Independent 100, 103, 104, 108, 116; Scottish National Party 105, 107, 111; Scottish National Party Photographic Libraries 112, 114; Turnbull 116; Mitchell Library 119, 142; Aberdeen City Council 131, 132, 133, 136; 'The Old Firm' by Bill Murray 140; Aberdeen FC Magazine 141; Sandeman's Whisky advertisement by kind permission of the Keeper of the Records, Scotland; National Archives of Scotland 147; Sunday Times Ecosse 144; Aberdeen University Library (George Washington Wilson Collection) 120, 144, 145, 146, 153; Rev. Archie McPhail 150, 151.

Every attempt has been made to contact copyright holders, but we apologise if any have been overlooked.

Democracy and the British People 1867–1928

WHAT YOU WILL LEARN

- The lack of democracy in Britain before 1850 and the attempts made to change the situation in the first half of the nineteenth century.

- The reasons for, and details of, the major changes which widened the franchise and extended democracy between 1867 and 1928.

- The effects of democracy on the political parties in the early twentieth century, focusing on the debate surrounding the rise of the Labour Party and the decline of the Liberals.

- The general effects of the growth of democracy on Britain's political identity.

LIVING IN A DEMOCRACY today, we take for granted the rights of citizens to participate in the political process, and to be properly represented at various levels of government, both national and local. These rights, however, hardly existed two hundred years ago and had to be won, often through the process of struggle by individuals, political parties and popular movements representing the interests of whole sections of society from women to workers. As a result, the system which has evolved is known as a Representative Liberal Democracy.

The main components of this system are adult suffrage for all men and women aged eighteen and over; the secret ballot, free from intimidation, bribery and corruption; the right of citizens to participate in the political process through voting in elections; the right to membership of a political party or pressure group; free elections at least every five years and occasional referenda on major national issues; government which rests on majority support in the House of Commons; a free press with the right to criticise.

The years between 1867 and 1928 were a time of major political change in terms of authority and of Britain's political identity. In the nineteenth century, the traditional authority of the Monarch and the landed aristocracy was eroded in favour of a limited form of democracy. The twentieth century brought in further change in the form of universal adult suffrage at the age of eighteen.

Background: Britain's Fledgling Democracy Before 1850

Until the *First Reform Act* of 1832, the system of Parliamentary representation had been largely unchanged since the sixteenth century. At the beginning of the nineteenth century, both Houses of Parliament were dominated by the landowning class. The House of Commons was elected at this time by 4.16 % of the population—that means four people out of one hundred had the right to vote.

Britain was, however, changing rapidly. The Industrial Revolution, in a relatively short space of time, changed the social and economic structure which underpinned the existing system of representation. The landowning classes were no longer the country's sole wealth creators. A new group of middle-class entrepreneurs, industrialists, merchants and traders could rightly claim to be the new wealth creators. These people argued that they should have the vote as a natural consequence of their economic power.

The outbreak of the French Revolution also led to an upsurge of interest in reform. During this period, Reform Societies were set up which discussed and wrote about some of the radical political ideas being popularised by writers such as Thomas Paine in his book *The Rights of Man*. However, the violence, disorder and war which the French Revolution brought, led to the introduction of repressive government in Britain. This state of affairs continued after the Napoleonic War until the early 1820s, as the government sought to deal with the problems of postwar economic readjustment, coupled with the increasing demands of the radical reformers for an extension of the franchise.

Attempts at Reform 1832–1850

The first real political reform came in 1829, when Roman Catholics gained the right to become MPs. Reform organisations such as the Birmingham Political Union, formed in 1830, worked for much wider reform than had been gained by the Irish Catholics.

Of the two political parties of the day, the Whigs and the Tories, the Whigs were more sympathetic to the idea of very limited political reform. Thus, concerned by support for groups like the Birmingham Political Union, and alarmed by the so-called 'Labourers' Riots' in

1830, the Whig government, under the leadership of Lord Grey, introduced a Reform Bill to the House of Commons in March 1831.

There was fierce Tory opposition as the Bill was debated in the House. Defeat at the Committee Stage led to the government's resignation. At the subsequent General Election, the Whigs were returned to power with a majority of one hundred and thirty six. A second Reform Bill then passed all of the stages in the Commons, but was rejected by the House of Lords.

The action of the Lords provoked popular discontent in some parts of the country with riots, disturbances and damage to property. A third Reform Bill passed all the stages in the House of Commons, but at the Committee Stage in the House of Lords it stalled due to Tory opposition. The Whigs resigned from government when the King refused Grey's request for the creation of fifty Whig peers to allow the Bill to become law. Once again, the reformers outside Parliament mounted a popular campaign in favour of the Bill.

At this point the King was forced to ask the Duke of Wellington, Leader of the Tories, to form a government. However, Wellington's efforts failed due to disunity within his own party and, once again, Grey and the Whigs returned to office. As a result, the Reform Bill became law in June 1832 due, in the end, to the deliberate absence of Wellington and other Tory peers from the Lords at crucial stages of the Bill's passage.

THE 1832 REFORM ACT
The Act covered two areas—the voters and the constituencies.

The Voters
Before the *Reform Act* the electorate was small—about 435,000 voters, with under 5,000 in Scotland. There were no uniform rules determining who could vote, resulting in many variations across the country. In some boroughs, every freeman could vote; in others only resident freemen had the vote; in other areas ratepayers could vote. In some parts of the country, local customs dating back to the Middle Ages determined the franchise and in yet other parts of the country, the local landowner nominated the voters. Naturally these voters always returned the candidate favoured by the landowner. In some country areas the landowner chose the MP—there was no election.

After the *Reform Act*, the electorate was marginally increased to 652,000 voters with over 60,000 in Scotland. On the surface, there seemed to be a more uniform franchise. For instance, in the boroughs every man owning or renting property worth more than £10 per year in rateable value got the vote. All of the ancient local customs were abolished. In the counties, owners of land worth £2 or more per year in rent got the vote. In addition, the vote was given to tenants who either rented land, paying more than £50 per year, or held land on a long lease of more than £10 per year. The limitations of the Act are demonstrated by the fact that five out of six males still had no vote; in the English counties there was one voter for every twenty four citizens; in Scotland there was one voter for every five citizens.

The Constituencies
Before the *Reform Act*, the total number of MPs was 658 of which Scotland had 45. There were two kinds of constituency: boroughs and counties. Most boroughs and all of the English counties sent two MPs to Parliament, while most Welsh and Scottish counties had only one MP. Large towns like Leeds, Manchester and Bradford had no MPs. Some constituencies had no voters or had ceased to exist, but still sent MPs to the Commons, eg. Old Sarum was one of the so-called 'rotten boroughs'. Other constituencies were known as 'pocket boroughs', as the local landowner nominated the MP.

Pocket boroughs were bought and sold as financial investments. Before 1832, it is estimated that one hundred and sixty landlords nominated almost half the MPs in the Commons.

After the *Reform Act*, the total number of MPs was still 658, of which Scotland had 53. Fifty six towns with a population of less than two thousand lost both of their MPs. Thirty towns with a population of between two and four thousand lost one of their two MPs. In addition, twenty two new two-member boroughs were created; twenty new one-member boroughs were created; six additional MPs were given to the larger counties; and Scotland gained eight new members.

Effects of the Reform Act
➤ Some of the anomalies of the old system were corrected.
➤ The size of the electorate increased to one in seven adult males entitled to vote (one in five in England).
➤ The trend of urbanisation was recognised.
➤ The Members of the Commons still came largely from the south and south-west of England, and continued to be dominated by the landed interest, as a person still had to own land to become an MP.
➤ There was still no secret ballot.
➤ Although the government did not envisage further reform, the Act created an expectation which led to further agitation for more widespread reform.

POPULAR MOVEMENTS FOR REFORM 1830s TO 1850
Clearly, the *First Reform Act* did nothing for the vast majority of people, who remained powerless. Thus, demands for reform by the radicals continued in the 1830s and 1840s. The most spectacular of the movements demanding further reform at this time was the Chartists. They originated in London, with the formation of the London Working Men's Association

for Benefiting Politically Socially and Morally and Useful Classes. The ideas embodied in Chartism became the focus for many democrats who had been disappointed by the 1832 *Reform Act*.

The Chartists campaigned in the 1830s and '40s for an extension of democracy to working people. They believed that this was the only way in which working and living conditions could be improved. Their strategy was to present petitions to Parliament demanding that the six points of the 'People's Charter' be enacted into law. Chartism attracted a large amount of support, particularly in the north of England, at times of economic recession.

Petitions were presented to Parliament in 1837, 1839, 1842 and 1848, all to no immediate effect. The Chartists organisation died out after the 1848 petition. Violence associated with the 1842 and 1848 petitions, a divided leadership, the lure of other causes such as trade unionism and the Anti-Corn Law League, and a general improvement in economic conditions all contributed to the failure of Chartism to achieve its aims.

However, the necessity for political reform and the movement towards democracy were not extinguished with the failure of Chartism. While

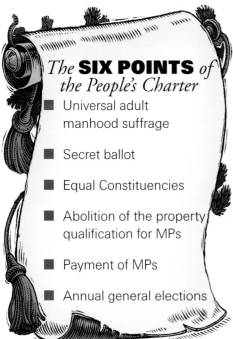

The **SIX POINTS** of the People's Charter

- Universal adult manhood suffrage
- Secret ballot
- Equal Constituencies
- Abolition of the property qualification for MPs
- Payment of MPs
- Annual general elections

many upper- and middle-class citizens saw Chartism as a dangerous menace to the stability of the country, gradual social and economic change combined to make further political reform not only desirable but inevitable.

REFORMS LEADING TO THE EXTENSION OF DEMOCRACY 1867–1928

Although the electoral system put in place by the 1832 *Reform Act* still remained intact in mid-Victorian Britain, it came increasingly under pressure in the 1850s. The passing of quarter of a century had brought increased urbanisation, industrialisation and general social change, yet the government of the country was still carried out by the middle and upper classes and was elected by a small minority of the population.

In Parliament, the two main parties, the Whigs and the Tories, had also changed during this period. The Tories, who were traditionally supported by the landed gentry, had split in 1846 over the repeal of the Corn Laws. Increasingly therefore, the Party moved towards the ideology of conservatism. The Whigs, on the other hand, were turning to the ideology of liberalism and, as a result, the property owning middle class came to identify with them. Thus, by the 1850s a number of leading Liberals, as the Whigs had become known, came to accept that further Parliamentary reform was necessary in order to take account of social change.

Between 1852 and 1860, four Reform Bills were presented to the House of Commons. Three of these Bills came from Lord John Russell, whose belief that the 1832 *Reform Act* was 'final', had earned him the nickname of 'Finality Jack'. Abandoning his position in 1852, Russell put forward proposals to lower and widen the property qualification in order to increase the electorate by giving the vote to working people who owned property and who had been educated.

BRITAIN IN 1865
Some Political Facts

- 116 MPs were sons of Peers and their relations.
- 109 MPs were sons of Baronets and their relations.
- 50% of MPs in the House of Commons (ie. 328 MPs) were elected by 20% of the voters in England and Wales.
- Many towns in the North and Midlands were like Leeds, which had a population of 200,000 but had only 7,000 voters.
- In Britain the total population was 30 million, of whom 1,430,000 could vote.

By 1860, all four Bills had failed to become law. However, by this time it had become clear that further measures of reform would be necessary, if only to take into account factors such as growth and movement of the population. In Parliament, Radical and Liberal MPs argued for limited reform.

Leading figures who supported reform became popular heroes, as public enthusiasm for political change grew in the early 1860s. Gladstone, the future Prime Minister, became a focus for attention in 1864 when he declared that "Every man who is not presumably incapacitated by some consideration of personal fitness or of political danger is morally entitled to come within the pale of the Constitution, provided this does not lead to sudden or violent or excessive, or intoxicating political change".[1]

Gladstone's argument was based on the idea of moral right, which caught the public imagination. Outside the Parliamentary arena, the writings of John Stuart Mill in his books *On Liberty* (1860) and

Representative Government (1861) served to underline the principles of democracy with the educated classes. At the same time, popular enthusiasm for democratic sentiment grew with support for the Northern cause in the American Civil War and the struggle for Italian liberty.

However, within the Liberal Party there was still a debate over the question of reform, and here it must be remembered that even the pro-reformers only wanted safe measures of limited reform.

Outside Parliament, public pressure in favour of reform mounted. In 1864, the National Reform Union was founded to promote the idea of a community of interest between the working and middle classes. It argued that the political aims of the two classes were similar and that they could work together in the political arena. Also founded in 1864, the Reform League was much more radical, working for manhood suffrage and a secret ballot. The League was numerically strong, attracting support from trade unionists, socialists and former adherents of the Chartists' cause. By 1866, the London Trades Council began to campaign for manhood suffrage.

While the 1865 General Election returned the Liberals to power under the leadership of Lord Palmerston, the issue of reform had remained dormant during the Election campaign. However, the death of Palmerston, who had consistently opposed political reform, brought the question back to life. Russell succeeded Palmerston as Prime Minister and Gladstone became Chancellor of the Exchequer. Both men now felt able to tackle the reform question, albeit in a cautious manner which they hoped would avoid dividing their party. Russell's strategy was therefore to play for time by proposing a Commission of Inquiry into the electoral system. This was to report in two years. Radical pressure from his own party, though, forced Russell to drop the idea of the Commission and set about drafting a Reform Bill.

THE 1866 REFORM BILL

This Bill aimed to add significant numbers of the working class to the electorate without threatening the establishment. It made the following proposals:

➤ Men owning or renting a property of £7 per year rateable value would get the vote in the boroughs.

➤ £10 lodgers in the boroughs would get the vote.

➤ County tenants who rented land and who paid more than £14 per year would get the vote.

➤ £50 bank depositors would get the vote.

➤ In all, an additional 400,000 would have got the vote. Thus the electorate would have been increased by 5%.

Russell's fears of Party disunity were confirmed when the Bill was published. The Radicals were disappointed because the Bill had not gone far enough, while the anti-reformers, led by Robert Lowe, vigorously opposed it. Lowe's supporters were nicknamed the 'Adullamites' by John Bright the reformer, after the Old Testament Bible story where David and his friends escaped from his enemies to the cave of Adullum. Working with the Tories in opposition to the Bill, the Adullamites forced the Government to accept an amendment to its proposals. With his party split, Russell resigned on 26 June 1866.

"Thus in June 1866 the Adullamite-Tory alliance succeeded. Disraeli had triumphed. Gladstone was humiliated and the Liberal Party hopelessly divided. Russell was too weak and tired to repair the split: Gladstone was too obstinate and inflexible. The former wished to drop the Reform Bill: the latter firmly refused ... When Russell failed to obtain pledged support in the Party for a Reform Bill in the next session he wearily decided to resign, and did so on 26th June. The Queen invited Derby to form a government."[2]

When Lord Derby and the Conservative Party were invited to form a government by the Queen, they did so reluctantly. In the House of Commons they were in a minority position, and in the country they had to deal with a cholera epidemic and popular demands for reform, underlined by marches, demonstrations and even rioting in Hyde Park.

The leading figure in Derby's Cabinet and in the House of Commons at this time was Benjamin Disraeli. His attitude to reform was different from that of his party colleagues. Disraeli favoured extending the franchise so long as it did not mean handing over political power to the working classes. While many Conservatives may have wished to leave the potentially divisive reform issue alone, Lord Derby chose to act. He believed that the agitation in the country for reform was now so strong that his government could not avoid the question. In addition, Derby took account of Queen Victoria's fear for the stability of the country in the absence of concrete reform proposals.

The Conservative Reform Bill was introduced to the Commons in March 1867 by Disraeli. Its proposals would have created an additional 400,000 voters by allowing household suffrage in the boroughs and by introducing so-called 'fancy franchises' for people with £50 in savings or who paid £1 in tax. It was also proposed to reduce the county franchise from £50 to £15. During the Commons debates on the Bill, Disraeli had to perform with great skill. He needed the support of the radicals within the Liberal Party as well as the anti-reformers within his own Party for the Bill to succeed. Disraeli convinced the Tory waverers that the Bill was essentially conservative, while the Radicals were led to believe that the proposals could become even more sweeping.

The case for increased Scottish representation in the Commons was made by the Edinburgh MP McLaren. He argued that the Scottish quota of MPs should be increased from fifty three to sixty eight since Scotland now contained one-ninth of Britain's population and contributed more than an eighth of taxation.

The Bill passed its third reading in the Commons without a vote and became law in August 1867, the House of Lords having made little alteration to its content.

THE SECOND REFORM ACT 1867

This Act increased the electorate by 1,120,000 voters to approximately 2.5 million.

The Vote

➤ In the boroughs, all householders with one year's residence and who paid rates got the vote.

➤ Lodgers living in accommodation valued at £10 annual rent got the vote.

➤ In the counties, the franchise was extended by reducing the £10 value for copyholders and leaseholders down to £5.

➤ Occupiers of premises which had a rateable value of £12 got the vote.

➤ Across the UK, one male in three now had the vote.

The Constituencies

➤ The Act, plus measures taken in 1868, led to a number of constituencies being disenfranchised.

➤ The available fifty two seats were redistributed as follows—twenty five went to the counties; nineteen went to the boroughs; one went to London University; two went to Scottish Universities; and five were allocated to Scottish constituencies.

Effects of the Second Reform Act

While it is clear that the *Second Reform Act* increased the numbers of men entitled to vote from one in seven in 1833 to one in three, it did not alter the balance of political power in Britain. The electorate still remained as before in both the boroughs and the counties, namely the middle classes—the shopkeepers and skilled workers, the landowners, tenant farmers, householders and local tradesmen. The most important change was the granting of the vote to occupiers in the boroughs. As a result, the electorate in some of the newer towns in England and Scotland increased dramatically.

The 1867 *Reform Act* gave the vote to many more men than had originally been intended by Disraeli, particularly in the towns. As a result, both political parties now understood that the traditional form of election campaigning would no longer be relevant. Thus, in order to mobilise the support of the urban working class, both the Liberals and the Conservatives developed national organisations which, in the future, managed party activities on a nationwide basis. Increasingly therefore, fewer genuinely independent MPs were elected to the Commons. To be elected to Parliament, a man re-

The Reform Debate

The Pro-Reform Lobby	The Anti-Reform Lobby
Main supporters—Russell and Gladstone	Main supporter—Robert Lowe
● *Efficient government needed the support of a wider electorate.*	● *Working-class people were selfish and ignorant.*
● *'Respectable' working-class men deserved the vote.*	● *They would use the vote in a self-seeking manner, destroying efficient government.*
● *Rewarding the working-class elite with the vote would lead to its 'moral improvement'.*	● *Empowering the working class would lead to attacks on property and the free market.*
● *The vote would turn working-class men away from Socialism.*	● *Power must remain in the hands of the elite who know how to use it.*
● *An extension of the franchise would break the power of the aristocracy.*	● *Extension of the franchise would lead to a form of tyranny with attacks on traditional institutions.*
● *It would push the Liberal Party in a more radical direction.*	● *Only men with property had the intelligence to participate in politics.*

The 1867 Reform Act

The Historical Debate

There are three different interpretations of the reasons for the passing of the 1867 Reform Act: the Whig school, the Socialist school and the Tory school.

The Whig School: *Stresses the idea that political reform came about as a response to economic and social change in Britain. 'Whig' historians also emphasise the notion that popular pressure for reform led to the passing of the Act.*

The Socialist School: *Argues that popular agitation in 1866 and 1867 was responsible for the timing of reform. 'Socialist' historians say that the Reform League's campaign in 1866 and the Hyde Park Riot all combined to push both Gladstone and Disraeli in the direction of reform.*

The Tory School: *Emphasises party competition in the years following Palmerston's death as the reason for reform. They argue that neither Gladstone nor Disraeli was interested in creating a truly democratic system, rather they were more concerned with outplaying each other.*

quired the support and organisation of a national party.

THE BALLOT ACT 1872

While the *Second Reform Act* gradually moved the nation closer to democracy, the electoral system still had to free itself from the crooked practices of bribery, corruption and intimidation. Although the Chartists demanded a ballot to replace the tradition of publicly declaring your vote from the hustings, a more democratic method of voting did not become an issue until the late 1860s. In the meantime, bribery during and between elections was rife. For instance, in 1865 £14,000 was spent on bribing the 1,408 voters in the constituency of Lancaster.

The idea of secret voting was criticised by individuals from both parties because, they argued, voting was a "privilege" and a "responsibility" which required to be carried out in public.

> "The motives under which men act in secret are, as a general rule, inferior to those under which men act in public."[3]

When a Parliamentary Inquiry into the 1865 General Election revealed the scale of electoral malpractice, Gladstone's Government brought in a Bill which, although rejected by the House of Lords in 1871, became law in 1872 as the *Ballot Act*.

Effects of the Ballot Act

➤ Once voting was done in secret, intimidation declined.

➤ Corruption was not completely wiped out. Between 1867 and 1885, four towns were disenfranchised due to corrupt practices. It took a further measure from the Liberals in 1883 to deal with the problem.

THE CORRUPT AND ILLEGAL PRACTICES ACT 1883

This piece of legislation plugged the gaps in the *Ballot Act* of 1872 by establishing:

➤ that candidates' election expenses were determined by the size of the constituency;

➤ what campaign money could be spent on;

➤ that election agents had to account for their spending;

➤ a detailed definition of illegal and corrupt practices;

➤ that a breach of the law disqualified a candidate for seven years;

➤ that active involvement in corruption was punishable by a fine or imprisonment.

WIDER ELECTORAL REFORM IN THE 1880s

Having dealt with the problem of corruption, Gladstone's second administration now turned its attention to wider electoral reform, against a background of falling popularity and division within the Liberal Party. In 1883, Joseph Chamberlain, one of Gladstone's Cabinet Ministers, drew up a legislative programme for the next election which he promoted in a series of speeches across the country. Chamberlain advocated land reform, fiscal reform to cut the burden of taxes paid by the poor, and measures to democratise local government. However, the central feature of Chamberlain's programme was a Reform Bill which would grant males in the counties equal voting rights with their borough counterparts.

While Gladstone was cautious about extending the franchise due to opposition within his own party, he was also well aware that an effective Reform Bill which removed electoral injustice could turn the tide of popular opinion in favour of his government. A Franchise Bill was therefore introduced to the Commons in 1884. Although the Bill passed all of the stages in the House of Commons, it was blocked by the House of Lords, which demanded that a scheme for the redistribution of seats be introduced at the same time. As protracted negotiations continued between government and opposition in both Houses of Parliament, there were some anti-peer disturbances in the autumn of 1884 in Birmingham, and protest marches in Scotland.

> "... These processions were pure street theatre, encapsulating more than anything else in the nineteenth century the character of proletarian Liberalism, and emphasising its civic and craft pride, its class feelings against landlords ... The Glasgow demonstration of 1884, intended to put pressure on an obstructive Tory House of Lords, involved 64,000 in the procession and another 200,000 gathering to greet them on Glasgow

The 1884 and 1885 Acts

"What had happened in effect was that the franchise had ceased, at last, in the counties as in the boroughs, to be a class privilege; and accordingly there seemed to be substance in the view that for the future Parliament would have to govern the country with an eye to the interests and wishes of the majority of the people."

(GDH Cole and Raymond Postgate, *The Common People* page 412.)

... The Historians' Verdict

"... the House of Commons, becoming more completely than ever the true focus of legislative power, changed fundamentally its electoral basis, and became more openly the organ of public opinion ... With secrecy of ballot after 1872, the workers of both town and country were able to use their vote freely without fear of reprisals from employer or landlord. Public opinion came to be more of a reality in politics."

(David Thomson, *England in the Nineteenth Century* page 175.)

"The *Third Reform Act* has been described as a 'bold and logical measure' granting manhood suffrage in town and country alike'. Had it achieved this end, or had been intended to do so, working-class radical support for the Liberals might appear totally justified in the perspective of its own tradition ... Unfortunately, due to the continued existence of groups who were not enfranchised ... the Act left some 40% of the adult males in the United Kingdom still unenfranchised in 1911, clearly concentrated in the poor and younger working class."

(TC Smout, *A Century of the Scottish People 1830–1950* page 246.)

Green. They carried countless pictures of Gladstone and many of Bright ...The French polishers, for example, carried a miniature wardrobe, first borne in 1832, and a flag inscribed, 'The French polishers will polish off the Lords and make the Cabinet shine' ... The basic message was clear – the 'class' obstructed reform, the 'masses' were here to demand it."[4]

Eventually it was agreed that there should be two Bills, one dealing with redistribution of seats and another which would tackle the extension of the franchise.

REPRESENTATION OF THE PEOPLE ACT 1884

The first of the two Acts dealt with extending the vote. The effects of this Act were as follows.

➤ The electorate was increased from 2.5 million to 5 million.
➤ In England and Wales two out of three men now had the vote.

➤ Male householders and lodgers in the counties with twelve months of occupation got the vote.
➤ Voting qualifications in the towns and counties were now identical, ie. all householders and lodgers paying £10 per annum in rent could vote.

REDISTRIBUTION OF SEATS ACT 1885

This piece of legislation aimed to construct constituencies of approximately equal size. The effects of this Act were as follows.

➤ Seventy nine towns with a population of under 15,000 lost both of their seats.
➤ Thirty six towns with a population between 15,000 and 50,000 lost one seat.
➤ Towns with populations between 50,000 and 165,000 kept two seats.
➤ Universities kept two seats.

➤ The remainder of the country was divided into single member constituencies.
➤ The total number of MPs was increased from 652 to 670.

In Scotland

➤ Representation at Westminster increased to today's number of seventy two MPs.
➤ The seven additional seats went to the counties.
➤ The County of Lanark's representation was increased from two to six MPs.
➤ The counties of Fife, Perth and Renfrew each had their representation increased to two MPs.
➤ In the Scottish cities, Glasgow's representation increased from three MPs to seven, Edinburgh's from two to four MPs, and Aberdeen's increased from one to two.

The *Third Reform Act* moved Britain closer to democracy, putting in place an electoral system which is very similar to that which presently exists for Westminister and local government elections. However, the country was far from being a democratic society. Women were still excluded from the system, as were male domestic servants, sons who lived at home, paupers on poor relief, soldiers living in barracks and those who had failed to pay their rates.

In addition, many other anomalies still existed, some of which are outlined below.

➤ Plural voting still existed. This meant that a man could have many votes if he owned property in different constituencies.

➤ Universities still elected MPs, a concept which seems rather odd today.

➤ While most MPs were elected by the 'first-past-the-post' system, university MPs were elected by a form of proportional representation called the single transferable vote. This situation persisted until 1950 when the university seats were abolished.

Therefore it is true to say that, "by

modern standards, Victorian democracy was undemocratic."[5] Between 1885 and 1918 there were few attempts to widen the franchise, despite the suffragette agitation prior to World War I. The 1918 *Representation of the People Act* at last removed the discrepancies in the male franchise and gave the vote to women aged thirty and over. Women eventually gained equal voting rights with men in 1928. Further twentieth century electoral reforms in 1948 and 1969 abolished university representation in Parliament and reduced the voting age from twenty one to eighteen.

Issue for debate
Did the rise of the Labour Party cause the decline of the Liberal Party?

The decline of the Liberal Party and the rise of the Labour Party has been a source of controversy among historians for many years.

George Dangerfield, in his well-written, but essentially misleading work, *The Strange Death of Liberal England*, published in 1936, was responsible for the view that the replacement of the Liberals by the Labour Party as the mouthpiece of the British working class was inevitable and that the rift between Liberal Leaders, Asquith and Lloyd George was merely an expression of and not the cause of this process. This view was to have considerable influence on later writers until the 1960s.

From a different standpoint, more recent historians such

as Paul Thompson and Henry Pelling have come to the conclusion that because Edwardian Liberalism was middle class, this made it essentially incapable of accommodating its working-class support at either national or local level. It was this factor which eventually ensured the triumph of the Labour Party. Thompson, in his book *Socialists, Liberals and Labour*, considered the radicalism of the Liberals in the 1900s to be an "increasingly outdated political concept". Pelling, an authority on the rise of the Labour Party, added that it, and not the Liberals, was better equipped "to take advantage of twentieth century political conditions".[6]

On the other hand, some historians, notably Trevor Wilson, have rejected this view. In his work *The Downfall of the Liberal Party, 1914–1935*, he argued that the Liberal Party was still in a healthy condition at the start of the war in 1914 when it was suddenly felled by the events of the war.

Kenneth O Morgan, in *The Age of Lloyd George*, concluded that during the diffi-

cult period of 1910 to 1914, "years of labour unrest, of the Ulster crisis and the Suffragettes' demonstrations", these challenges were directed more against the British constitutional system than against the Liberal Party itself. Moreover, the Liberals, with Lloyd George in a key reforming position, were nowhere near exhausted. Morgan's conclusion was that "to view these years as a kind of Indian summer for a party on the verge of imminent collapse is a basic distortion of political history".[7]

In 1974, Ross McKibbin, in his work *The Evolution of the Labour Party 1910–24*, reinforced Pelling's view in addition to adding fresh research. McKibbin argued that the growth and expansion of trade unions in the late nineteenth and early twentieth centuries led to the rise of the Labour Party. Also, as union membership increased after 1910, Labour's national structure and local campaigning changed, thus improving the Party's electoral position. Furthermore, the Labour Party was a real threat to the Liberals by 1914 and

could have done even better had it not been hindered by legal impediments which affected the Party's ability to organise, and a restricted electoral system which continued to prevent large numbers of potential working-class Labour supporters from voting.

A recent work by Duncan Tanner, *Political Change and the Labour Party 1900–1918*, reassessed all of the evidence and clarified the issues. He argued that the success of the Liberal Party was due to its ability to attract working- and middle-class voters, rather than to the ideology of the 'New Liberalism'. He also argued that the Liberals were only under threat from Labour pre-1914 in specific areas of the country and that the experience of war enhanced Labour's reputation in these areas. Overall, the Liberals were defeated in 1918 due to their attitude to the war. His final argument was that although Labour became the major anti-Tory party after 1918, the Liberals still had a place in a new, developing, three-party system.

Changing Britain 1850–1979

FORCED FELLOWSHIP.
SUSPICIOUS LOOKING PARTY. "ANY OBJECTION TO MY COMPANY,
GUV'NOR? I'M AGOIN' YOUR WAY"—(aside) "AND FURTHER."

FACTORS PROMOTING THE DECLINE OF THE LIBERALS AND THE GROWTH OF LABOUR

● **The Liberals split in 1886 when Gladstone, the Liberal Prime Minister, proposed Home Rule for Ireland.** Ninety three Liberal MPs voted against the Bill and many of them, calling themselves Unionists, gradually moved over to the Conservative side. The loss of Joseph Chamberlain, in particular, was a severe blow to the Liberals as he was their most radical spokesperson and was regarded as a natural successor to the ageing Gladstone. The Whig gentry, who had been a crucial element in Gladstonian Liberalism, were already shaken by the passing of the 1884 Reform Bill. They regarded the Irish Bill as the last straw and left the Party. Support was also lost in the centre of the Party among professional and academic opinion such as historians Arnold and Dicey. Gladstone, himself, seemed to be the only unifying factor in a party which was deeply split and disillusioned.

● **The attempt by the Liberal Party to remould itself in the late 19th century was another source of problems.** With the adoption of the Newcastle Programme in 1891, which committed the Liberals to a vast range of reforms, there were now two contrasting views in the Party— 'Old Liberalism' and 'New Liberalism'. The former advocated the traditional individualism of Liberalism and the latter proposed the new collectivist or government interventionist thinking.

● **Imperial affairs, particularly the Boer War in South Africa, helped to weaken the Liberals in the 1890s.** While the Conservatives were united in their approach to the war, the Liberals were split into three factions. Those who were opposed to the war, including Lloyd George, were called the National Liberal Federation; the faction which supported the war, including Rosebery and Asquith, were called the Liberal Imperialists; and the third faction, which observed an embarrassed neutrality, comprised the majority of the Party and included Campbell-Bannerman. The ending of the war in 1902 concluded the most painful phase of Liberal disunity.

● **The Liberal landslide victory, the biggest since 1832, gave a misleading picture of Liberal popularity and strength in 1906.** Although the Party was now united under Campbell-Bannerman, historians and contemporaries have found difficulty in explaining the reasons for this surprising election result. To a large extent the Liberals owed their triumph to the electorate's negative reaction to Conservative mistakes over the previous ten years. For example, the Conservative plan to end 'free trade', which had been the basis of Britain's industrial wealth until that point, and to introduce import duties on goods from non-imperial countries, split the Party and alienated many voters. Voters thought that this would put up the cost of living as the cost of goods would have to be increased. Other important vote losers for the Conservatives were the importing of 'Chinese slaves' to South Africa, which upset humanitarians, and the 1902 *Education Act* which upset non-conformists.

Although the Liberals retained office in the two elections of 1910,

Changing Britain 1850–1979

The Electoral Fortunes of the Liberal and Labour Parties 1906–1929

Year	Liberals	Labour
1906	*377	29+24 Lib-Labs
1910 (Jan)	*275	40
1910 (Dec)	*272	42
1918	133[1]	4[2]
	28[3]	59[4]
1922	57[5]	142
	60[6]	
1923	159	*191
1924	40	151
1929	59	*288

Note
* Indicates the party forming the government.
[1] Coalition or Lloyd George Liberals
[2] Coalition Labour
[3] Asquith Liberals
[4] Labour
[5] Lloyd George Liberals
[6] Asquith Liberals

Table 1.1

their majority was greatly reduced. Indeed, they relied on the support of the Irish Nationalists and the new Labour Party to keep them in power.

● *In spite of the achievements of the greatest of all Liberal governments, they were a struggling party in 1914.* The Liberal government was besieged on three fronts by an escalating militant suffragette campaign (see Chapter 3), an increasing number of industrial disputes (see Chapter 2), and by the twin possibilities of civil war in Ireland and the resultant mutiny of British army officers in Dublin.

Undoubtedly at this point the government's reputation was badly shaken. Its record in by-elections was poor and the Conservatives anticipated victory at the next general election. Nevertheless, the Liberal Party was very far from being dead as most contemporaries would have agreed. After all, the different challenges facing the Liberal government were directed more at the constitutional system than at the Party. Moreover, Asquith's ministry was still overtly united and, with Lloyd George in the Cabinet and a new generation of younger men like Masterman and Simon, there were no signs of exhaustion.

● *The arrival of the Labour Party in Parliament from 1906 meant that the eventual demise of the Liberal Party was a strong possibility.* On the one hand, the middle-class character of Edwardian Liberalism and its basic incapacity to accommodate working-class support at local and national level would have made it difficult for the Liberals to hold on to the working-class vote. On the other hand, the potentially strong appeal of the new Labour Party to the working class on such important issues as social reform and trade union legislation made them, and not the Liberals, better equipped to profit from twentieth century political conditions. (See Chapter 2.) However, this shift in the balance of working-class support from the Liberals to Labour was likely to be a gradual process.

● *Some historians have argued that World War One accelerated social and political changes rather than causing them.* The Great War is often cited as having precipitated the decline of the Liberals and, conversely, the rise of Labour. Before 1914 the Liberals had won the three previous elections but after 1918 never held office again. Indeed, by 1923 they had slumped

to being the third party in the country. The demands of total war and Asquith's apparent inability to provide strong and effective leadership led to his resignation in December 1916. Lloyd George formed a fresh coalition government with the support of most of his Liberal and Conservative colleagues. However, lasting damage had been done to the Liberal Party as Asquith and his supporters felt betrayed from within by the new Prime Minister who, in their view, had conspired with the Conservatives. Unfortunately for the Party, the gulf between 'Asquithian' and 'Lloyd George' Liberals in the House of Commons extended to the constituencies. The growing rift continued in the 1918 Election when Lloyd George and his Liberal supporters stood for Parliament on a platform of continuing the coalition government with the Conservatives. Asquith and his supporters opposed him but were no match for the coalition parties. (See Table 1.1.) Indeed, in the course of this Ministry, Lloyd George was to become a prisoner of the Tories as they were the largest single party with 389 MPs.

Although the war had caused problems within the Labour Party due to the different reactions of various groups, it gained Cabinet experience much earlier than could have been expected. Arthur Henderson became a member of the small war Cabinet, with eight other Labour members in the government.

ONGOING ISSUES OF DEMOCRATIC CHANGE
Although the question of the franchise was largely settled by 1928, other areas of the constitution became the focus for reform and innovation. This is not surprising, since democracy implies that change is necessary and ongoing, and that it is carried out by consensus through elected representatives who are empowered by the voters and who are ultimately accountable to them.

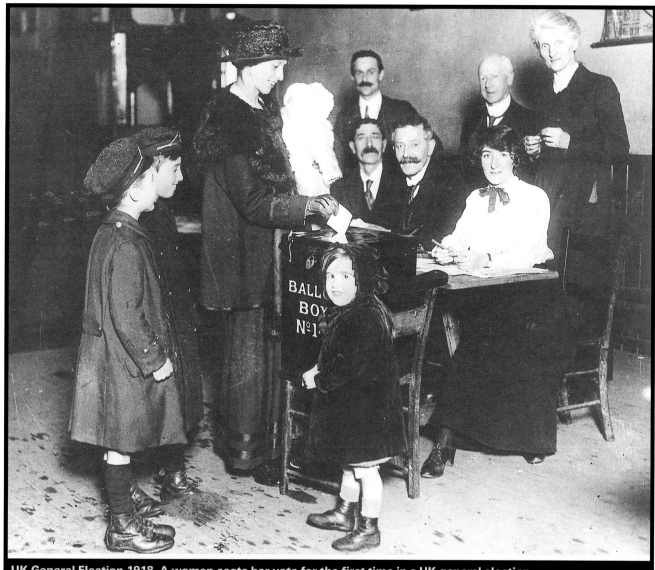

UK General Election 1918. A woman casts her vote for the first time in a UK general election.

Apart from the vote, there are two areas where change was sought in order to enhance democracy. These are the House of Lords and the electoral system.

Reform of the House of Lords

Parliament is made up of two chambers, the House of Commons and the House of Lords. The constitutional relationship between the two Houses was the focus of attention at various times during the twentieth century.

As constitutional precedent dictated, this relationship, until the late nineteenth century, was one in which an elected House of Commons initiated most legislation. The function of the largely hereditary House of Lords was to examine, criticise and revise un-

tidy parts of legislation. The position of the Lords was recognised as being 'subordinate' to that of the Commons because the latter was elected by the people.

While the 1867 *Reform Act* had underlined this position of subordination, increasingly the Conservative-dominated House of Lords became unwilling to pass Liberal legislation. As we have already seen, the Lords refused to pass the 1884 Franchise Bill without a redistribution scheme, and in 1893 it rejected the Home Rule Bill. After 1906 the Lords rejected Liberal legislation on education, land valuation and Scottish smallholdings, and in 1909 rejected Lloyd George's famous 'People's Budget' in which the rich were to be taxed to pay for naval rearmament.

The Liberals perceived the behaviour of the Lords over the Budget as an attack on democracy and were determined to meet the challenge head on. In a famous election speech in 1910 Asquith described the Lords as a "doormat second chamber" which only woke up when "democracy votes Liberal." After two general elections in the space of two years, the Liberals, in 1911, introduced a Parliament Bill which only became law when the House of Lords was threatened with the creation of enough new peers to ensure a government majority. The resulting *Parliament Act* (1911) took away the Lords' power over Bills which concerned taxation and government spending—money Bills. They were left with the power to amend or reject other Bills, but

13

only had the power to delay them for two Parliamentary sessions.

Since then, the Lords have only rarely used their power, fearful that if they did so the Commons would cut their authority completely. Further reform, which was on the political agenda in 1920 and 1922, came to nothing.

The Electoral System

Although the electoral system which evolved in the nineteenth century was simple and easy to administer, it was unfair to minor parties. The system, as it stood in the twentieth century, was overgenerous to the dominant parties, Labour and the Conservatives, leaving parties like the Liberals, despite a broad base of support across the country, with very few seats in Parliament.

While electoral reform is perceived as a contemporary issue, it has, in fact, been on the political agenda since World War I. In 1918 an all-party 'Speaker's Conference' proposed a form of proportional representation (PR) as a method of election which would more accurately reflect the wishes of the people. Although this proposal was dropped due to the 1918 Election, proportional representation was again proposed in 1931 by the minority Labour government as an inducement for Liberal support. The Liberals have been enthusiastic supporters of PR as a means of reviving their political fortunes since 1922.

The development of liberal democracy in Britain has been slow and piecemeal. The system which had evolved by 1928, while retaining many of the traditions, had in place most of the apparatus necessary to satisfy the democratic aspirations of the nation. Nevertheless, the essence of democracy is that of a system of government which promotes and encourages political change from below. Thus, issues such as electoral reform, devolution, the protection of human rights, the right to privacy and the promotion of equality continue to be debated, explained and acted upon as part of our everyday, ongoing democratic political culture.

REF**O**RM *timeline*

1832   First Reform Act
Extends franchise (£10 householder in boroughs) giving vote to the middle classes; redistributes parliamentary seats.

1834   The Monarch dismisses Ministers despite their parliamentary majority
He is forced to reappoint Ministers shortly afterwards. It never happens again.

1867   Second Reform Act
Extends franchise and further redistributes seats.

1872   Ballot Act
Introduces secret voting to end intimidation.

1883   Corrupt and Illegal Practices Act
Tackles corruption by setting strict and effective limits on election campaign spending at a constituency level.

1884   Third Reform Act (Representation of the People Act)
Further extends the franchise to give two out of three men the right to vote, but still leaves many anomalies.

1885   The Redistribution of Seats Act
A further redistribution of seats establishing many single member constituencies.

1911   Parliament Act
Powers of House of Lords limited; life of a Parliament limited to five years.

1911   Payment for Members of Parliament

1918   Representation of the People Act
The vote is given to all men aged twenty one and over and all women over thirty. General elections to be held on one day. First-past-the-post system of election confirmed.

1928   Equal Franchise Act
All women aged twenty one and over get the vote, putting them on an equal footing with men. All adults over twenty one now have the vote except peers, the insane and felons.

THE GROWTH OF DEMOCRACY:
EFFECTS ON BRITAIN'S POLITICAL IDENTITY

"True democracy is government 'for', as well as 'of' and 'by' the people."[8]

The growth of democracy in nineteenth and twentieth century Britain radically affected the country's political identity. In this section we will examine how this has changed with reference to popular control, the party system inside and outside Parliament, voting in elections and choosing a government, and the scope of government activity.

Popular Control
At the beginning of the nineteenth

century, Parliament was not representative in terms of social class as a percentage of the population, gender or by geography. The reforms of the nineteenth and early twentieth centuries saw many of these problems resolved. As the franchise widened during the nineteenth century, increasing numbers of men got the vote, and by 1928 all men and women had the vote on an equal footing. After 1949, there was 'one person, one vote'.

Following on from the 1832 *Reform Act*, the new industrial towns of the North and Midlands received representation in Parliament, and successive Acts during the nineteenth century began to take account of both population growth and urbanisation as seats were redistributed. From 1885, each constituency contained roughly the same number of voters, thus greater equality was introduced into the representative system. Before these reforms, a small constituency with a few thousand inhabitants returned the same number of MPs as a city with a population numbering hundreds of thousands.

The 1911 legislation, which introduced payment of MPs is important in making Parliament more representative, because for the first time it enabled working-class people to become MPs. Prior to this, Parliament was exclusively middle or upper class as intending MPs had to be 'of independent means'. The 1911 *Parliament Act* effectively curtailed the power of the hereditary House of Lords in the legislation process, placing power firmly in the hands of the popularly elected House of Commons.

Despite the enfranchisement of women in the twentieth century, and the payment of salaries to MPs, Parliament has yet to become absolutely representative.

By 1979, the House of Commons was still mainly white, male and middle class. The net result of these nineteenth and twentieth centuries reforms is that the House of Commons, which legislates (makes laws), and to which the Executive (Prime Minister and Cabinet) is accountable, is itself properly elected and therefore ultimately answerable to the people.

The Party System
As the franchise was extended and, consequently, the number of voters increased, the modern party system developed inside and outside Parliament. Until 1832, there was only a very loose kind of party organisation. MPs generally cooperated more as individuals than as disciplined members of an organised party whose policies were underpinned by an ideological vision of society. The situation changed as the electorate began to grow after 1832. As the number of voters in a constituency increased from,

The Spitalfields soup kitchen, East London, 1867.
Despite increasing democracy and the extension of the franchise distress and poverty remained.

Changing Britain 1850–1979

in some cases, a few hundred to tens of thousands, local landowners found that they could no longer dominate the voters. As a result, party leaders had to find ways of persuading the electors to vote for their candidates. This became a really urgent matter after 1883 when the *Corrupt and Illegal Practices Act* cracked down on election spending.

During the second half of the nineteenth century, party leaders devised two methods of dealing with this problem. Firstly, they began appealing to the electorate as a whole on a nationwide basis with a 'programme' or manifesto. This contained a series of measures or policies which they promised to carry out if the voters returned enough of their candidates to give them a majority in the House of Commons. Secondly, each party developed a national organisation, with a party headquarters and full-time paid staff. At a local level, they developed local constituency associations, consisting of devoted local people who lived in the constituency. Under the guidance of a professional party agent, these local associations began the task of fundraising for the party. At election time, it was their job to get the party's message over to the voters by putting up posters, delivering leaflets and organising meetings at which their candidate would speak.

These developments were all in place by the end of the nineteenth century, and had the effect of turning political parties outwards from Westminster into nationwide organisations aimed at trying to serve the people, albeit with their own vision of society.

Over the last two hundred years, Britain has had what commentators describe as a 'two-party system'. This means that politics has been dominated by two major po-litical parties. Despite the growth in democracy this has been the case over the past two centuries. During the nineteenth century, Whigs and Tories, later to become Liberals and Conservatives, were in the ascendancy. Although there was a brief experience of a 'three-party system' in the early 1920s, the 'two-party system' returned at the end of World War II and has dominated since then.

During the twentieth century, the main political parties became increasingly driven by ideology. Voting reinforced the ideological basis of party policies as increasingly people voted on the basis of social class. Recent research is beginning to show that voting on the basis of class went into decline in the 1970s.

Choosing a Government

When individuals voted two hundred years ago they were choosing someone as their own, sometimes personal, representative in Parliament. Today when we vote, we are not just electing a representative, we are also electing a government. This in turn determines certain policies covering the vast area of government such as taxation, health, education, defence and the environment. We are also voting to choose someone to lead the country for the next five years. This is a direct consequence of the effect which the growth of democracy has had on party organisation.

In earlier times there were many MPs who did not belong to any of the parties in Parliament, or who did not commit themselves to any party until they had been in the House of Commons for some time. It was therefore often difficult for the voters to know exactly what they were voting for, or to be sure about what kind of government might be formed. Today the vast majority of candidates are members of a political party. Once the result of the general election is known, the voters know whether their MP will be sitting on the government or opposition side of the House of Commons.

At the beginning of the nineteenth century it was relatively easy for a man of means to become an MP. Today, because the political process is dominated by the parties, it is virtually impossible, due to cost and organisation, for an independent candidate to be elected.

The Scope of Government Activity

At the beginning of the nineteenth century, the main aim of government was to maintain law and order, secure trade, and maintain the defences of the country against foreign enemies. The growth of democracy, however, led directly to a gradual increase of government influence on the lives of its citizens. Increased democracy meant that MPs could be held accountable for their actions every five years. Thus an MP who did little to meet the needs of his constituents would be unlikely to be re-elected. Parliament, during the nineteenth and twentieth centuries, gradually became more representative of the needs of the country as a whole. Some outstanding individual MPs pressed the government for intervention in certain areas eg. poverty, education, public health. The development of the modern party system meant that the political parties had to compete for the votes of the whole country. They could no longer simply appeal to their own constituency or section of society. To get elected, they had to be seen to be addressing the needs of the country as a whole. As a consequence of the growing electorate, politicians were forced to abandon the nineteenth century principle of laissez-faire in favour of state interventionism. Increasingly, the government intervened to meet the needs of the poor.

The Growth of the Labour Movement 1890–1922

WHAT YOU WILL LEARN

- **The ways in which the labour movement attempted to influence the development of democracy in Britain between the 1890s and 1922.**

- **The nature and development of the labour movement to the 1890s.**

- **The individuals, organisations and ideas which shaped the Labour Party.**

- **The growth and development of the Labour Party and trade unions between 1900 and 1918.**

- **The effects of World War I and its aftermath on the growth of the labour movement up to 1922.**

THE LABOUR MOVEMENT is made up of two distinct but interrelated parts: the industrial wing and the political wing. The industrial wing of the movement is represented by the trade unions, while the political wing came to be represented by the Labour Party. Since the 1850s, the labour movement has aimed to "negotiate a place for the working class within the framework of a capitalist democracy; the unions bargaining, the party reforming".[1]

The development of the movement is thus a history of struggle which always aimed at changing the existing political and social order.

> "What constituted Labour as a movement was the belief that each struggle was, or could be linked into a larger social purpose. Embodied in the network of working-class institutions and practices was a sense of class identity and interest, of membership of an oppositional culture whose common objective was the creation bit by bit of a fairer and a more cooperative social order."[2]

Background

The existence of organised groups of workers dates back to long before the Industrial Revolution. The fact that such bodies existed is emphasised by the amount of legislation which came into being in the seventeenth and eighteenth centuries to regulate the activities of such combinations of workers.

Industrialisation in the late eighteenth and early nineteenth centuries had the effect of bringing together large numbers of workers in a single place of employment. The emergent factory system gradually awakened some groups of workers to their common plight, thus bringing the need for workers to combine more sharply into focus. When workers did begin to band together, the governing classes often reacted with hostility. They saw these early trade unions as organisations with primarily political rather than economic aims. Thus, until the second half of

the nineteenth century, the development of workplace representation and bargaining was slow.

TRADE UNIONS–KEY EVENTS 1799–1890

1799 and 1800 The Combination Acts

These made it illegal for workers to join together to form a union. Despite these laws, there is good evidence of a growth in trade union activity, notably against the introduction of machinery in some trades, and in certain areas of the country, particularly London.

In 1824 *The Combination Acts* were repealed. As a result there was an unprecedented explosion of industrial action across the country.

1825 Combination Act

This confirmed the legal status of unions to work peacefully to improve wages, but curtailed their ability to use violence to interfere with the mode of production and made union members liable to prosecution under common law. While trade unions could now operate more openly, it was still easy for the employers to restrict their activities.

The 1830s marked a period of intense political and industrial activity for sections of the working class. The 1832 *Reform Act*, while granting democratic rights to the entrepreneurs, financiers and small businessmen of the Industrial Revolution, ignored the organised sections of the working class. The historian Henry Pelling describes the 1830s as a time when intelligent working men, in their disappointment and frustration at failing to get the vote in 1832, threw themselves into activities which attempted to raise and emphasise the status of the "work of the artisan or labourer" by setting up a "new system of cooperative production." The 1830s became the decade in which attempts were made to form general unions on a national basis, and also a time when industrialists such as Robert

Owen began to articulate the ideas of workers' cooperation and socialism.

"It is well known that during the last half century, Great Britain ... increased its powers of production; the natural effect of the aid thus obtained from science should be to add to the wealth and happiness of society ... and that all parties would thereby be substantially benefited ... On the contrary ... the working classes, which form so large a proportion of the population, cannot obtain even the comforts which their labour formerly procured for them."[3]

1834 Grand National Consolidated Trades Union
This general union attempted to put Owenite principles into practice. However, the GNCTU collapsed in ruins within twelve months of its formation, despite achieving a membership of almost half a million at its peak. The GNCTU failed for four reasons. Firstly, the leadership all held differing views from one another. Secondly, poor communication made coordination of the union's activities difficult. Thirdly, Owen's vision of a shared community of interest amongst working men proved to be flawed. Local and sectional interests dominated. Finally, the intervention of the authorities in bringing about the case of the 'Tolpuddle Martyrs' proved to be decisive in 'frightening off' working men from the GNCTU.

Trade unions did not, however, collapse with the demise of the GNCTU. At a local level, most trades continued to have some form of workers' organisation, although these unions were usually small and were confined to skilled workers. Far from being intimidated by the events of the mid-1830s, these unions continued to press for improved pay and conditions. In some trades though, the employers forced the workers to sign the so-called 'Odious Document', an agreement that individuals would cease to be union members.

In mid-Victorian Britain most unions, while operating satisfactorily, were small and were limited to skilled workers, although there were some larger unions, notably the Miners' Association of Great Britain.

The historian James Hinton describes the economy at this time as "an anarchic mixture of the old and the new." Some industries had embraced the new technology of the industrial revolution, whereas other areas of human endeavour, such as building and construction, were relatively unaffected.

1850s–1870s–Model Unions
At this time, only a small minority of workers belonged to trade unions, these being the relatively skilled craftsmen. These so-called Model Unions saw their role as one of maintaining the pay and conditions of their members, while maintaining the division between their members and the rest of the unorganised and unskilled working class. These men are described by some historians as an 'élite' within the working class. Although they did not approve of the capitalist system, they had made a temporary accommodation with it. Suspicious of socialism, they concentrated their efforts on amalgamating their smaller local craft unions into large national craft unions, the most famous of which was the Amalgamated Society of Engineers.

These unions came into being when the economy was booming. Their members earned high wages and could therefore afford the relatively high dues, sometimes as much as 1/6 ($7^1/_2$p) per week. In return, the unions employed paid, full-time officials whose job was to negotiate agreements on pay and conditions with the employers. In addition, they provided sickness, retirement, unemployment and injury benefits to their members. Five of these Model Unions made their headquarters in London and their leaders met regularly, form-

ing the London Trades Council. The leaders of this moderate group became known as the 'Junta', and it came to have a good deal of influence on national trade union development.

1860s Local Trades Councils
These were formed by craft unions and were a lot less moderate in their views than the London 'Junta'. As a result, there were clashes at a local level between employers and groups of workers anxious to have trade union organisation in the workplace. Occasionally these clashes became violent, involving lock-outs and the use of 'blackleg' labour. The police and local magistrates usually took the side of the employers.

1867 Royal Commission of Inquiry into Trade Unions
This followed outbreaks of violence during a file-grinders' strike in 1866 in Sheffield, and the questioning of the legal status of trade unions which was raised during a case involving the Boilermakers Union. The Commission heard evidence from the 'Junta' and also from representatives of the Manchester and Salford Trades Council who were keen to get all trade unions acting together rather than being dominated by the 'Junta'.

1868 First Trade Union Congress held in Manchester
The 'Junta' did not attend, perceiving the Congress as a rival to their own power base. Thus, the first historic meeting of the TUC went ahead without them.

1869 Report of Royal Commission on Trade Unions
This gave approval to the National Craft Unions for their organisation, benefits to members and absence of violence and strikes. As a result, Gladstone's Liberal Government passed two important pieces of legislation in 1871.

1871 Trade Unions Act
Trade Unions were given a status in law which they had not previ-

The Forth Bridge. Construction began in 1882 and was completed in 1890, providing employment for thousands of men.

ously enjoyed. Their funds were also given legal protection from dishonest officials.

1871 The Criminal Law Amendment Act

The practice of 'peaceful picketing', which had been legalised in 1859, was outlawed, with severe penalties proposed for the guilty.

> "The Junta's own moderation had betrayed them. They had presented their own organisations as friendly societies rather than Trade Unions. Now Gladstone gave them what they had asked for more laterally than they had anticipated."[4]

1871 The TUC Parliamentary Committee

The aim was to demand the total repeal of the *Criminal Law Amendment Act*. Meanwhile, the courts used this Act to pursue poorly organised workers. In one notorious case, seven women were sent to jail for saying "bah" to a blackleg. This and other events merely served to strengthen the resolve of the TUC to campaign harder for the removal of the Act. During the ensuing 1874 General Election, the TUC ran a campaign to pressurise candidates to reveal where they stood on the matter. Trade union members were urged to vote only for those who supported the TUC's demands. The miners even put up independent

candidates in some constituencies. Union support led to Conservative victory in 1874 and, in the following year, Disraeli's government introduced two Bills which were important for trade unions.

The first Bill, which replaced the *Master and Servant Act*, meant that breach of contract was now a civil rather than a criminal matter, and was punishable by a fine rather than by imprisonment. The second repealed the *Criminal Law Amendment Act*, and so once again legalised 'peaceful picketing'. By 1875, after a period of intense union activity in the early 1870s, it seemed that the Model Unions had achieved an accommodation with capitalism—but not without a struggle. Historians' opinions differ about the strategy of the 'Junta'. Some assess their approach of setting themselves limited but realistic aims and pursuing them in a statesmanlike manner as being the only viable strategy at the time, while others view them less charitably as "the servile generation."

In the early 1850s, it is estimated that the British trade union movement had about 100,000 members. By 1874 membership had shot up to over 1 million. However, from

then until the mid-1880s membership declined due to economic recession, only to rise again by 1888 to about 750,000. These years saw hard times for the unions which often had to fight campaigns against wage reductions while facing dramatic membership losses. Some smaller unions went out of existence altogether.

THE NEW UNIONISM

'The decades of the New Unionism' is the way in which historians describe the period between the 1880s and the turn of the century. During this period, it is clear that trade unionism was gradually changing, becoming more political with a much wider vision of its role in society. How did the unions begin to change at this time?

Existing unions, such as the Amalgamated Society of Engineers, began to admit semi-skilled workers. New general unions, which were prepared to organise all who wished membership, were being formed. Furthermore, trade unions began to associate themselves with the ideology of socialism, looking outwith the established political parties as a means of winning demands for state intervention. Finally, as it gained a wider membership, the growing trade union movement became more assertive.

During this period, the state took union activity more seriously. The Labour Department of the Board of Trade began to record and measure levels of industrial unrest. In addition, a Royal Commission on Labour was established. Publishing fifty eight volumes of evidence between 1892 and 1894, the Commission was concerned that conciliation procedures be set up

Membership of Seven Largest New Unions	
Year	N° of Members
1890	320,000
1992	130,000
1906	80,000

Table 2.1

on a local basis, hoping that the new unions which had not adopted such practices would quickly do so.

The leaders of the New Unionism were younger men with strong socialist principles such as Tom Mann and Ben Tillet.

> "... we repeat that the real difference between the 'new' and the 'old' is that those who belong to the latter and delight in being distinct from the policy endorsed by the 'new', do so because they do not recognise, as we do, that it is the work of trade unionists to stamp out poverty from the land ... A new enthusiasm is required, a fervent zeal that will result in a sending forth of trade union organisers as missionaries through the length and breadth of the country. Clannishness in trade matters must be superseded by a cosmopolitan brotherhood, must not be talked of but practised ... We ... are prepared to work unceasingly for the economic emancipation of the workers."[5]

THE ORIGINS OF THE LABOUR PARTY
People, Organisations and Ideas

This section will examine the events, various ideological traditions, organisations and personalities which influenced the Labour Party's development in the last quarter of the nineteenth century.

Although the nineteenth century saw a gradual move by governments away from laissez-faire policies in the area of social issues, the pace of change was slow, and was limited in meeting the needs of the working classes. Towards the end of the nineteenth century, various factors came together to bring about change in the established two-party system of government.

The *Reform Acts* of 1867 and 1884 together added about eight million working-class voters to the electorate who, after the *Ballot Act* of 1872, were able to vote independently without fear of pressure from their employers. Radicals in both the Conservative and Liberal Par-

ties perceived the need to capture this working-class vote, and in this area both Conservatives and Liberals were successful for a time.

The leaders of the TUC, which was formed in 1868, adopted the strategy of campaigning to persuade Parliament to secure the rights of trade unions and their members. To this end, the Labour Representation League was set up in 1869, and by 1874 had succeeded in getting two ex-miners elected to Parliament. These men sat with the Liberals in the House of Commons and took the Liberal Whip. By 1885, there were eleven such working-class Lib-Lab MPs in the House of Commons.

The development of unions for the unskilled, led by socialists who saw the role of unions as being wider and more political than just workers' welfare organisations, provided fresh impetus to the trade union arm of the labour movement. The decline of political radicalism towards the end of the nineteenth century left a void which came to be filled by socialism.

> "The decline of the Radicals was not due to the misadventures or treacheries of a few leaders. It was in part due to the faults of the programme itself ... the levying of 'ransom' on capitalists is possible only so long as they are willing and able to pay it. But it was due also to the emergence of a new movement which demanded and promised a great deal more than the Radicals had ever done—the Socialist Movement."[6]

What were the major elements of this "Socialist Movement" which gave birth to the Labour Party at the turn of the century? Clearly the unions, as has been shown, were a major element, but there were other organisations, groups and individuals who can legitimately claim a place in the history and traditions of the Party, notably the Social Democratic Federation, the Fabian Society and Keir Hardie.

The Social Democratic Federation (SDF)

Founded in 1881 as the 'Democratic Federation', it became the SDF in 1884.
Leaders: *HM Hyndman*, Old Etonian and London Stockbroker who wrote the classic *England for All* which tried to popularise the ideas of Karl Marx; *William Morris*, poet; *HH Champion*, former military man; and *RB Cunninghame Graham*, Scottish laird and Liberal Crofters MP.

The SDF was the first socialist body in Britain since the phenomenon of Owenism in the 1830s. Its ideology was Marxist and its objective was to build a mass working-class political party. Hyndman and his colleagues in the SDF actually fixed the year of 1889, the centenary of the French Revolution, as the beginning of "the complete International Social Revolution." The SDF was temporarily important in the labour movement during the 1880s, although it was dogged by internal disputes. Fairly early on, Morris quarrelled with Hyndman. Morris left the SDF along with other prominent personalities to form the Socialist League.

During the eighties and early nineties, the SDF attempted to organise the unemployed. Some SDF activists even went as far as drilling the unemployed. For many socialists in the labour movement, the SDF's revolutionary line was far too extreme. The SDF, however, argued that socialists in the mainstream labour movement were weak and indecisive.

By the end of the decade when trade revived, the SDF went into decline. Although it failed to gain any real electoral support, the SDF contributed much to the development of socialist thought.

New Unionism in Action

The London Dock Strike 12 August–14 September 1889

DOCK LABOURERS were unorganised, unskilled, casual workers whose job was to load and unload the ships in Britain's ports. The chance of getting work was affected by the weather and the time of year. There were always more men than there was work available. In 1888, the socialist Ben Tillet founded the Tea Operatives and General Labourers Union. It was not very successful. In the same year, Tillet led a strike at Tillbury Docks which failed due to lack of interest from the dockers themselves. Tillet and his colleagues, however, took heart from the success of the match girls' and gas workers' strikes.

MAIN CAUSE

The immediate cause of the 1889 strike centred around the unloading of a cargo vessel 'The Lady Armstrong' at West India Dock. Once the ship's cargo was unloaded, a dispute arose between the dockers and the Dock Superintendent over bonus payments. Will Thorne, leader of the gas workers, spoke to the dockers, urging them to refuse to work. They did this, and the strike had begun.

With help from Tillet's union, the strikers demands were:
- Pay to be raised to 6d (2$\frac{1}{2}$p) per hour (the 'Docker's Tanner').
- The minimum length of employment should be 4 hours.
- Overtime should be paid at 8d (3p) per hour.
- The contract system should be abolished.

COURSE OF THE STRIKE

With only seven shillings and sixpence (37$\frac{1}{2}$p) in his union's funds, Tillet first of all set about persuading other dock workers to join the strike. Eventually, the strike spread throughout the London docks, involving boiler-makers, stevedores, coal heavers, ballastmen, lightermen, painters and carpenters. The problem of financial relief for the families of striking dockers was tackled through collections, and morale was maintained by organising daily marches with banners and bands. Money came in from a wide spectrum of the community, including a donation from fellow dockers in Australia. The strike committee, comprising Ben Tillet, Tom Mann, Eleanor Marx, John Burns, Harry Orbell and Henry Champion, organised what became a massive relief operation.

Eight relief centres were established and it is estimated that at the height of the strike 25,000 people were being fed per day.

A Mediation Committee was eventually set up by the Lord Mayor of London, comprising the Lord Mayor and his Deputy, the Bishop of London, Sidney Buxton MP, Sir John Lubbock (President of the London Chamber of Commerce) and Cardinal Manning.

After protracted negotiations between the dockers and the employers, an agreement was signed on 14 September ending the strike. The dockers won their demand for 6d per hour, with 8d per hour for overtime.

EFFECTS OF THE STRIKE

The victory of the dock workers proved that unskilled and unorganised groups of workers could win concessions from their employers. Secondly, the early victories of the 'new unions' led to a rapid growth of membership. In addition, previously unorganised groups of workers began to form unions. Most historians agree that the success of New Unionism between 1884 and 1892 was based on low unemployment, good militant leadership, the strike weapon, police tolerance of vigorous picketing and the failure of the employers to unite in opposition.

However, as the economic boom of the late eighties and early nineties came to an end, so did the growth of New Unionism as the figures in Table 2.1 illustrate. Nevertheless, this period is significant in the history of the labour movement because it allowed individual socialists and early socialist organisations to carry their message to the working class in a practical way by providing leadership and organisation where none had previously existed. Consequently, the political arm of the labour movement came into being.

"The expansion of socialist influence in the working-class movement represented by the formation of the ILP, was very largely a result of the activity of socialists in the trade union explosion. The subsequent development of the new socialist party however, owed as much to the limitations and failure of the New Unionism as to its successes."
(James Hinton *Labour and Socialism* page 58.)

The Fabian Society

Founded 1884.
Leaders: *Sydney* and *Beatrice Webb, George Bernard Shaw, HG Wells, Frank Podmore.*

This small socialist society, whose middle-class intellectual membership came from around the London area, played a key role in developing the ideology of British socialism. Originally the word 'Fabian' was used by Podmore when describing the strategy which he believed socialists should adopt. He said that "For the right moment you must wait, as Fabius did most patiently when warring against Hannibal, though many censured his delays: but when the time comes you must strike hard, as Fabius did, or your waiting will be in vain and fruitless".[7]

In the early days the Fabians opposed the more revolutionary views of the SDF, choosing to concentrate on the production of tracts and essays, which have become a notable contribution to socialist thought.

In 1888, a series of lectures entitled 'The Basis and Prospects of Socialism' were given in London's Radical/Liberal clubs. These were published in 1889 as *The Fabian Essays in Socialism*. Pelling, the historian, describes these essays as

Sydney and Beatrice Webb photographed at their home in Hampshire.

"the most important literary product of the Society, or for that matter the indigenous socialist movement as a whole."

The conclusions of these essays are as follows:

- Webb argued that the ideas of socialism were already winning, and that socialism meant that there should be public control of the means of production.

- William Clark said that Britain would follow the USA in the creation of large industrial combines and the existence of these would make an easy transfer to state control.

- Graham Wallas and Annie Besant looked to a decentralised socialist Britain, stressing the implementation of a socialist programme through local government.

- George Bernard Shaw emphasised that the extension of democracy would advance the cause of socialism. He stressed a gradual approach towards ending private property with owners receiving compensation.

Like the SDF, the Fabians never had a large membership, numbers being in the hundreds rather than in the thousands. Nevertheless, the society had a profound influ-ence on the history and development of the British labour movement.

"... it was not for their immediate political tactics, but for their success in formulating a long-term evolutionary programme, that the Fabians were to be important in the eventual foundation of the Labour Party."[8]

James Keir Hardie

"The major achievement of Keir Hardie was to bridge the gap between official politics and the trade unions, and to 'politicise' the labour movement."[9]

Hardie was born at Legbrannock, near Holytown in Lanarkshire in 1856, the illegitimate son of Mary Kerr who later married David Hardie, a ship's carpenter. As the eldest child in the family, he started work at the age of eight, first as a message boy then as a trapper down the mines. He received his education at night school.

As a young man, he became a strong temperance supporter and joined the Evangelical Union, despite the fact that his family was not at all religious. Gradually he became involved in trade union activities where, in common with most people, his political sympathies lay with the Liberal Party.

Hardie was sacked from his local pit for trying to organise trade union activities. He earned a living for four years as a local correspondent with the *Cumnock Advertiser* while continuing with his trade union activities. By 1887, he had succeeded in setting up the Ayrshire Miners Union and the Scottish Miners Federation.

During these years, Hardie read the works of Marx, William Morris, HH Hyndman and Henry George. He visited London in 1887 with a delegation of miners. Here he made contact with socialists and attended several SDF meetings. In the end, he rejected the revolutionary class war analysis of the SDF.

"His views had already developed by way of Henry George from Liberalism to Socialism; but these views were assimilated into the background of his own life and experience, which was something that the London Socialist could not share."[10]

In the autumn of 1887, Hardie was adopted as the Parliamentary candidate for North Ayrshire on behalf of the miners, and in early 1888 when the mid-Lanark seat became vacant he stood at the by-election. Despite vigorous campaigning, and standing on a platform of representation for the working man, he came bottom of the poll with 617 votes out of 7,000. In 1888 the power of the existing parties was still too strong, even for a local candidate.

Convinced of the need for a separate political party with a distinctive socialist identity, Hardie and others formed the Scottish Labour Party in 1889. At the same time he resigned from the Liberal Party.

At the 1892 General Election Hardie was elected as the independent MP for the constituency of West Ham, having been adopted as a candidate by a local Radical club. At the same time, John Burns was elected as MP for the constituency of Battersea. These two men were the first Labour MPs, marking a significant milestone in the

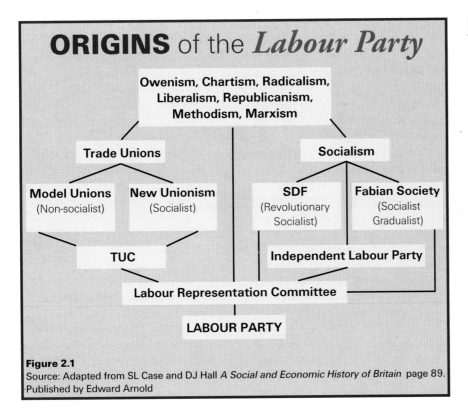

ORIGINS of the *Labour Party*

Owenism, Chartism, Radicalism, Liberalism, Republicanism, Methodism, Marxism

Trade Unions

Socialism

Model Unions (Non-socialist)

New Unionism (Socialist)

SDF (Revolutionary Socialist)

Fabian Society (Socialist Gradualist)

TUC

Independent Labour Party

Labour Representation Committee

LABOUR PARTY

Figure 2.1
Source: Adapted from SL Case and DJ Hall *A Social and Economic History of Britain* page 89. Published by Edward Arnold

history of the labour movement. In 1893, Hardie was instrumental in forming the Independent Labour Party (ILP) which, in 1900, became part of the Labour Representation Committee which became the Labour Party as we know it today.

By the early 1890s, it was becoming clear that there was a need to bring the various traditions and organisations of British socialism together. Keir Hardie called for such a meeting at the TUC in 1892. At what became the founding conference of the Independent Labour Party at Bradford in 1893, the delegates adopted a gradualist programme of social reform which sought to win the eight hour day, state benefits for old age and sickness, free education and the abolition of all indirect taxes.

> "Proclaiming a Socialist system as their objective, both the Fabian Society and the Independent Labour Party set out in practice to get not Socialism, but social changes pointing in a Socialist direction."[11]

Neither the gradualists, nor the SDF, were satisfied with the birth of the ILP. The Fabians tried and failed to persuade the TUC to set

up its own Labour Party, and in the short-term saw the future of socialism in the Liberal Party. The SDF believed that the ILP would water down socialist principles in order to gain votes and funding from the unions. Unlike the established political parties, the ILP did not have a centralised organisation, which was a major weakness. In addition, it was always short of funds as local branches regularly failed to pay their subscriptions to the national headquarters which employed one secretary and an assistant. The ILP appealed to the unions for financial support, but in the early 1890s the movement was still dominated by the skilled unions whose leaders supported the Lib-Lab perspective.

At the 1895 General Election, the ILP put up twenty eight candidates, none of whom was successful, Hardie himself losing his seat at West Ham. However, the ILP did have some success in the 1890s in local elections and by the turn of the century could claim one hundred and six local councillors and a good representation on School Boards and Poor Law Boards of Guardians.

BIRTH OF THE LABOUR PARTY

Towards the turn of the century, changes in the trade union movement itself, added to economic uncertainty and a growing realisation that the Conservative and Liberal Parties had little to offer the poor, turned many skilled workers in the direction of socialism. In addition, the employers' 'counterattack' of the late 1890s persuaded the unions that a political defence through Parliament was needed. Accordingly, at the 1899 TUC, the Railway Servants Union proposed a conference of all "cooperative, socialistic, trade unions and other working organisations ... to devise ways and means for securing the return of an increased number of Labour Members to the next Parliament."

The historic Conference (now regarded as the birthplace of the Labour Party) took place on 27 February 1900 in London. At the Conference the SDF called for the new organisation to have clearly defined socialist aims, whereas those of the Lib-Lab viewpoint supported more limited aims. The ILP took a middle course.

The Conference accepted a resolution from Hardie which proposed that:

- A distinct Labour group in Parliament be set up.
- Such a group would have its own Whips and distinct policies.
- It would legislate "in the direct interests of labour."

Thus, the Labour Representation Committee (LRC) was set up. It became simply the Labour Party in 1906. The LRC had an Executive Committee of twelve, seven from the unions, one from the Fabian Society, and two each from the ILP and the SDF. From the outset, the LRC was going to be dominated by the unions.

> "The foundation of the LRC was a triumph for the advocates of independent labour representation, but it did not overnight transform the character of working-class politics."[12]

The LRC was now, however, a distinctive political party. Each group put forward its own candidates at elections and was responsible for their expenses. The LRC had no national party organisation because it was a coalition of organisations which already existed. Individuals became LRC members by joining an organisation like the ILP or the SDF. Nevertheless, the LRC was the base from which a national Labour Party could be formed in the future.

THE LABOUR MOVEMENT 1900–1918

As we have seen, in the year 1900 many of the different strands within the labour movement came together with the formation of the LRC. However, the years 1900–18 were far from easy for the labour movement.

On the industrial front, the ability of the unions to strike was attacked in the courts when a legal precedent was set in the Taff Vale Case of 1901.

The Taff Vale Railway Company of South Wales sued the Amalgamated Society of Railway Servants for damages caused by a strike. The case went to the House of Lords and, against expectations, the company won damages of £23,000 from the union. This was a crushing blow to all trade unions since it meant that strike action would be impractical if their funds were not protected by law. Nevertheless, while the Taff Vale case limited union freedom of action, it unexpectedly helped the LRC. Unions which had failed to affiliate in 1900 now rushed to do so. By 1903 individual membership had doubled, bringing in workers from the older skilled unions as well as from the new general unions.

Politically, Labour made some notable gains. Victories at by-elections in 1902–3 increased Labour's representation in Parliament from two to five. However, the LRC's candidates only did well in areas where the Liberals did badly or

even withdrew their candidate. With a general election looming, both the LRC and the Liberals realised that it would be electoral suicide to fight each other in certain constituencies. In the light of this, the parties concluded an electoral pact by which the LRC was unopposed by the Liberals in thirty constituencies.

In the 1906 General Election, the LRC fielded fifty candidates and twenty nine were elected. Added to the thirteen miners MPs, four unaffiliated trade union MPs and seven Lib-Lab MPs, Labour's total representation in the House of Commons increased to fifty three.

Although the Liberal Party had won a crushing victory, Labour was now in a stronger position than ever before to influence events. Thus, the years 1906–14 saw Labour cooperating with the Liberals to bring into being the social legislation which is generally regarded as having laid the foundations of the modern welfare state. In addition, Labour was able to persuade the Liberals to pass the *Trade Disputes Act* of 1906, which benefited the trade unions by setting aside the Taff Vale judgment.

Between 1906 and 1914, the Labour leadership concentrated the Party's efforts on building up its strength across the country. This policy brought considerable success. In 1909 the Miners Federation affiliated to the Labour Party, immediately bringing in an additional sixteen former Lib-Lab MPs.

During this period finance became a problem for Labour and progress was hindered for a time by the Osborne Judgment of 1909. When a union affiliated to the Labour Party, it used part of a member's weekly dues to help fund the Party. This was known as 'the political levy'. WV Osborne, a member of the Railman's Union and a Liberal, objecting to his union's support for Labour, took his complaint to court. In 1909 the case reached the House of Lords, where it was de-

cided that, under the Trade Union Acts, unions could not use their funds for political purposes. As a result, the Labour Party was faced with financial disaster. It was partly saved by the *Parliament Act* of 1911 which made provision for the payment of MPs. The Osborne Judgment was finally reversed in 1913. The *Trade Union Act* of that year permitted a political levy to be charged by unions if a majority of members agreed and so long as those who objected were allowed to 'contract out'.

Many socialists, both inside and outside Parliament, were far from happy with Labour's progress at this time. The ILP tried to get the Party to incorporate into the constitution resolutions stating that socialism was the ultimate goal. This move was not successful before the war. Socialists were also sceptical of the Liberal welfare reforms which Labour had supported. These reforms, they asserted, did little for the poor, and the welfare bureaucracy which was set up only rewarded the 'deserving', while punishing the 'undeserving' poor.

SYNDICALISM: THE RADICAL SOCIALIST ALTERNATIVE

Socialists within the labour movement wanted more rapid change. They pointed to the failure of Labour to win any of the fourteen by-elections contested between 1910 and 1914 as evidence that a more radical approach was required. For people like Tom Mann and Ben Tillet, and Scottish socialists such as William Gallacher, the answer to the problems of the working class lay in Syndicalism, a brand of radical socialism which advocated workers' control of industry and direct action by the unions.

"… Syndicalism had come into Scotland with the formation in 1903 of the Socialist Labour Party, a breakaway from the SDF which took away the majority of the Scottish branches. Syndicalism was basically a plan for turning trade unions from organs of defence into organs to attack capitalism. The trade unions

Number of Workers on Strike 1909–1914

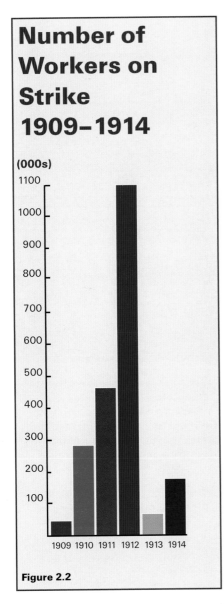

(000s)

Figure 2.2

action in 1912. In the same year 850,000 miners stayed out on strike for five weeks. Government intervention eventually guaranteed the miners a minimum wage. Also in 1912, three rail unions combined to form the National Union of Railwaymen, and the following year the 'Triple Alliance' of transport, mining and rail unions was formed.

Unfortunately for the syndicalists, the three unions remained separate entities, but they did agree to act together in presenting their demands to employers simultaneously, and to go on strike together if necessary.

The coming of war in 1914 ended the unrest, but the period 1910–14 did demonstrate the impatience of many socialists in the trade union movement with the Labour Party in Parliament. In its own way, each arm of the labour movement had achieved significant advances for the working class. However, on the eve of war in 1914 Labour was still not a comprehensive working-class political movement. It had failed to organise two significant elements of the working class—women and the poor. It was still in a minority position in Parliament and, more seriously, it believed that the working class was not yet strong enough to bring about radical change in society.

THE LABOUR MOVEMENT AND THE WAR

When war broke out in August 1914, the labour movement was initially divided. The movement as a whole supported the war, but the ILP took an anti-war stance. With pacifists and revolutionaries in its ranks, it was in a difficult position. Ramsay MacDonald, a member of the ILP and chairman of the Parliamentary Labour Party, opposed the war. He was removed from his position and was replaced by Arthur Henderson. Eventually, the ILP leadership resolved its dilemma and joined the coalition government.

Keir Hardie's anti-war sentiment stemmed from both his Christianity and his socialism. In the last years of his life he argued vigorously against the war fever which he saw gripping the country in 1914. His last article for the *Labour Leader*, shortly before his death, vividly portrayed his despair.

"When a set of selfish and incompetent statesmen have plunged nations into shedding each others' blood, it is the worker who is called upon to line the trenches; to murder his fellow worker with whom he has not, and never had, any quarrel; it is the worker who is commanded, under the penalty of being branded a traitor, to carry woe and desolation into the hearts of womenfolk and children."[14]

Overall, the labour movement supported the war, some sections with 'jingoistic fervour', other sections giving just enough support to demonstrate their patriotism. During the war the TUC called an industrial truce with the employers, accepting that they would have to give up many hard-won rights. The TUC accepted:

- Dilution of labour—the use of unskilled men and women in place of skilled workers.
- The provisions of the *1915 Munitions Act* which effectively reduced the possibility of strike action.
- Compulsory arbitration of disputes.
- Direction of labour.

Number of Working Days Lost by Strike Action 1909–14

Year	Days Lost
1909	660,000
1910	8,796,000
1911	4,974,000
1912	34,226,000
1913	3,937,000
1914	5,154,000

Table 2.2

were to take over industry and run it themselves in the interests of the workers, bypassing orthodox political action which was regarded as worse than useless ... It was hostile to trade or craft unions, and wanted the workers to organise in industrial unions, ultimately to be joined in one big union which would be the instrument of social revolution."[13]

The years 1910–14, as well as being years of general social unrest and economic uncertainty, were a time of trade union militancy and unprecedented industrial unrest, as Figure 2.2 and Table 2.2 demonstrate.

The syndicalists aimed at creating large industrial unions. In 1910 Ben Tillet founded the Transport Workers Federation, which was unsuccessfully involved in strike

A shell filling factory during World War I.

Before the war, it was believed that workers in South Wales and on Clydeside would actively oppose any conflict. However, when war came, opposition was confined, in all but a few cases, to the effects of the war on workers, rather than to the war itself.

On Clydeside, socialist activists who were disillusioned with the ILP came to dominate the unofficial Clyde Workers Committee. Some members of the Committee, notably John Maclean, Harry McShane and William Gallacher, were Marxists who wanted to stop the war. For them, the vital struggle was not for better conditions, or against dilution of labour for which the Clyde Shop Stewards Committee was fighting, but the war itself. Others, such as David Kirkwood, were more concerned about defending the position of skilled workers.

In South Wales the miners came out on strike in 1915 and, refusing arbitration, they only went back to work when Lloyd George, at that time Minister of Munitions, gave in to their demands. In Sheffield, the shop stewards led by JT Murphy brought the engineers out on strike to prevent the conscription of engineers into the forces.

The strike succeeded in temporarily winning exemption for some skilled men. Most of the industrial unrest took place in 1915 and 1916. The government became sufficiently alarmed at the situation to order the arrest of members of this Clyde Workers Committee. John Maclean was arrested in 1917 and sentenced to five years in jail. His colleague, Harry McShane, described Maclean's trial in his book *No Mean Fighter*.

"... John Maclean turned his trial into a political forum. He conducted his own defence and spoke for over an hour in his final summing up. He said: 'I am not here to be accused. I am here as the accuser of capitalism, dripping with blood from head to foot.' He indicted international capitalism for what it had done in the war, and was preparing to do against the Russian Revolution. But he also attacked those workers who had been prepared to give record output for the war."[15]

The pre-1914 expectation of war resistance did not become a reality.

"The Clyde workers' movement, and the Shop Stewards movement in England even more so, were about resistance to the effects of war (dilution, wages, rents), not the war itself."[16]

"The most militant workers were often also the most patriotic—South Wales and Clydeside, the two centres of industrial discontent, also provided the highest proportion in the country of recruits to the army."[17]

Although socialists like Murphy, Gallacher and Kirkwood were always a minority in the labour movement, they are important because their views represent a continuing strand in socialist tradition. They saw the Workers Committees acting as the vanguard of socialism, gradually undermining and defeating capitalist control of industry.

In 1916, the Labour Party and trade unionists were brought into the coalition government. Arthur Henderson became Minister of Education, John Hodge (Secretary of the Steel Smelters Union) became Minister of Labour and George Barnes (Secretary of the Engineers Union) became Minister of Pensions. As part of the government, these men argued for the nationalisation of key industries in the post-war period.

Changing Britain 1850–1979

LABOUR 1918–22: FROM PARTY OF PROTEST TO OFFICIAL OPPOSITION

The years 1918–22 were watershed years for the Labour Party. Prior to 1914, "it was a specialised interest group: it represented not the nation or a cross-section of the nation, but the trade unions, to which less than half of Britain's working population belonged".[18]

By 1922, the Labour Party had a national organisation, owned several local and one national daily newspaper (*Daily Herald*), had polled almost 30% in a general election and was the official opposition in Parliament. The following section examines some of the factors which contributed to Labour's success. During the war, the Labour Party produced two documents, which were of great importance for the future: the *Labour Party Constitution* and *Labour and the New Social Order*. From its inception the Labour Party had been at a disadvantage because it was a federation of local societies. *The Labour Party Constitution*, written by Arthur Henderson and Sydney Webb, changed the situation. They produced a document of values, principles, rules and procedures to which all Party members would have to agree. It was accepted by the 1918 Party Conference.

Clause IV outlined the socialist aims of the Labour Party:

> "to secure for the workers by hand or by brain the full fruits of their industry and the most equitable distribution thereof that may be possible, upon the basis of the common ownership of the means of production, distribution and exchange, and the best obtainable system of popular administration and control of each industry or service."

A new national Party organisation was set up to recruit individual members who could identify with the constitution and programme of the Labour Party.

Labour and the New Social Order This was the title of the Labour

---

WORLD WAR I AND ITS AFTERMATH

THE EFFECTS ON THE LABOUR MOVEMENT UP TO 1922

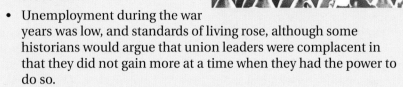

THE WAR strengthened and changed the labour movement in the following ways.

- Trade union membership almost doubled between 1914 and 1920.
- The percentage of unionised women workers increased from 9% to 24%.
- Unemployment during the war years was low, and standards of living rose, although some historians would argue that union leaders were complacent in that they did not gain more at a time when they had the power to do so.
- Employers' recognition of trade unions increased.
- The experience of war served to draw the working class together as never before.
- The achievement of a foothold in government served to enhance a general mood of assertiveness in the labour movement.
- The ILP lost a lot of its influence within the Labour Party because of its opposition to the war.

Party's programme published in 1918. It aimed to broaden Labour's appeal to the new electorate enfranchised by the 1918 *Reform Act*. Like the constitution, this historic document set Labour on the path of socialism, committing it to policies for:

- The nationalisation of land, and the fuel and transport industries.
- A planned economy.
- Full employment.
- The provision of adequate social welfare.

Following the armistice in November 1918, Labour withdrew from the coalition, in order to fight the ensuing election as an independent party.

On the industrial front, after the end of the war, the country enjoyed a brief period of economic prosperity. This lasted from 1918 until the spring of 1920. During this period, the Miners Federation made demands for a six hour day, nationalisation of the mines, and a

30% increase in pay. To avoid a strike, the Coalition Government appointed the Sankey Commission to investigate the industry. The Commission's report was rejected by the government which at that time was dominated by the Conservatives. It had recommended pay increases for the miners and nationalisation of the pits. By 1920, the railwaymen and the miners had been on strike. In addition, the dockers had been awarded higher wages after a Commission of Inquiry. In Scotland, the so-called '40 hours strike' in 1919 had led to troops and armoured cars being deployed on the streets of Glasgow.

By the time the slump came in 1920 the government, in anticipation of industrial conflict, had already made preparations. The *Police Act* of 1919 prevented the Police Federation from associating with other unions or the TUC, and the *Emergency Powers Act* of 1920 gave the government sweeping powers to deal with all-out strikes.

In early 1921, unemployment had increased to over two million with some areas, notably South Wales, Lancashire, Northeast England and Clydeside, being particularly badly affected, due to their reliance on traditional industries which could not now compete with foreign goods. The coal industry, still run by the government, was particularly badly hit by the recession.

The government saw a solution to the problem in returning the pits to their pre-war private owners, a bitter blow to the miners who wanted nationalisation. While accepting the return of their assets, the owners stated that wage reductions would be necessary. When the leaders of the Miners Federation refused to accept these pay cuts, a coal strike began on 1 April 1921.

The miners called on other members of the Triple Alliance for support and a General Strike was organised, originally for 12 April. The government intervened at this point and the leaders of the Triple Alliance negotiated with Lloyd George. Hodge, the secretary of the Miners Union, accepted a deal by which the government would subsidise the miners' wages at their old rate while negotiations continued with the mine owners, but it was rejected by his union executive. Meantime, the leaders of the rail and transport unions used Hodge's acceptance of Lloyd George's offer as an excuse to call off the threatened General Strike, only hours before it was due to start on the new date of 15 April.

Thus the miners were left to fight alone and were eventually forced back to work on much less favourable terms than they had been initially offered. On that occasion the power of the Triple Alliance turned into a debacle. The date of 15 April 1921 became known as 'Black Friday', a day in trade union history now associated with betrayal, although in reality it was more a failure of the three leaders of the Triple Alliance to work out properly an effective mechanism for their alliance.

In order to prevent the same scenario repeating itself, the TUC took a hand in matters and formed a General Council, whose aim was to coordinate the labour movement's 'industrial muscle', thus avoiding the future isolation of a single union in an industrial dispute.

On the political front, the Labour Party fought the 1918 General Election against the coalition on a socialist platform. Fielding 360 candidates, it gained 2,385,472 votes, 22.2% of the total vote, and won 63 seats. One disappointing feature of the election was the failure of leading Party figures such as Arthur Henderson, Ramsay MacDonald and Sydney Webb to win seats. Nevertheless, Labour had, for the first time, contested an election without the cushion of a pact with the Liberals and had increased its representation in Parliament. As the reforms in national Party organisation, linked to the growth of active local constituency associations, began to take hold, so Labour was able to increase its share of the vote throughout the early 1920s.

The 1922 General Election saw Labour massively increase its Parliamentary representation to 142 and increase its vote to 4,237,769, a share of 29.2%. Ramsay MacDonald was re-elected to Parliament, and was elected by the Labour MPs as Party Leader. He took his seat in the House of Commons as official Leader of the Opposition.

The Movements for Women's Suffrage 1850–1928

THE STRUGGLE FOR women's rights and the development of a feminist ideology have a long history. In 1792 a book by Mary Wollstonecraft became the first work to be published on the subject. In her book, *Vindication of the Rights of Women*, she clearly challenged a society dominated by men by arguing that if women were endowed with the gift of reason, they should be treated equally with men. Such radical ideas did little to improve the position of women at the time. The social and economic effects of the Industrial Revolution proved to be a more potent force affecting the role and status of women.

The Social and Economic Position of Women in 1850

Industrialisation fundamentally changed the importance of women and their economic worth. It meant the end of the home-based cottage system of manufacture, centred around the family unit, where women played a central role. Working-class women now had to go 'out' to work in the factory, while at the same time attending to their domestic duties of wife and mother after a long day of drudgery. Some married women remained at home to do paid work such as sewing or childminding. This work was entirely different from the family craft work which was done before the Industrial Revolution. Payment was extremely poor, hours were long and the end result was mere subsistence for the family.

As the process of industrialisation accelerated into the nineteenth century, there emerged a new entrepreneurial middle class of businessmen, professionals and rich landowners. Their values were founded firmly on the rocks of hard work, thrift and the sanctity of the family. By the 1850s, the stereotypical image of the family in Britain was very much that of the middle-class family, with the male as breadwinner/decision maker/protector, and the wife as carer and provider for the husband and children. This image was reinforced by the religious and cultural values of the day.

Lack of education was a major handicap to the progress of women in the first half of the nineteenth century. For the majority of women who belonged to the working class, there was little chance of any education. The role of working-class women and girls was to work, either in the factory or at home. Education for them was seen as being unnecessary and by some as being dangerous. The conventional wisdom of the day was to encourage working-class women to be content and to behave themselves in the station of life in which providence had placed them.

Prior to 1850, little real attempt was made to give middle- and upper-class girls any serious education. In most cases, girls were brought up at home where they were educated by a governess. They learned to read, knit, sew, play the piano, paint in water colours and speak a little elementary French. Serious educational study which might lead to future employment was very rare. The first duty of a well-to-do girl was to get married. Education served only as a means to that end. Nevertheless, there were notable exceptions to the norm in the first half of the nineteenth century. These women of ability and independence were all from the middle and upper classes and in various ways attempted to assert their independence. Notable examples are Elizabeth Fry who worked for prison reform, Mary Carpenter who founded the first reform school for girls, and distinguished novelists such as the Brontë sisters and George Eliot.

The position of women around 1850 is well described by the historian Angela Holdsworth.

> "As many manual and professional jobs were closed to them it was a struggle for single women to support themselves. All they could

hope for was marriage to a good man and a lifetime of keeping his house and rearing his children. Once married, women's property and income became their husband's by law. Circumstances forced them to depend on the goodwill of a father, husband or brother. Independence, a fulfilling career, even a decent job were not for them. Women were not allowed to vote, nor to stand for Parliament, nor to hold any kind of public office. By necessity, their horizons were limited to their own private world at home."[1]

SOCIAL AND ECONOMIC CHANGE: WOMEN 1850–1914

'The Feminist Movement' or the 'Women's Movement' is the name used by many historians to refer to the efforts of women in the nineteenth century to improve their rights in law and society. Nineteenth century feminists had many aims: they wanted to train for work to enable them to take jobs outside the home; they wanted equal educational opportunities with men; they wanted equal rights with men in law; and they wanted equal voting rights with men.

The 'Feminist Movement' had no real organisation until the early twentieth century, and had no real starting date. The leaders were women from the upper and middle classes who had the material resources and sufficient leisure time to enable them to pursue their various causes. Their aims were wider than simply advancing the cause of women's rights. What they were attempting to do was to put right some of the many general social problems of the day.

It would be incorrect to attribute the success of the various feminist causes solely to outstanding female leaders, of whom there were so many. While people like Florence Nightingale, Josephine Butler and the Pankhursts played key roles in bringing about change, it is important to note that their efforts were undertaken against the backdrop of a society in which

WOMEN *in Employment*
1851

OCCUPATION	NUMBER EMPLOYED
Domestic Service	1,135,000
Textiles	635,000
Clothing Manufacture	491,000
Agriculture	229,000
Professional	106,000
Food, Drink, Tobacco	53,000
Metalwork	36,000
Paper, Printing	16,000
Bricks, Pottery etc.	15,000
Mining, Quarrying	11,000
Wood Furniture	8,000
Skins, Leather	5,000
Chemicals, Soap	4,000
Others	88,000

Table 3.1

there were fundamental forces of social, economic and political change at work between the 1850s and 1918.

From the middle of the nineteenth century to the end of the Great War, the cause of women's rights made progress, despite the fact that Britain was a male dominated society with a woman on the throne (Queen Victoria) who was little disposed to the many feminist causes. The period to 1918 saw significant changes in the balance of power between men and women in the areas of employment and trade union membership, marriage and the family, education and working rights.

Employment and Trade Union Membership

As has already been stated, the idea that a woman's place is in the home is firmly rooted in Victorian middle- and upper-class society. This idealised picture of women in Victorian Britain is far from the truth, and is a measure of the hypocrisy which existed at the time. The first proper census, taken in 1851, revealed the extent of women's employment outside the home. Almost 29% of women of working age were in some form of

paid employment. In addition, women made up 33% of the nation's total workforce.

The figures in Table 3.1 show that approximately 1.14 million women were in domestic service. They worked in the homes of the middle and upper classes expending a vast amount of physical energy in order to maintain their employers in a lifestyle which was alien to their own personal experience. Domestic service was the main form of women's work. Most servants 'lived in', worked long hours, and had severe restrictions placed on their own social lives by their employers. Where families employed male servants (a sign of great affluence), women were paid less than their male counterparts for doing the same work. The wages recommended for female domestic servants in 1861 are shown in Table 3.2. Low pay was a problem for most women in work. Women generally earned half or less than half of a man's wage for doing the same job and this picture was common to most areas of employment.

Low wages were often the least of women's concerns in the industrial workplace. Throughout the nineteenth and into the twentieth century, they endured the worst ills of the factory system such as long hours and poor conditions in terms of light, heat, ventilation and protection from dangerous and toxic substances and machinery. In addition, they ran the risk of sexual assault from male supervisors. Many women were even worse off than those in the factories. Pay and conditions in 'sweat shops' and in the 'sweated trades' were even worse than in regular factory work. Sweat shops were small workshops where women were employed doing jobs such as making hats and jewel boxes for very low wages. The sweated trades were those where women worked from their own homes for a middleman. Those women were paid according to the amount of work they did or the goods produced. Woman in both areas of employment were ruthlessly exploited in Victorian times and beyond.

Although the aforementioned patterns of work continued into late Victorian times, changes in the pattern of the nation's economic life meant new forms of employment for working-class women. Seebohm Rowntree in *Poverty, a Study of Town Life, 1901*, noted that in York, "The number of girls who enter domestic service, except as nurses, is small and decreasing. They prefer to become dressmakers, shop assistants or clerks, or find employment in the confectionery factories".[2]

Towards the end of the nineteenth century, as Britain evolved into an advanced industrial society, the numbers of jobs available to non-manual workers increased. The people to fill these jobs came mainly from those who had benefited from the increased educational opportunities after 1870. In the years between 1861 and 1911, there was a 307% increase in the employment of women in non-manual work.

Technology opened up the way for women to make a career in office work. The development of shorthand and the invention of the typewriter transformed office work from a task to which young men were apprenticed for a number of years, to one in which much less training was required and which was therefore deemed to be suitable for women. As office technology developed, increasing numbers of women were sought to operate the new calculating and duplicating machines. Employers considered that women were more suitable than men for the new keyboard skills which the modern office demanded. In reality, the truth was that rather than being better at office work than men, women were preferred by employers because they could be paid less. In 1909, 97% of women in office work earned less than men. Furthermore, many areas of clerical work, and indeed other forms of non-manual work for women, operated a marriage bar which meant that when a woman married she had to leave her job. In the civil service,

the marriage bar was written into the law, underlining the legal and institutional discrimination against women in Victorian and Edwardian times. To get round the marriage bar, some women concealed their marriage from their employers for fear of losing their job.

Nevertheless, office work was a much sought after form of employment for women, being seen as more respectable than factory work and offering a better quality of life.

While the field of women's employment was undergoing change in the latter decades of the nineteenth century, it was also clear that the attitudes of women towards pay and conditions were also changing. These attitudes were, in turn, influenced by changes taking place both in industry and in society in general which were to affect the lives of working women.

Trade unions became legal in 1824 and were a vehicle through which women were able to work to improve their overall status, pay and conditions in the workplace. There was, however, no great influx of women into trade unions until the 1870s. This was due to the fact that women had the double burden of work and home to bear, the relatively unskilled nature of their employment, and most importantly, the opposition of men to women union members.

Men opposed female union membership because, it was argued, the wages earned by a man were used to support an entire household. If women worked and became trade union members, it would destroy this argument and undermine efforts to secure higher wages for men. Female union membership was also opposed as men saw increased numbers of women on the labour market as a threat to their jobs. Yet in spite of these impediments, women's trade union membership increased dramatically between 1870 and 1914.

AVERAGE WAGES COMPARED

Occupation	Men	Women
Thimblemakers (Brass) 1851	15–21s per week	7–9s per week
Surface Workers in Tin Mines*	2s per day	1s per day
Tailoring Machinists*	22s 6d per week	11s per week
Office Work*	£2 per week	£1 per week
Domestic Service*	£35 per year	£10–£17 per year
Carpet Weavers, 1890s	£1 15s per week	£1 per week
Civil Service Typists 1914	£3 per week	£1 per week

*1880s

Table 3.2
Source: *Votes for Women* by Diane Atkinson. Published by Cambridge Educational 1988.

WOMEN in Unions

Year	Number
1877	21,085
1886	36,900
1892	142,000
1913	433,000
1914	437,000

Table 3.3

It is not difficult to understand why female trade union membership increased during this period. As increasing numbers of women sought work, it was clear that opportunities for women were limited, and that in whatever job a woman chose to do, pay and conditions were usually worse than for men. Thus women had an equal if not greater need than men to join together and campaign for improved rights in the workplace. Although there was a strong tradition of female membership in the Lancashire Cotton Unions, overall, women were not being recruited into the individual male craft unions. Thus, until mid-century women were excluded from most general trade union activity.

The formation of the Women's Trade Union League in 1874 was an early attempt to persuade women to join or organise their own trade unions. Although the League succeeded in setting up some small unions in London, many of these failed to survive for any length of time. Nevertheless, the League did serve to raise the awareness of women to their working conditions and particularly to issues of health and safety. Trade unionism, however, failed to make any impact on domestic service.

The 1881 census revealed that more than 1.5 million women were in some form of domestic service. Attempts at forming unions for domestic service workers and those in other service industries (hotels, restaurants, etc.) failed in the nineteenth century, although it is clear

from the many accounts of 'life below stairs' that unionisation was needed. The main reasons for failure were rooted in the nature of domestic service.

➤ Women had little time off work.

➤ Women in service were isolated from each other, unlike those who worked together in factories sharing a common experience.

➤ Women in service were set against each other by the system of rank in the middle- and upper-class households. There was, therefore little chance of the domestic staff in a household uniting against their employers to secure improved pay and conditions.

Within the trade union movement women were beginning to assert themselves. In 1875, the first woman delegate attended the Trades Union Congress and by 1881 there were ten women delegates. This was an important step for women, because by attending the TUC "they staked a claim for equality with men in Union policy making and leadership."[3]

As in many other areas of life, women had to struggle for acceptance at the TUC. Some men reflected the prevailing attitudes of the day, namely that women should not be working in factories but should be at home. The nineteenth century TUC tended to have a paternalistic attitude towards women. This can be seen in the debate over the issue of protective legislation—the laws which governed the conditions under which women and children could work.

Women were overwhelmingly defeated in the TUC over the issue of protective legislation and the organisation stepped up its efforts to secure laws solely aimed at protecting women's working conditions. As a result, the Women's Trade Union League turned its attention to campaigning for the appointment of female factory

inspectors who, it was hoped, would ensure that employers complied with existing legislation. The first woman factory inspector was appointed in 1893 and subsequent reports from female inspectors brought to public attention the conditions under which women worked.

In the early years of the twentieth century, women in the trade union movement turned their attention to lobbying for protective legislation for workers (mainly women) in the sweated trades. Low pay and extremely poor conditions were still the hallmarks of this type of work, and because most of the women worked from home, it was virtually impossible for them to be organised into unions. Their case was taken up by the National Federation for Women Workers, founded in 1906, whose secretary was Mary McArthur.

To publicise conditions in the sweated trades, an exhibition was staged which shocked Edwardian public opinion and led to the formation of the Anti-Sweating League. Through the activities of the League, the *Trade Boards Act* of 1910 was passed, setting up Wages Boards, whose job was to set minimum wage levels in trades where there was no effective union organisation. Like many other pieces of well-intentioned legislation, it took some time and a good deal of struggle by trade unionists, male and female, before it became effective.

From the setting up of the Women's Trade Union League until the end of World War I, there was a good deal of debate amongst women on the question of separatism. The debate centred around the wisdom of having separate unions or sections of unions for women. In the 1870s and '80s, when opposition to female union membership amongst men was still strong, it is understandable that separatism was an attractive argument for many activists. As the trade union movement grew,

Housekeeper and domestic servants, 1886.

and with it the membership of women, separatism became less of an issue.

By 1918 there were approximately one million women trade unionists in three hundred and eighty three unions, only thirty six of which were all-female unions. Although separatism still remains an issue for some women to this day, the real struggle in the early years of the twentieth century was for pay, conditions and union membership. There is no doubt that between 1850 and the outbreak of World War I, women workers had achieved great improvements in their pay and conditions, but by comparison with men they still lagged far behind in those areas. For Mary McArthur the crux of the matter centred around union membership when she said, "Women are unorganised because they are badly paid, and poorly paid because they are unorganised".[4]

Marriage and the Family

In the middle of the nineteenth century, Queen Victoria and her family represented the ideal model of family life to the nation. Both Church and State emphasised the family as the cement which held

TOWARDS THE end of the 1880s, there was a considerable increase in industrial action by women. The reasons for these strikes varied. Some were undertaken to resist pay cuts, others for pay increases, while others still were about health, safety and discipline (the system of fines) in the workplace. The best known strike was that of 'The Match Girls' of the Bryant and May factory in London in 1889. This strike received a lot of publicity at the time and the successful outcome served as a milestone to encourage other women to organise and press their employers for improved conditions.

CASE STUDY

The Match Girls' Strike

Members of the Match Makers Union, 1888.

the magazine, help was sought from the Women's Trade Union League, which rapidly led to the formation of the Match Makers Union.

Media interest in the strike was strong, with the *Times* condemning strike leaders, particularly Annie Besant who had become the Secretary of the Union, as "socialist agitators". The publicity, however, won a good deal of support for the women, including funds of £400 which were sufficient to sustain their action. The strike lasted a fortnight, ending when the London Trades Council intervened and negotiated a settlement with the directors of Bryant and May. The resulting agreement was a victory for the women with all employees being reinstated, higher wages gained, fines abolished and the Match Makers Union being established and accepted.

Many industries employing large numbers of working-class women put the health of their employees at considerable risk. In the white lead industry in the North of England, many women suffered illness and death from the lead poisoning contracted at the workplace. The 'laissez-faire' attitude of the state to health and safety matters and the desire for profit meant that most industrialists paid little heed to such issues. Some employers in the white lead industry were considered to be 'enlightened' because they provided their girls with breakfast at the workplace. At this time, poisoning was thought to be caused through working with toxic materials on an empty stomach.

The Match Making industry inflicted equally hazardous conditions on its women workers. These were highlighted in a left-wing magazine called *The Link* which was edited by the socialist reformer Annie Besant. The *Link* article was the result of a campaign by a group of Fabian socialists, notably Sidney Webb, Bernard Shaw and Annie Besant, to publicise the horrifying conditions at Bryant and May's factory in the East End of London. Not only did the article emphasise the low pay and poor conditions which existed in the factory, it graphically brought public attention to the disease called necrosis of the jaw or 'phossy jaw' which workers in the factory risked contracting. Literally gangrene of the jaw, 'phossy jaw' was caused by exposure to the phosphorous used in the manufacture of matches.

The management of the factory responded to the article by asking their employees to sign a document stating that, contrary to the allegations in *The Link*, they were well treated. When one woman was sacked for refusing to sign the document, 1,400 of her colleagues came out on strike. Immediately, the strikers went to the offices of *The Link* in Fleet Street in search of advice and leadership. Through

The Match Girls' strike was a famous victory for working-class women and it had widespread effects. Firstly, both male and female workers came to realise that only by joining together could they secure improvement in their pay and conditions. Secondly, and perhaps more importantly, the great new general unions of dock workers, gas workers and many other general labourers began to recruit women on an equal basis with men.

society together in a rapidly changing and increasingly technological world. The family was particularly important to the middle and upper classes. The husband was head of the family and the wife was subject to her husband, just as in society women were under the authority of men. Thus, the aim of all respectable women was to marry an honest man of even temperament and have his children. Unmarried women were often viewed as having 'failed', becoming a source of pity and ridicule.

In order for a middle- or upper-class woman to acquire a husband, her education and upbringing had to be geared to fit her for the role of the dutiful wife.

"The respectable woman must live up to an ideal created by man. She must be gentle, pure and ladylike and at least appear to be less intelligent than her husband. She must be perfectly mannered and very modest in her behaviour and speech. She must be talented in the drawing room ... despite her fashionable frailty she must manage her household efficiently, bear a large family willingly, and be utterly faithful to her husband."[5]

Most working-class women in mid-Victorian Britain would have wished to aspire to the middle-class ideal of marriage, but were prevented from doing so for several reasons. Poverty and poor housing conditions condemned them to a life of drudgery, endless toil, and childbearing. Cruelty towards working-class women was rife, many working-class men having a particularly brutal attitude towards their spouses. Two of the main causes of this were overcrowding and drink. Lack of education and basic legal rights prevented working-class women from escaping from an unsatisfactory marriage.

On the surface, the Victorian middle-class family presented an image of stability, happiness and contentment. However, there was a good deal of moral hypocrisy in

Victorian Britain. Beneath the images of domestic bliss lurked the evils of pornography and child prostitution which were popular with the men of the middle classes.

Marriage as an institution was popular with Victorian women of all social classes because they perceived that it would enhance their identity. This was another Victorian myth. Once the marriage bond was sealed, a woman literally became the 'goods and chattels' of her husband. In the mid-nineteenth century, the legal position of married women left much to be desired.

"Legally, a married woman's status was that of an infant. She had no rights before the law and everything she owned was her husband's, even her own earnings and her children. For a woman, divorce was almost impossible. If she no longer wished to live with her husband she could apply to the Church courts, and might obtain a separation on the grounds of cruelty, adultery or unnatural practices. Her chances of getting a divorce were very slender, since that could only be granted by an Act of Parliament. It was, however, very much easier for her husband to obtain a divorce on, for

instance, the grounds of his wife's adultery, for the wife in a divorce suit could not be a defendant, a plaintiff, or a witness."[6]

Many of the changes brought about in family law came from the efforts of middle-class feminists. These women were educated and had sufficient time, resources, and social connections to campaign for improved legal rights for women within marriage. Moreover, they were highly motivated by the sheer inequality of a woman's position before the law. The issues of divorce, custody of children and maintenance attracted a good deal of attention. The main changes made in family law are outlined below.

Although divorce had been obtainable by law from 1857 with the setting up of the Divorce Court, social convention in Victorian and Edwardian times was disapproving. Divorce was viewed as scandalous, ruining careers and bringing disgrace on those involved. For a woman, there was the added burden of supporting herself after the divorce. An Act of Parliament in 1866 gave divorced women the

CHANGES *in Family Law*

Matrimonial Causes Act (1857)
This law gave mothers increased access to their children after divorce. In addition, wives could now keep any post-divorce earnings and keep or inherit property from the marriage.

Matrimonial Causes Act (1873)
This law continued the unequal treatment of women over grounds for divorce. A husband could still sue for divorce on the grounds of the wife's adultery, whereas a wife had to be able to prove cruelty by the husband in addition to adultery as grounds for divorce.

Additional legislation gradually, but not completely, improved the rights of married women.

Married Women's Property Act (1870)
This law allowed married women to keep their own earnings up to a maximum of £200 per annum.

Married Women's Property Act (1882)
By this law, husbands lost their automatic right to claim their wives' property as their own.

DIVORCE

In the early years of the twentieth century, a Royal Commission investigated the whole question of divorce, producing two reports in 1912.

Report 1

✝ No major changes to be made in the law. Divorce should only be granted on the grounds of adultery.

✝ Restricted press reporting of divorce cases.

✝ Equal rights for men and women seeking divorce.

✝ Divorce to be made possible for the poor.

Report 2

✝ Major changes recommended. Divorce should be granted on the grounds of insanity, cruelty, adultery, drunkenness, desertion for three years.

✝ Restricted press reporting of divorce cases.

✝ Equal rights for men and women seeking divorce.

✝ Divorce to be made possible for the poor.

right to claim maintenance up to a level of £2 per week from their ex-husbands. By 1895, women had the following additional rights in law.

- The right to become the sole guardian of their children on the death of their husband.
- The right to claim maintenance from the husband even if it was the woman who sued for divorce.
- The right to obtain a separation order if the husband was consistently cruel or in prison.

The fact that the Royal Commission on divorce (see above) was forced to produce two reports illustrates the controversial nature of divorce at this time. Nevertheless, significant legal rights for women had been achieved by the outbreak of World War I. Marriage still remained popular, and although divorce was now easier for women, the notion that a woman had a duty to 'suffer in silence' in an unsatisfactory relationship still prevailed.

'Suffering in silence' was indeed the lot of many working-class women. Escape from a failed marriage was out of the question for them. Their duty was seen as looking after the children of the marriage for, despite the wider use of birth control, working-class families remained large. In the 1890s, working-class girls married in their late teens and had at least ten pregnancies in their child-bearing years. It is little wonder, therefore, that the life expectancy of working-class women was only forty six years.

By the beginning of the twentieth century, feminists were starting to turn their attention to the role of women within the family, and to the inequalities which existed there. Despite the extension in a woman's legal rights, the Victorian and Edwardian marriage relationship was very much a one-sided affair.

Campaigning for change, feminists raised issues like:

- The maternal responsibility of women for the upbringing of children.
- The duty of a wife to 'submit to her husband'.
- The question of large families and the burden they placed on a woman.
- Women's health issues.

Opposition to feminists who campaigned on these issues was fierce. Nevertheless, the picture of marriage which emerges prior to World War I is one in which women were gradually beginning to work out an individual identity for themselves.

Education

England's education system in the middle of the nineteenth century lagged well behind that of some other European states, notably France, Prussia and Scotland. Education at this time remained the privilege of the middle and upper classes. Two religious societies, the National Society and the British and Foreign Society, accounted for the entire provision of education for the working classes. Few working-class parents were, however, in a position to enable their children to take advantage of what was available. Most working-class children, therefore, grew up unable to read or write. If the general state of education at this time was poor, opportunities for girls were extremely limited.

In mid-century, middle- and upper-class girls were educated to be good wives, mothers and homemakers. The curriculum offered to these girls emphasised 'accomplishments' such as social etiquette, music and dancing. Male educationalists believed that the stress of a conventional education could damage the health of a girl in adolescence. They argued that adolescent girls needed rest, not an education which would tax the mind.

> "Women were thought to have smaller brains and, it followed, less intellectual potential than men. It was also a common belief that women were behind men in evolution, as their prime function, motherhood, kept them closer to nature. In short, they were inferior. An educated woman was a paradox, and if she showed she had brains, might frighten off potential husbands."[7]

Women were therefore educated for a life of subordination. Early feminists who questioned this view of women were criticised in the press and in periodicals.

Much of the pioneering work in the field of women's education came in the second half of the nineteenth century. It began in 1848 with the founding of Queens

College, London, as a training institution for women teachers. The early graduates from the college set new standards of education in girls' schools. However, good girls' schools were few and far between.

The scandal of middle-class girls' education was fully revealed in 1868 when the Taunton Commission on Education made its report. The Commission was set up by the government to enquire into the education of boys and only included girls' schools at the last moment due to the campaigning of Emily Davis, a feminist whose aim was to bring girls' education up to the standard available to boys.

The School Inspectors who reported to the Commission noted that, in many cases, they had great difficulty getting information due to "unrelenting hostility" from a number of schools. Overall, the Commission found that the "general deficiency of girls' education can be stated with absolute confidence." It found that almost everywhere, the emphasis of the curriculum for girls was solely on domestic skills plus 'accomplishments' like embroidery or playing the piano. The lack of academic achievement and the physical conditions in which many girls were taught also merited heavy criticism from the Inspectors.

Nevertheless, the picture was not entirely gloomy. There were some good girls' schools. The first academic schools for girls were set up in the 1850s when the North London Collegiate School for Ladies and Cheltenham Ladies College were founded by the early feminist pioneers, Dorothea Beale and Franchesca Buss. Such schools were, however, very much in the minority in offering girls subjects like mathematics, science, Latin and Greek.

There was universal agreement that girls' education needed to be reformed. A debate then arose among feminists over the nature of reform. One school of thought wanted the reforms to make education for girls as good as but different from that available to boys. The opposing group argued that equality was the only way forward: girls' education, it was said, should be identical in all essentials to that given to boys. Emily Davis argued that a different education for girls meant an inferior education. All were agreed that there should be an increase in the number of good schools for girls.

The logical conclusion to the extension of education for girls was that they would demand access to higher education at university level. Emily Davis campaigned to gain women the right of admission to university. In 1866, in her book *The Higher Education of Women*, she argued that women should have the opportunity to "find out what they could do." Educationalists of the day were less than charitable towards Miss Davis's attitude to the education of women. In the face of opposition, she opened a school for women students in Hitchin in 1869. In 1874, the school moved to Cambridge where it became Girton College, and was soon followed by the establishment, by Anne Jemima Clough, of a second women's college, which became known as Newnham Hall.

The aims of Emily Davis and Jemima Clough illustrate the difference in attitude to change which divided early feminists. Miss Clough adopted a gradualist approach over university recognition of women's colleges, being prepared to accept "lesser recognition" as a stepping stone to full and equal status with other colleges.

Emily Davis, on the other hand, aimed for full recognition of women's colleges which would have an identical curriculum and examinations to men's colleges. Miss Davis adopted an uncompromising attitude, arguing that the only way forward for women was to meet men on level terms. Partial or lesser recognition, she argued, would only serve to mark women's colleges as inferior institutions.

The opening up of higher education proceeded steadily as the twentieth century approached, with women's colleges being founded at Oxford University in 1879 and increasing numbers of universities, including the four in Scotland, enrolling women as students on an equal footing with men.

By the turn of the century, small but increasing numbers of middle-class women were going on from school to higher education and from there into professions which had previously been male preserves. Some of these professions, such as nursing, teaching and social work, were areas where able women were extremely successful. In addition, the legal and medical professions, after a long and arduous struggle, had opened their doors to women practitioners.

Thus, by the end of the Victorian era there is no doubt that the cause of women's rights had made significant progress. Yet in the key areas of voting rights, and participation in the political process, women remained as outsiders, powerless with no rights. This lack of political rights simply served to underline the inferiority of women in spite of achievements in other areas.

THE CAMPAIGN TO WIN THE VOTE TO 1914

'The cause' was the phrase used by many nineteenth century feminists for the whole movement for women's social, economic and political rights. By the close of the century, 'the cause' required an issue which would bring women of all shades of opinion together. The issue of the vote became the focus of women's struggle for equality.

The nineteenth century was the battleground for the extension of the franchise to the male members of the working classes. In the

A London Suffragette campaigning for votes for women..

struggle, men who already had the vote took the lead in fighting for the rights of their peers. However, in their struggle for the vote, women had to fight for themselves, getting very little help from men. Yet the struggle itself provided women from many different social, cultural, political and religious backgrounds with a sense of solidarity which previous issues had failed to provide.

The issue of votes for women was taken up by the Chartists in the early years of their campaigning, but was subsequently rejected. It re-emerged in the debate which preceded the passing of the Second Reform Bill in 1867. It was raised by John Stuart Mill the economist, who in 1865 was elected to Parliament. He was in favour of widening the franchise to include women, and to that end introduced an amendment to the Reform Bill. Although it was defeated, seventy three MPs voted for it. In the years following the *Second Reform Act*, women house-

holders gained the right to vote in local elections.

The question of votes for women was again raised in the debate preceding the Third Reform Bill in 1889. Again an amendment to the Bill was moved, this time by a Mr Woodall (Liberal). The Prime Minister of the day, Gladstone, spoke against the amendment and again it was defeated, although this time one hundred and thirty five MPs voted for the amendment to grant women's suffrage.

By the 1890s, as it became clear that women were playing a more important role in society, there was a steady majority in favour of Commons' resolutions declaring that women should have the right to vote. However, it was a far cry from giving support to a Bill which would enfranchise women. Indeed, it is more probable that at the turn of the century only a minority of the population wanted women's suffrage.

Why were people opposed to women's suffrage at this time?
Firstly, and most obviously, politicians were against the idea. The Conservatives were against it, although former Prime Minister Disraeli had argued in favour of women's suffrage. The main fear of the Conservatives was that women, once enfranchised, would vote for the Liberals, or even worse, the Labour Party.

The Liberals, although in favour of women's suffrage, voiced similar concerns to those of the Conservatives, namely that women might vote for the opposition parties. The Leader of the Liberal Party and Prime Minister from 1908 to 1916, HH Asquith, was against votes for women. The disapproval and opposition of a Prime Minister proved to be a formidable hurdle for the cause of equal voting rights. The newly formed Labour Party gave qualified approval to women's suffrage. It wanted all adults to have the vote and argued that, if only property-owning women gained the vote, the Conservatives and Liberals would be the sole beneficiaries.

Secondly, in society at large prevailing attitudes were against giving votes to women for the following reasons, many of which were spurious, but which were nevertheless taken seriously at the time.

🢖 If women became involved in politics, it would threaten the family and therefore the stability of society.

🢖 Politics would have a corrupting influence on women, making them less feminine.

🢖 Women, being highly emotional, would be totally unsuited to making logical political decisions.

🢖 Women were not educationally equipped to make proper use of the right to vote.

Those who accepted the above arguments came from all social classes and from all parts of the political spectrum. The movement to gain votes for women had two wings, the suffragists whose origin went well back into the nineteenth century, and the more militant suffragettes who came into being in 1903.

The Suffragists
The suffragists proudly traced their roots to the nineteenth century movement for social reform.

> "The early suffragists were a well-connected group of women who used their influence to try and persuade powerful men to take up their cause."[8]

They became a national movement in 1887 when, under the leadership of Millicent Fawcett, various suffrage societies formed themselves into the National Union of Women's Suffrage Societies (NUWSS). The methods employed by the NUWSS were similar to those employed by the separate suffrage societies for the preceding thirty years, namely peaceful persuasion and education, always working within the law. Suffragists wrote pamphlets, held meetings, and sent out trained speakers, all with the aim of changing public opinion.

The leadership of the suffragists was exclusively middle class, yet it was acknowledged early on that the movement needed to have the support of working-class women. Radical suffragists as they became known, led by the Gore-Booth sisters, worked in the mills of Lancashire to gain the support of working-class women for their cause.

Many of these mill workers, who had involved themselves in trade union activities but found themselves to be 'voices in the wilderness', turned to the suffragist movement as an outlet for their frustrations with the male-dominated trade union movement. Diane Atkinson in *Votes for Women*, argues that the "NUWSS, of all the women's suffrage societies, had the most to offer to working-class women." What is clear is that the issue of the vote was drawing women together as never before, and giving them an identity which they had hitherto lacked.

The Suffragettes
The suffragettes were born out of the suffragist movement in 1903. Mrs Emmeline Pankhurst, who had been a member of the Manchester suffragist group and who had been involved in the campaign to seek support from working-class women in Cheshire, decided to break with the NUWSS and form a separate society. She had grown impatient with the middle-class, respectable, gradualist tactics of the NUWSS. The new suffragette organisation was called the Women's Social and Political Union (WSPU). Its motto was 'Deeds, not Words'.

Strategy and Tactics 1903–1914
Both suffragists and suffragettes wanted votes for women. Where they differed was over strategy and tactics. The suffragists always kept their efforts within the law while the suffragettes were prepared to break the law.

In 1906, a deputation of suffragettes, suffragists and politicians met the new Liberal Prime Minister, Campbell-Bannerman. He informed the group that, although he was personally in favour of women's suffrage, his Cabinet colleagues were divided. Suffragist members were disappointed at this attitude as many were Liberal supporters. Their response to the Prime Minister was to mount a campaign of petitions, leaflets and meetings targeted at Liberal politicians to try to persuade them to change their minds on the issue of women's suffrage. Later in the same year, they adopted a new and more aggressive tone by threatening to put up independent candidates to run against Liberal politicians who were against votes for women.

Meanwhile, the suffragettes campaigned in a much more robust manner. HH Asquith, the new Chancellor of the Exchequer and a leading opponent of women's suffrage, was heckled in the House of Commons. Marches and demonstrations were organised with women being arrested when they tried to demonstrate at the Commons. In 1907 the suffragettes split into two groups following conflict between Mrs Pankhurst, her daughter, and other members of the WSPU's executive. Those who left formed the Women's Freedom League (WFL), while the Pankhursts and their supporters established an even firmer grip on the WSPU, foreshadowing even more aggressive tactics in the future.

In spite of internal bickering over strategy and tactics, the three women's groups continued to work together most of the time. Certainly their message was beginning to have some influence on

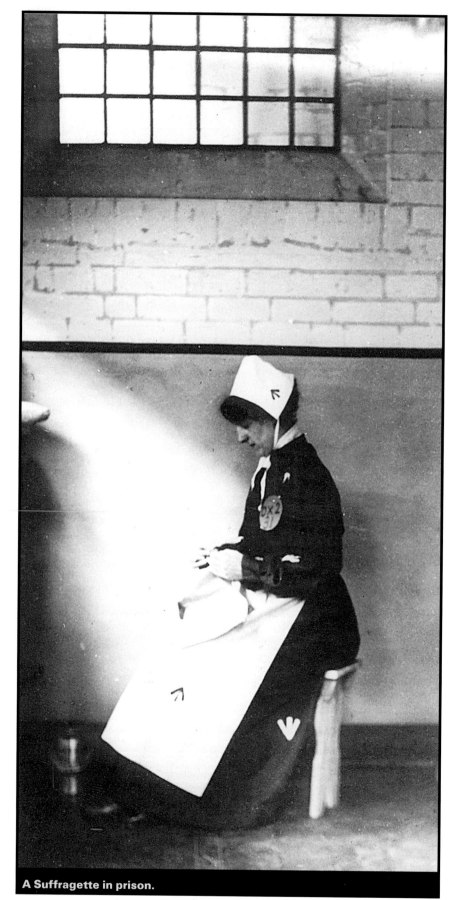
A Suffragette in prison.

the 'antis'. In 1906 Beatrice Webb, the Fabian Socialist, explained to Millicent Fawcett how she had become a convert to women's suffrage.

Women ... "in my opinion are rapidly losing their consciousness of consent in the work of government and are even feeling a positive obligation to take part in directing this new activity. This is in my view, not a claim to rights nor an abandonment of women's particular obligations (bearing children and the advancement of learning), but a desire to fulfil their functions by sharing the control of State actions in those directions."[9]

As time went on, demonstrations increased. In London, Mrs Pankhurst and her daughter were arrested for trying to 'rush the House of Commons'. The WFL founded the Women's Tax Resistance League in 1909, and some of its members chained themselves to a ventilation grille in the House of Commons, shouting 'votes for women' through it, until it was removed. All of these efforts gained the cause publicity. As a result, people began to think more seriously about the issue of women's suffrage.

By 1909 tactics had become more militant: politicians opposing women's suffrage were frequently interrupted; Winston Churchill was attacked by a woman with a dog whip; the new Prime Minister HH Asquith, the 'bête noire' of the suffragettes, had his windows broken. Increasingly he and other 'anti' politicians were relentlessly pursued the length and breadth of the country by women prepared to disrupt political meetings.

As the suffragette campaign intensified, the opposition from press and public also increased. In 1908, the leader writer in the *Daily Express* warned that "the time for dealing gently with idle mischievous women who call themselves militant suffragists has gone by", and demanded that "these women who unite to disorder and riot,

Emmeline Pankhurst arrested outside Buckingham Palace, 2 May 1914.

shall be punished with the utmost severity." The popular press cruelly lampooned both suffragists and suffragettes in cartoons, describing the women as unfeminine, masculine, frustrated spinsters.

Despite the opposition from politicians, press and public, the organisation for women's suffrage seemed to be prospering. By 1909 the WSPU had branches all over the country, seventy five paid office staff, and a newspaper, *Votes for Women*, which sold twenty thousand copies per week but was read by many more. The NUWSS was also doing well. Its membership was thirteen thousand in 1909 and it had an efficient and well-run organisation nationwide. Increasingly, however, the two organisations were growing apart, with the NUWSS becoming particularly concerned that the growing militancy of the WSPU was losing the movement support from both MPs and public.

In the summer of 1909 there was an outbreak of window smashing by suffragettes. This usually meant a jail sentence, the women being classed by the authorities as common criminals. The WSPU consistently claimed that, since its members were involved in a political struggle, offences committed by them should be judged as political acts, and those who were imprisoned should have the special status of political prisoners. In July 1909, Miss Wallace-Dunlop went on hunger strike to gain political status. She was soon followed by others. At first the government released hunger strikers, fearing the adverse publicity that the starvation of imprisoned women would bring, but after a few months the decision was taken to feed them by force. However, force-feeding backfired on the government in that the militant suffragettes began to win back support which their tactics had previously lost for them.

The Conciliation Bill and Its Failure

During the General Election of January 1910, Asquith promised that MPs would have the opportunity for a free vote in Parliament on a Bill for Women's Suffrage. A Conciliation Bill was drafted by an all-party Commons Committee in response to the Prime Minister's undertaking and was introduced in the House after the Election.

It was given its Second Reading in July 1910, and in the debate thirty nine speeches were made for and against. Winston Churchill and Lloyd George both spoke against the Bill, on the grounds that, since it was designed only to give the vote to female property owners, it would automatically favour the Conservatives. The Bill passed its Second Reading with a majority of one hundred votes, whereupon Asquith curtailed further discussion by suspending Parliament until November. There was initial violence by members of the WSPU after Asquith's announcement, but once this had died down, both the NUWSS and the suffragettes resumed peaceful campaigning in the hope that the Conciliation Bill would eventually become law in 1911. In the meantime, Mrs Pankhurst went on a speaking tour of North America. The NUWSS continued its attacks on the militants of the WSPU while defending its own constitutional approach.

In 1911 another Conciliation Bill, which proposed to give voting rights to women whose husbands were already voters, got no further than a Second Reading. The Bill was presented to the House again in 1912, but failed to get a majority at the Second Reading. Later in the same year, Asquith brought in a Bill to widen the franchise to all men, and proposed that the Commons could introduce an amendment to it in order to add votes for women. As in 1844 and 1867, when the amendment was proposed the Speaker ruled it out of order on the grounds that it would change the nature of the Bill.

Mrs Pankhurst returned from the USA in 1912 and immediately committed the WSPU to a new phase of violence and outrage which went far beyond the law-breaking which had taken place since the beginning of the campaign. Suffragettes felt that they had been tricked and outwitted by Asquith, and now aimed "to create an intolerable situation for the government, and if need be, for the public as a whole." Thus, the eighteen months prior to World War I are rightly described by historians as the 'wild period' of suffragette actions. Paintings were slashed, houses and business premises were firebombed and telegraph wires were cut. During this period the suffragettes gained a martyr in Emily Davison who, on 4 June 1913, threw herself in front of the King's horse 'Anmer' at the Derby. Suffragettes turned her funeral into an immense propaganda exercise for their cause. However, there is a great deal of evidence to show that the campaign of violence did the cause more harm than good. Churchill was of the opinion that "their cause had marched backwards."

Suffragettes sentenced to prison continued to go on hunger strike in pursuit of the demand for political status. In 1913 the government passed legislation which, it was hoped, would strengthen the hand of the prison authorities in dealing with hunger strikers. The so-called 'Cat and Mouse Act' enabled the authorities to release hunger strikers on licence, then rearrest them once they had recovered their health. The aim of the Act was to demoralise the suffragettes, but it only succeeded in strengthening their resolve. Some women simply resorted to further lawbreaking while on licence, and in the end force-feeding was reintroduced.

Why were men attracted to the women's suffrage movement ?
This interesting area has, until recently, received scant attention from historians. Research shows that sympathetic men played a significant, but auxiliary, role in the campaign. From 1908, when women were banned from Liberal Party rallies, men took on the role of interrupting speakers on behalf of the 'cause'.

"Many brave men, from that day, risked insult and broken heads, and even their livelihood, by challenging delinquent Liberal leaders on the issue of votes for women."[10]

Some men were thrown out of meetings, were imprisoned, went on hunger strike, and were forcibly fed. George Lansbury, a future leader of the Labour Party and Hugh Franklin, a nephew of a government minister of the day were both forcibly fed while in prison. Members of the Men's Political Union (one of seven men's organisations) played the unusual role of being phantom husbands to suffragettes who managed to get invited to government social functions. Invitations were always made out to 'Mr and Mrs', and so in order to attend and therefore disrupt these functions, suffragettes had to have a husband. The WSPU called for both men and women to 'rush' the Houses of Parliament. In 1914, an NUWSS rally in London for male supporters was filled to overflowing.

"Notions of chivalry and 'fair play' often underlaid the motivations of male sympathisers with women's suffrage ... feminists of the period found ways of working with men without losing control of their struggle. For some sympathetic men the experience of a women-defined struggle was a distressing one. Other men, however, understood that their role could only be an auxiliary one, and respected the autonomy of the women's movement.

The image of advice proffered and rebuffed is indicative of the tensions between men and women within the suffrage camp. Yet some male support could be retained even though its 'advice' might be rejected. This suggests that the women's movement had found ways to create an alliance which strengthened its effectiveness."[11]

Did the coming of war delay the franchise for women?
In the early summer of 1914, amid impending civil war in Ireland and the possibility of large-scale industrial unrest, Asquith agreed to receive a deputation from the East London Federation of Suffragettes. This group was led by Mrs Pankhurst's other daughter Sylvia, who had been expelled from the WSPU earlier in 1914, due to her mother and her sister Christabel's disapproval of her work with working-class women. Asquith seems to have recognised that these women had genuine social grievances which could have been more effectively tackled if they had had the vote. Although the Prime Minister was not going to change his mind on the question of women's suffrage overnight, there is a good deal of evidence to suggest that in time he would have brought in a Bill to provide for universal adult suffrage. War, however, intervened and the whole movement immediately scaled down its activities in the face of a greater threat to the nation.

Recent research suggests that:

- "in many ways the war may have delayed the franchise rather than expedited it".

- "the pre-war suffrage movement prepared the ground for votes for women".

- "two weeks before the outbreak of war, negotiations between suffragists were taking place".[12]

In addition, the Liberal leadership seemed ready to make women's suffrage part of its Party programme. This, of course, is mere speculation. Negotiations between the government and women suffragists had taken place before but had never provided votes for women. There is no guarantee that it would have been the case this time.

FROM WAR TO EQUAL VOTING RIGHTS
There was a varied response within the women's suffrage movement to the outbreak of war.

"The movement lost its impetus and its leaders went their separate ways. Christabel and her mother became super-patriots vigorously supporting the war effort, while

Sylvia Pankhurst sided with the pacifists. Millicent Fawcett and the suffragists on the other hand, continued to lobby politicians while making themselves useful to the war effort by funding ambulances for women to drive to France, and organising women's voluntary work."[13]

What the war did was to highlight the economic and strategic value of women to the State. This, however, did not happen immediately. In the first year of the war women were, by and large, unaffected, although in certain areas of women's work, notably the cotton and clothing industries, the level of unemployment amongst women actually increased as imports fell and people bought fewer clothes. The first propaganda slogan of the war was 'business as usual', and as far as everyone was concerned, war was a man's business. Professor Arthur Marwick notes in *The Deluge* that in the first year of the war, "the overall picture was one of willing women finding no outlet for their desire to serve."

Eventually economic necessity, rather than the demands of Mrs Pankhurst and other feminists for the 'right to serve' drove the government to recruit women, first of all into the munitions industry, then into many other sectors of the economy. The figures show a dramatic increase in 1916 with the introduction of compulsory military service for men, and again in 1917 when National Service was introduced. (See Table 3.5.) The nation was involved in total war, and the nation as a whole had to be mobilised. Many other areas of employment show significant increases in the numbers of women employed. Although mainly from the working class, the war brought increasing numbers of women from all social classes into employment.

Marwick maintains that the war served to accelerate a process which had started well before 1914.

"The growth of large-scale industry and bureaucracy would undoubtedly have brought this development eventually, but it was the war, in creating simultaneously a proliferation of government committees and departments and a shortage of men, which brought a sudden and irreversible advance in the economic and social power of a category of women employees which extended from sprigs of the aristocracy to daughters of the proletariat."[14]

In addition, women in the medical services served with distinction during the war, bringing credibility to the cause. This was further magnified in 1917 when the government formed the various women's paramilitary organisations into the Women's Auxiliary Army Corps and later the WRENS and the WRAFS. Marwick makes the point that the war heightened women's own self-image and their individual identity.

"Above all, in their awareness that they were performing arduous and worthwhile tasks and were living through experiences once confined only to the most adventurous males, they gained a new self-consciousness and a new sense of status."[15]

During the war, the government made positive moves towards the introduction of votes for women. Britain's war propaganda, much of which was directed at the USA, stressed the fact that the Allies were fighting for democracy, which implied universal suffrage. The government, therefore, had to be seen to be acting in this direction.

Women and the War Effort: Some Myths Exploded
The long-held popular image is that the contribution of women from all social classes 'pulling together' for the war effort in areas of work like the munitions industry and the land helped to secure the vote in 1918. Recent research shows that this picture is incomplete for various reasons. Initially the war caused redundancies in

A group of munitions workers at a factory in Holton Heath, England 1914–1918.

WOMEN Employed in the Munitions Industry	
Year	N°· Employed
1914	212,000
1915	256,000
1916	520,000
1917	819,000
1918	919,000

Table 3.5

Changing Britain 1850–1979

industries dominated by women. When there was a labour shortage in 1915, the government targeted unemployed males to fill the vacancies rather than women. Suffragette activists like the Pankhursts did not see factory work as attractive work for women. They argued that vacated clerical posts were more suited to women.

When the female workforce expanded there was no social class harmony. Few middle and upper-class women worked in the factories. In the munitions industry they formed 9% of the female workforce in skilled and supervisory positions. The shell fillers (the most dangerous work) were young working-class women. Female middle-class supervisors "maintained constant vigilance against unwholesome entertainments: women workers were reprimanded for spending too much time on the street or for attending the cinema too often. But one positive aspect of the work was that supervisors guarded against sexual harassment on the shop floor".[16]

The extent to which the war was a contributory factor to the winning of women's new found rights is a matter for debate amongst historians. Some argue that the government could not refuse to grant voting rights to women because they had contributed so much to the war effort. John Ray, in *Britain Between the Wars*, contends that "women proved by their work that they deserved the vote equally with men. Thus their war efforts succeeded where the suffragette campaign had failed."

Other historians argue that the picture is much more complicated. Women were already campaigning for and winning new rights before 1914. Stevenson, in *British Society*, argues that "although the First World War has usually been taken as marking a turning point both in the acquisition of the right to vote and in wider opportunities for women, it is clear that the war was as much the occasion as the cause of growing female emancipation." AJP Taylor in *English History 1914–1945* simply argues, "War smoothed the way for democracy—it is one of the few things to be said in its favour."

.
Question One
Why did women get the vote in 1918 rather than in 1914?
The historian Martin Pugh argues that women were granted the vote in 1918 because the pre-war agitation had paved the way. By 1913, "the lines of the precise solution to the problem had already emerged. The question was one of detail: on what terms were women to be enfranchised? The answer emerged in WH Dickinson's 1913 Bill which included the vital proposal to enfranchise wives. This was the element incorporated into the 1918 Act which removed the fears of Liberal and Labour politicians about the potential danger of

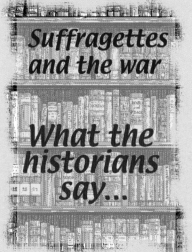

Suffragettes and the war

What the historians say...

creating more Conservative voters by confining the qualification to single or propertied women."[17]

Yet another explanation is that people simply changed their minds about votes for women during the war.

"Male prejudice against women melted in the face of revelations about their capabilities during wartime and their contribution to the war effort."[18]

Question Two
Why did women fail to get complete equality with men in 1918?
The 1918 *Representation of the People Act* meant that 12,913,166 men and 8,479,156 women had the vote. It is now clear that the enfranchisement of women in 1918 came about because politicians were concerned with ensuring that all men had the vote. The 1918 Act was the result of the deliberations of the 1917 all-party Speaker's Conference.

"Towards the end of their work they dealt with women's suffrage, anxious not to throw away their achievements by disagreement over one item. By fifteen to six the members voted in favour of the principle of giving some votes to women: they rejected equal suffrage with men by twelve votes to ten ... fearful about the dangers of women becoming a majority, they also thought it prudent to add a further control in the form of a maximum age limit, suggesting either thirty or thirty five."[19]

It can therefore be argued that the Act failed to reward a significant proportion of women for their war effort. Young working-class women who worked on the land and in the munitions factories were, by and large, excluded from the vote.

Shell filling was a common occupation for women before the war because it did not require much skill. By the end of the war, approximately 83% of women in factories were doing work which had been previously categorised as women's work.

The popularity of the Women's Land Army is a myth. The response from women was small with only 16,000 women taking part in the 1918 harvest. Women experienced a prejudiced welcome from farming communities who viewed them as 'outsiders'. Their propaganda value to the government was, however, enormous.

The Representation of the People Act 1918

The establishment of a coalition government during the war helped the cause. There were no longer the rigid party divisions which in the past had hindered the cause of women's suffrage, and as the war proceeded more men who were well disposed to the cause came into the government. The question was eventually referred to an all-party committee of the House of Commons which was chaired by the Speaker. This so-called Speaker's Conference made its report on 30 January 1917. Its recommendation was not unanimous, but by a majority decided that "some measure of women's suffrage should be conferred ... Any woman on the Local Government Register who has attained a specified age, and the wife of any man who is on that register, if she has attained that age, shall be entitled to be registered and to vote as a parliamentary elector." Eventually the "specified age" was agreed to be thirty and ironically HH Asquith, the former Prime Minister, moved that the recommendations be drafted into a Bill. This was passed on its Third Reading by 385 to 55 and became law in June 1918.

All men over twenty one gained the vote provided they had resided in Britain for six months. Women over the age of thirty who were householders or who were married to householders or were university graduates gained the vote.

Campaigners for women's suffrage were disappointed by the age bar. They wanted complete equality with men. Nevertheless, most activists were prepared to wait.

THE EFFECTS OF REFORM

There was uncertainty about how politics would be affected by the reforms. The new electorate numbered 12.9 million men and 8.5 million women. As a result, some politicians began to pay more attention to women's issues and this was evident in the campaigns of 1918 and 1924.

With the extension of the franchise to women over thirty in 1918 came measures which, for the first time, enabled women to become Members of Parliament. Opponents of female suffrage had sounded dire warnings of the creation of a women's party, and of Parliament being 'swamped' by women. Seventeen women were Parliamentary candidates in the Election of 1918 and all were defeated except Constance Markiewicz who, although elected, never took up her seat as she was against Irish representation in Parliament. The first woman to take her seat in the Commons was Nancy Astor who was elected for the Conservatives at a by-election in 1919. Mrs Astor was an American by birth, and at the time of taking her seat in Parliament, to the cheers of veteran suffragettes, she had never campaigned for women's rights. This situation was soon rectified as she became an effective voice on behalf of women.

Equal voting rights remained on the political agenda during the 1920s, although there was no return to the pre-1914 militancy by the suffragettes. With the collapse of organised opposition to female suffrage in 1918, it was not long before members of all three parties started to introduce proposals for equal voting rights into the House of Commons. When Stanley Baldwin, Leader of the Conservative Party publicly promised equal suffrage for women in the 1924 Election campaign, it was only a matter of time before it became a reality. Nevertheless, he had to defy leading members of his own party such as Austen Chamberlain, Winston Churchill and the press baron Lord Rotheremere who used his power through the *Daily Mail* to discredit Baldwin's proposal. The *Mail* repeatedly warned of the dangers of the 'flapper vote' going to Labour at subsequent general elections, in a final bid to cause division within the Conservative Party. This tactic failed, and in 1928 the Conservatives joined with the Labour and Liberal Parties to pass the Bill through Parliament.

Representation of the People Act 1928

All women over twenty one gained the vote, provided they had resided in Britain for six months.

When women achieved equal voting rights with men in 1928, it was again expected that there would be a large influx of women into

WOMEN MPs
Elected Between the Wars

General Election	Conservative	Labour	Liberal	Other	Total	(%)
1918	–	–	–	1	1	0.1
1922	1	–	1	–	2	0.3
1923	3	3	2	–	8	1.3
1924	3	1	–	–	4	0.7
1929	3	9	1	1	14	2.3

Table 3.4

Parliament. This did not happen, although in 1929 the first female Cabinet Minister, Margaret Bondfield, was appointed by Labour. During the interwar period, women MPs reached their maximum of fifteen after the 1931 Election. (See table 3.4.)

Between the wars, the very small number of female MPs were virtually forced into confining themselves to speaking for women and women's problems, which were perceived to revolve around prices, social policy and domestic matters.

Were women effective in politics during this period?
More women attempted to get into politics at this time. In the 1918 General Election there were seventeen female candidates of whom one was elected. By 1929, the number of candidates had increased to sixty nine of whom fourteen were elected. Despite this increase, the overall numbers of women candidates remained low. Local party selection committees still tended to look upon women as 'high risk' candidates, and even the Labour Party, whose selection record was better than that of both the Conservatives and the Liberals, rarely selected women to stand in safe seats. Angela Holdsworth, in *Out of the Doll's House*, argues that although women made little impact, "sixteen acts protecting women's interests were passed in the early 1920s ... these changes in the law may well have had more to do with politicians' awareness of women's voting power than the lady MPs." These new laws positively affected the position of women in politics, employment and the family.

Sex Disqualification (Removal) Act 1919
This Act removed legal restrictions on women entering the professions, particularly the law. As a result there were four thousand female magistrates, mayors and local councillors in Britain by 1923.

The Matrimonial Causes Act 1923
This Act removed from the wife the need to prove cruelty or desertion in addition to adultery as grounds for divorce.

Guardianship of Infants Act 1924
This gave guardianship of infant children jointly to both parents. If they disagreed, the courts would decide who got custody.

New English Law of Property 1926
Women now had the right to dispose of their own property on the same terms as men.

Women continued to make steady progress in the interwar period, although the advances made were less spectacular than those made between 1850 and 1918. In the employment field, women had managed to gain a foothold in areas formerly reserved for men. However, in terms of pay and promotion they still lagged well behind their male colleagues. They were typically employed in unskilled, non-unionised jobs in the distributive, clerical and service industries.

Socially, women began to establish an identity of their own by breaking free from the conventions of the past. The pioneering work of former suffragette Dr Marie Stopes on birth control began to give working-class women control over their own bodies. Family size could be planned and so the poverty and health problems associated with continual childbearing could be reduced. Better education and increased employment opportunities also provided more scope for women to break away from their conventional 'kitchen sink' image. Nevertheless, prejudice still remained deep within the social and cultural fabric of British society.

WHY DID IT TAKE SO LONG FOR WOMEN TO GET THE VOTE?
The campaign for women's suffrage began in 1866 and it took a further sixty two years for full

equality to be achieved in 1928. In 1866 one man in five had the right to vote. John Stuart Mill argued in 1867 that, if it was accepted that men who paid rates and taxes should get the vote, then women who were in a similar position should have the same rights. Politicians of the day were, however, reluctant to start giving women equal voting rights when so few men had the vote.

This view was underpinned by the cultural values and issues of late Victorian Britain, which have little relevance today. What were these anti-feminist values and issues which at the time defined the reaction to demands for reform?

At that time Britain had an Empire which it wished to maintain and extend. In Africa, Asia and the Middle East, this Empire rested on the illusion of British cultural supremacy. Politicians argued that this could not be maintained if there was the possibility of women in government.

Christianity had a major influence on Victorian society. Many politicians drew their values from the Bible on matters such as the family, marriage and divorce. They believed that women and men had been designed by God for different roles. Hence, politics would merely distract women from their God-given roles as homemakers, mothers, wives and moral guides.

At this time, there were more women than men in Britain's population, and a higher proportion than today were single. Men feared that increased opportunities would further alienate young women from marriage and domestic life.

In the years leading up to the turn of the century, those who opposed women's suffrage argued that there was no demand from women themselves for the vote. This argument was based on the small size of the suffragist movement at the time, and the lack of evidence of a mass demand for the vote. As opinion polling did not come into being in Britain until the 1930s, it is difficult to test this argument.

In 1892 Gladstone argued that, despite the demands of the suffragists, women in general were indifferent to the issue. A petition presented to Parliament in 1897 containing 257,000 signatures was seen at the time as being too small. Anti-suffragists such as Winston Churchill argued that women did not see the vote as essential since their needs were already catered for by Parliament, citing as evidence legislation such as the *Married Women's Property Acts* of 1870 and 1882 and the *Contagious Acts* of 1886.

Prominent female anti-suffragists, notably Queen Victoria, described the issue of women's rights as a "mad wicked folly". These people, especially the Queen, were, at the time, role models for many women. Thus anyone who challenged the accepted female role of wife, mother, and homemaker would be received with scepticism, if not outright antagonism.

In the face of such entrenched attitudes from both men and women, the suffragists employed the methods of Victorian pressure groups to bring about change between the 1860s and the early twentieth century. On the surface it would seem that their campaign was a failure. How effective and realistic was their strategy?

The suffragists were realists because they recognised that only Parliament could deliver the vote, so MPs had to be persuaded that their cause was just. The suffragists were successful in quietly persuading many MPs that some women should have the vote. The suffragists can, however, be criticised for their excessive cau-

tion. By the late nineteenth century they were proposing that the vote be granted in the first instance to one million women who were unmarried heads of households and who were ratepayers. It can be argued that this was a serious error in tactics because governments were more interested in married women than single women.

The middle-class membership and cautious approach of the suffragists alienated working-class women and Socialists who argued that they were only interested in getting the vote for wealthy women. Indeed, this approach went a long way towards delaying the formation of a mass movement.

Both the suffragists and the Pankhursts failed to see the necessity of forging an alliance with the labour movement which would have had more credibility with the public and the government. Such an alliance could have demanded votes for the adults of both sexes, thus further enhancing its democratic credentials. If the suffragists can be criticised for their overcautious middle-class approach, what of the suffragettes under the leadership of the Pankhursts? They were excellent propagandists, but it is arguable that their militant campaign after 1905 scared off as many potential supporters as it attracted. How realistic and effective was their strategy?

The suffragettes aimed to force the government to grant votes for women by whipping up public support for the cause. While succeeding in gaining a lot of support and publicity, the suffragettes failed to make a real impact on the government. The tactics of sporadically attacking private property, heckling politicians, setting fire to postboxes in an uncoordinated manner and so on suc-

ceeded in creating a public nuisance, but failed to scare the government. Had the suffragettes mounted organised attacks on major economic targets like railways, docks, factories and other public utilities, they might have succeeded in frightening the government. Sacrifices by suffragettes such going on hunger strike, or by individuals like Emily Davison, were seen at the time by some as self-promotion.

The suffragettes were never able to maintain their issue at the top of the political agenda for any length of time. Other issues intervened such as the budget crisis in 1909; impending civil war in Ireland; various industrial relations crises in the years prior to 1914.

Finally, while the outbreak of war in 1914 proved to be advantageous to the long-term cause of women's suffrage, in the short-term, it removed the reform issue from the political agenda. As a result both the suffragists and the suffragettes could be criticised for ending their campaigns too quickly and too readily. The Pankhursts accepted an amnesty for suffragette prisoners in return for a cessation of their campaign, and Mrs Fawcett, the suffragist leader, declared in 1915 that there was no chance of gaining reform while a coalition government was in power.

In the end, the war killed off the momentum of the reform campaign, and probably delayed women's suffrage. The issue returned to the political agenda in 1917 when the Speaker's Conference recommended the granting of the vote to women over the age of thirty. Thus in 1918 a partial franchise was granted to women. It took yet another ten years of delay before they had equal voting rights.

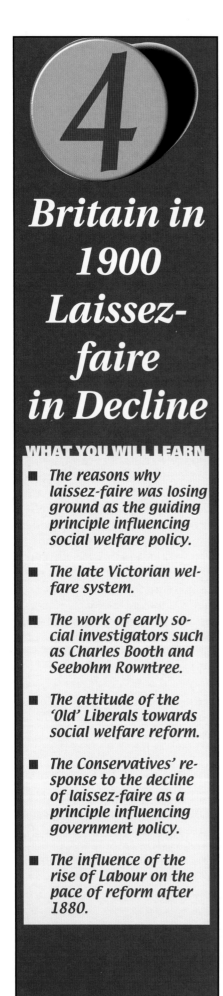

4

Britain in 1900 Laissez-faire in Decline

WHAT YOU WILL LEARN

■ The reasons why laissez-faire was losing ground as the guiding principle influencing social welfare policy.

■ The late Victorian welfare system.

■ The work of early social investigators such as Charles Booth and Seebohm Rowntree.

■ The attitude of the 'Old' Liberals towards social welfare reform.

■ The Conservatives' response to the decline of laissez-faire as a principle influencing government policy.

■ The influence of the rise of Labour on the pace of reform after 1880.

FOR MOST OF the nineteenth century, British governments held firmly to the 'laissez-faire' principle, namely that the state should not interfere in the lives of the people or in the workings of the market economy. The individual should be free to run his or her own life unhindered by the tyranny of the state. If people were destitute, it was their own fault and due to their own moral failings. Poor relief in the workhouse or poorhouse was deliberately made so harsh that most of the poor shunned it. However, from 1870 the principle and practice of laissez-faire or 'individualism' came under increasing challenge. Britain was entering an 'age of collectivism' when governments began to accept the need to regulate and care for their citizens in certain limited areas.

In the 1870s and 1880s, there had been several periods of severe economic depression. During these times, it became clear that neither the state apparatus nor voluntary effort was able to cope with the mass ranks of unemployed poor. Social investigations also began to reveal the extent of poverty. These factual reports, as well as the more sensational journalistic accounts of slum life, stirred middle-class consciences. Many began to realise that the combined efforts of public and private poor relief were woefully inadequate. Political thinkers, like TH Green, provided the intellectual ammunition for the 'New' Liberals to challenge the traditional individualist ideology of their party. Socialist or collectivist ideas were being spread through groups such as the Social Democratic Federation and the Fabian Society. Out of all these pressures for change emerged new social welfare legislation in the areas of public health, education and poor relief.

THE LATE VICTORIAN WELFARE SYSTEM

The late Victorian period saw a gradual move away from the theory and practice of individualism towards collective action by national and local authorities. It was a period of transition and, therefore, it is understandable that many people clung to established ideas of self-reliance in an age increasingly facing

Whitechapel, London, 1907. A 'down-and-out' lady on a bench.

London, 1908. Unemployed sleeping rough.

problems and demands no longer capable of being left in the private domain. The urban middle class were becoming aware of how inadequate the Poor Law was when it came to dealing with the mass of people at the bottom of the social heap. However, the typical humanitarian response of the wealthy was to dispense private charity rather than to call for more public welfare. Philanthropy, not state-sponsored 'socialism' was the preferred middle-class remedy for the social ills of the day.

Although this acceptance of the need for private, voluntary giving was inspired by the individualist rather than the collectivist impulse, it also marks a perceptible shift away from the first principle of laissez-faire—self-help. It was an unspoken admission of the inadequacy of the Poor Law and of the inability of many, including the able-bodied, to provide for themselves. To fill the gap in the welfare system, a host of charitable bodies sprang up in the nineteenth century, such as the YMCA (1844), the Salvation Army (1866), Dr Barnardo's Homes (1869) and the RSPCC (1884).

Many of these charities were motivated by a Christian or humanitarian desire to care for the suffering humanity only too evident in the industrial towns and cities. It is rather ironic that at a time when social 'Darwinism' was becoming fashionable (the belief that only the fittest survive), evangelicals,

Christian Socialists and humanitarians were also practising compassion for the weakest members of society. Moreover, few of these charities investigated very thoroughly the needs of applicants for relief. The Salvation Army, for example, did not accept the Poor Law categories of 'deserving' and 'undeserving' poor.

By the 1870s, hundreds of organisations were striving to provide the sorts of social services for which governments were unwilling to take responsibility. The problem was that the 'private sector' welfare system lacked coordination and supervision. In 1867, the Charity Organisation Society (COS) was founded. Its aim was to attack the problem of poverty in a more coherent and rigorous way than before. The leading figure in the COS was CS Loch. He had no truck with the "indiscriminate alms-giving" practised by some charities.

> "We have to use charity to create the power of self-help."[1]

According to Loch, aid should only be given to the deserving poor and then only after a detailed investigation into the character and circumstances of the applicant. Financial assistance should help to restore the person's independence; indiscriminate aid, on the other hand, would only serve to demoralise the individual, robbing him of self-respect and initiative.

By the 1890s even the COS had to moderate its hard-line, laissez-faire approach in the face of widespread economic distress. By advocating temporary job creation schemes to tide people over during periods of economic depression, the COS was tacitly admitting that at least some poverty was unavoidable and could not be blamed on individual workers.

Despite these improvements, only a tiny percentage of those in need were willing to undergo the rigours of the workhouse and, as a result, poverty remained largely untreated. In the 1880s, about 3% of the population were in receipt of relief at a time when something like 30% of people were in dire poverty. Furthermore, the workhouse was still a grim and forbidding place which was feared and hated by the poor.

As time went by, it became evident that the Poor Law was the wrong instrument for solving the social problems of an industrial nation. Above all, its approach to unemployment was fundamentally wrong, for it was no use trying to frighten an unemployed worker into finding work when no work was available. It was also failing to deal with the mass of untreated poverty revealed by the journalists and social investigators at the end of the nineteenth century.

POOR LAW Statistics

Year	% of paupers relieved
1834	8.8
1850	5.7
1860	4.3
1870	4.6
1880	3.0
1900	2.5

Table 4.1

Changing Britain 1850–1979

BOOTH'S *Classification of People*

A	The lowest class—occasional labourers, loafers and semi-criminals.			
B	The very poor—casual labourer, hand-to-mouth existence, chronic want.			
C&D	The poor—including alike those whose earnings are small, because of irregularity of employment and those whose work, though regular, is ill-paid.			
E&F	The regularly employed and fairly paid working class of all grades.			
G&H	Lower and upper middle class and all above this level.			

The proportion of the different classes shown for all London are as follows:

A (lowest class)	37,610	or	0.9%
B (very poor)	316,834	or	7.5%
C&D (poor)	938,293	or	22.3%
E&F (working class comfortable)	2,166,503	or	51.5%
G&H (middle class and above)	749,930	or	17.8%
Inmates of Institutions	99,830		

Table 4.2 Source: C Booth, *Life and Labour of the People in London* (1892) Vol 11 pages 20–21

THE INVESTIGATION OF POVERTY

Middle-class consciences were aroused by the undeniable facts of poverty discovered through painstaking investigation by Charles Booth and Seebohm Rowntree. Booth was a wealthy Liverpool shipowner who took an interest in the poor. When he settled in London, he enjoyed walking through the East End, visiting pubs and music halls. He even lodged for a few days at a time with working-class families and developed considerable respect for them. He was spurred into action by the wish to disprove the Marxist HM Hyndman's assertion that the wages of a quarter of working men were insufficient to keep them in health. The 1880s were years of economic depression and Booth was aware of it, but he was determined to collect precise statistical evidence about the extent of poverty in London. The first essential was a definition of poverty. Booth stated at the outset in very precise terms what he meant by 'the poor' and in doing so invented (almost by accident) the concept of a 'poverty line'.

Booth said, "by the word 'poor' I mean to describe those who have a sufficiently regular though bare income, such as 18s (90p) to 21s (£1.05) for a moderate family, and by the words 'very poor' those who from any cause fall much below this standard ... My 'poor' may be described as living under a struggle to obtain the necessaries of life and make both ends meet; while the 'very poor' live in a state of chronic want."[2]

Booth's problem was to discover exactly how many people in London fell into each of these categories. He originally intended to use the census returns of 1881 but they proved to be useless for his purpose. In the end he turned to the School Board Visitors for information. Their reports, checked in various ways, formed the basis of his results.

Over one million families were investigated by Booth's team and the monumental task took seventeen years to complete (1886–1903). The results were contained in seventeen volumes entitled *Life and Labour of the People in London*. Booth was shocked to find out that Hyndman's figures were an underestimate of the extent of poverty since about 30% of people in London were living below his 'poverty line'.

Booth had been able to show with devastating clarity that decades of private philanthropy and charitable effort had made little impact on the problem of poverty in London. His figures also challenged the Poor Law statistics, which seemed to imply that poverty had been steadily reduced to almost insignificant proportions. However, the reality was that about 3% of the people in London at the turn of the century were being relieved through the Poor Law at a time when 30% of the people were in poverty. In other words, only about 10% of the poor were being helped by the Poor Law, the other 90% having to fend for themselves. Although Booth did attribute some of the blame for this poverty to moral failings (for instance, the 'loafers'), it was clear that casual labour, poor pay and unemployment caused most of the distress. These factors were outwith the control of the individuals concerned.

Seebohm Rowntree, related to the cocoa and chocolate manufacturers, who were known to have a charitable attitude towards the poor, carried on the investigation of poverty in his own town of York. He came up with a more satisfactory working definition of poverty:

● "Families whose total earnings are insufficient to obtain the minimum necessaries for the

maintenance of merely physical efficiency. Poverty falling under this head I have described as 'Primary Poverty'.

● Families whose total earnings would be sufficient for the maintenance of merely physical efficiency were it not that some portion of them is absorbed by other expenditure, either useful or wasteful. Poverty falling under this head is described as 'Secondary Poverty'."

Rowntree determined the poverty line at 21s 8d (£1.08). He said that this was the minimum necessary for food, rent, clothing, light, fuel etc.—just enough "for the maintenance of merely physical efficiency". He was surprised to find that York had 27.8% of its population living in poverty in 1899.

While Booth and Rowntree were using careful investigation to define and quantify urban poverty, several other writers were publicis-

ing, in more colourful and emotive language, the squalor in which much of the working class existed. The cumulative effect of all this literature was to create a greater awareness of poverty by the middle class. The climate of opinion was gradually drifting away from the individualist concern for renewed hard work and self-help by the lower class towards a 'collectivist' belief in social reform. Some of this drift was motivated by fear of working-class agitation. The extension of the franchise to working-class men in 1867 and 1884 also forced the two established parties to take account of the new voters.

THE 'OLD' LIBERALS AND SOCIAL REFORM
The overall record of the Liberal governments under Gladstone for introducing social reform in the closing three decades of the nineteenth century was a disappointing one. This was partly due to three factors.

'The results of free trade'—a postcard by T B Kennington circa 1910.

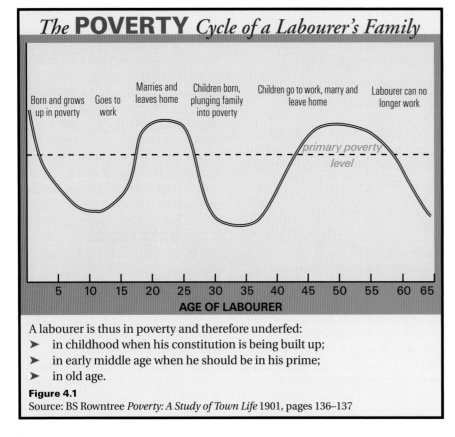

The POVERTY Cycle of a Labourer's Family

Born and grows up in poverty

Goes to work

Marries and leaves home

Children born, plunging family into poverty

Children go to work, marry and leave home

Labourer can no longer work

primary poverty level

AGE OF LABOURER
5 10 15 20 25 30 35 40 45 50 55 60 65

A labourer is thus in poverty and therefore underfed:
➤ in childhood when his constitution is being built up;
➤ in early middle age when he should be in his prime;
➤ in old age.

Figure 4.1
Source: BS Rowntree *Poverty: A Study of Town Life* 1901, pages 136–137

● Gladstone's desire to keep down public expenditure.

● His firm belief in individual self-help.

● His preoccupation with the Irish Question which was to have unfortunate repercussions on his party. The Irish Question undoubtedly helped to split the Liberals and to place them in the political wilderness from 1886 to 1906 during which time they only held office briefly between 1892 and 1894.

Apart from a few exceptions, the 'Old' Liberalism of the Gladstone era, with its emphasis on the preservation of personal freedom by lack of government intervention, was still very much in evidence.

There was little movement away from the Poor Law principle. Some of the harsher features of the system were modified, but the system itself remained in place. For example, the provision of job creation schemes represented a relaxation of the rules in exceptional times, not their abandonment. The no-

tion that many of the poor were in that position due to unemployment, which was no fault of their own, was still anathema to the Local Government Boards. Even the term 'unemployed' had not entered common usage.

Nevertheless, the state was beginning to take more responsibility for the weakest members of society and those whom it thought to be deserving. On the other hand, we must be careful to avoid making too extravagant a claim for the Britain of 1900. This was still what we might call the 'enabling state' rather than an early prototype for the Welfare State. Voluntary action, private charity and self-help were still very much in vogue, but now local and national government were beginning to play a more positive part in enabling people to get back on their feet, while at the same time deterring the 'undeserving poor' from abusing the system. The real turning-point was to come with the Liberal governments' social welfare reforms between 1906 and 1914.

THE CONSERVATIVES AND SOCIAL REFORM

In the twentieth century, the Liberals (1906–14) and Labour (1945–51) both contributed significantly to the development of the Welfare State. What about the Conservatives though? They were in power for most of the last thirty years of the nineteenth century. The main hope for change lay with Lord Randolph Churchill. In a speech at Dartford in October 1886, Churchill had advocated an impressive list of social reforms including "improvement of public health and housing, compulsory national insurance, smallholdings for agricultural labourers, reform of parliamentary procedure, and the provision of parks, libraries, art galleries, museums and public baths and washhouses".[3] These proposals were far too radical for the Conservative leadership and when Churchill tendered his resignation over a disagreement concerning the Budget in December 1886, it was accepted.

Another Conservative reformer who was highly critical of the Party's poor record on social reform was JA Gorst. Not surprisingly, Gorst failed to make any progress towards the top of the Conservative Party hierarchy. With Churchill and Gorst sidelined, Lord Salisbury was able to lead the Conservative Party along traditional lines. Consequently, the 1880s and 1890s saw few social reforms and little was done to improve the lives of the working class, although three significant reforms were introduced.

Housing Act (1890)
This Act further extended the provisions of the 1875 Act for clearing slums and erecting new dwelling houses.

Education Act (1891)
Free elementary education was introduced by increasing government grants to Church and Board schools.

Workmen's Compensation Acts (1897, 1900)
An employee could now obtain compensation for injury at work without having to prove negligence on the part of his employer. However, both Acts only covered a small number of occupations.

DID THE RISE OF LABOUR FORCE THE PACE OF SOCIAL REFORM?

From the 1880s onwards, the Liberals and the Conservatives had to contend with and respond to the appeal of socialism. For the previous thirty years, Marx and Engels had been asserting that the real cause of poverty lay with capitalism itself. Only when the capitalist system had been destroyed would the workers really enjoy the fruits of their labour. The Social Democratic Federation, founded by HM Hyndman, took a Marxist revolutionary line. Hyndman was suspicious of reforms which aimed to take the harsh edge off capitalism. Social welfare measures were only sops to the working class and helped employers to keep wages low.

The Fabian Society was a more moderate and gradualist organisation which included among its leading members the writers Sidney and Beatrice Webb and the playwright George Bernard Shaw. They were in favour of more state intervention to relieve poverty. The Webbs helped to influence contemporary thinking on social problems through their books, pamphlets and frequent contacts with the political and academic establishment.

By 1900, the Labour Party had been established. Like the Fabians, Labour did not seek the overthrow of capitalism. In the early years, the programme of the Labour Party was based on the protection of trade union rights and interests. As Labour was the party of the working class, the Liberals and Conservatives would feel growing pressure to compete for working-class votes by proposing measures of social reform.

Historians disagree about the importance of the working-class and socialist organisations in forcing the pace of social reform.

● "... socialism and the organisation of labour represented a threat to the other two parties in view of the more democratic franchise that existed. Though socialists were an infinitesimal minority of the electorate they had an influence far beyond their numerical strength."[4]

● "... the pressure for social reform from the working class was politically negligible before the First World War."[5]

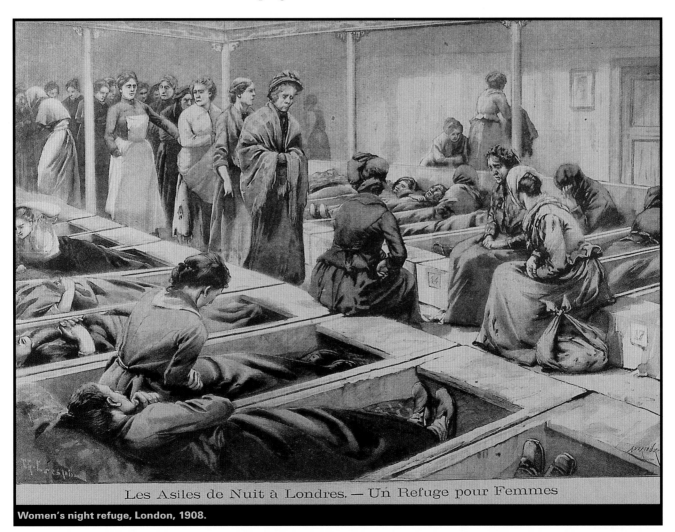

Les Asiles de Nuit à Londres. — Un Refuge pour Femmes

Women's night refuge, London, 1908.

The Liberal Welfare Reforms 1906–1914

WHAT YOU WILL LEARN

- The differences between 'Old' and 'New' Liberalism.

- The origins of the Liberal social welfare reforms.

- The nature and purpose of the legislation as it related to the young, old, sick, unemployed and employed.

- The opposition faced by the Liberals as they introduced their reforms.

- The extent to which these reforms went towards solving social problems in Britain.

- The extent to which the government had taken responsibility for the welfare of the people by 1914.

- The contrasting views of historians towards the Liberal social welfare reforms, 1906-1914.

THE LIBERALS swept into power in January 1906 with a massive majority of three hundred and fifty six (including Labour and the Irish Nationalists). They had defeated a Conservative Party which had been in government for most of the previous twenty years.

However, it would be wrong to imagine that the Liberals had won the election on a wave of 'New' Liberalism. In 1906, most Liberals were still committed to the primary cause of traditional or 'Old' Liberalism—to preserve personal freedom by opposing governmental interference in either everyday life, or the workings of the market economy (laissez-faire). During the election campaign their main concern was Free Trade. Furthermore, Campbell-Bannerman, the new Liberal Prime Minister (1906–8), still very much believed in the virtues of 'Old' Liberalism.

Nevertheless, from the turn of the century onwards, a small group of Liberals began to campaign for more state action to help to improve the conditions of the poor. Although the exponents of 'New' Liberalism were small in number, their influence was eventually to prove decisive in committing the Party to a series of social reforms. Extensive pressure was exerted from below by a group of highly influential individuals: Junior Ministers like Charles Masterman; journalists with the *Nation* newspaper, such as HW Massingham, HN Brailsford, LT Hobhouse and JA Hobson; social reformers like Sidney and Beatrice Webb; and civil servants like Robert Morant and William Beveridge.

"What then is the matter with the Liberals? ... The political force of this Old Liberalism is spent. During the last twenty years, its aspirations and its watchwords, its ideas of daily life and its conceptions of the universe,

Liberal Welfare Legislation 1906–14

Group	Assistance Given	Legislation
YOUNG	School meals	*Education (Provision of Meals) Act 1906*
	Medical inspection	*Education (Administrative Provisions) Act 1907*
OLD	Pensions	*Old Age Pensions Act 1908*
SICK	Health Insurance	*National Insurance Act Part I 1911*
EMPLOYED	Compensation for injuries sustained at work	*Workmen's Compensation Act 1906*
	Eight-hour day for miners	*Coal Mines Act 1908*
	Minimum wages for 'sweated industry' workers	*Trade Boards Act 1909*
	Half-day off for shop assistants	*Shops Act 1911*
UNEMPLOYED	Help to find work	*Labour Exchanges Act 1909*
	Unemployment insurance	*National Insurance Act Part II 1911*

Key LIBERAL MINISTERS

Prime Minister	*Chancellor of the Exchequer*	*President of the Board of Trade*	*Home Secretary*
Sir H Campbell Bannerman 1906–8	H Asquith 1906–8	D Lloyd George 1906–8	H Gladstone 1906–10
H Asquith 1908–15	D Lloyd George 1908–15	WS Churchill 1908–10	WS Churchill 1910–11
	S Buxton 1910–14	R McKenna 1911–15	

have become increasingly distasteful to the ordinary citizen ... Its worship of individual liberty evokes no enthusiasm. Its reliance on 'freedom of contract' and 'supply and demand' ... now seems to work out disastrously for the masses, who are too poor to have what the economists call an 'effective demand' for even the minimum conditions of physical and mental well-being ... The principles were fresh once—in the last quarter of the eighteenth century. Their exponents' minds were fresh too—about the middle of the nineteenth century. But Adam Smith is dead, and Queen Anne and even Sir Robert Peel; while as to Gladstone, he is the deadest of them all."[1]

In line with arguments from the New Liberals that Old Liberalism was out of date and could not cope with the present social problems, the achievements of the Campbell-Bannerman administration proved to be quite disappointing. Most of the period up to 1908 was concerned with traditional Liberal measures such as the Education Bill. The two main excep-

tions were the School Meals Act (1906) and the Medical Inspection of Schoolchildren (1907). It was only with the advent of Asquith as Prime Minister in 1908 and the appointments of Lloyd George and Churchill to the Cabinet that the mood began to change.

During its lifetime, the Liberal government brought in a series of new laws directed towards the young and the old. It insured many of those in work against unemployment and sickness and improved conditions for millions of vulnerable workers. We will now look at the key social reforms undertaken during these years and attempt to gauge their significance as steps on the road to the welfare state.

THE YOUNG

The first social reforms to be undertaken by the Liberals were concerned with children and in particular dealt with the provision of school meals and the medical inspection of pupils. Now that education was compulsory, it was

all too obvious to teachers and the education authorities that large numbers of children were coming to school hungry, dirty and/or suffering from ill health. Concern about the problem was widespread and efforts to provide school meals on a voluntary basis can be traced back to the 1860s. Arguments in favour of these reforms fell into two categories.

There were the philanthropic or humanitarian arguments based on the adage 'Feed the stomach, then the mind'. One of the most fervent advocates of school meals was Margaret Macmillan in Bradford.

"The state compels the children to work (in school)—it makes the demand for sustenance urgent, intolerable. But it does not compel parents to feed their children. Hence it is certain to some of these hungry little ones that free education is less of a boon than an outrage.

Here, for example, is a group of very hopeful children. They have known what hunger is all their lives, but

General ELECTION *Results* 1906–1914

Parties	JANUARY 1906		JANUARY 1910		DECEMBER 1910	
	Seats	Votes	Seats	Votes	Seats	Votes
Conservatives	157	2,451,454	273	3,127,887	272	2,420,566
Liberals	377	2,757,883	275	2,880,581	272	2,295,888
Labour	29	329,748	40	505,657	42	371,772
Lib-Labs	24	–	–	–	–	–
Irish Nationalists	83	35,031	82	124,586	84	131,375

Table 5.1
Source: D Butler & J Freeman *British Political Facts 1900–1968*

CAUSES OF REJECTION
of Army Recruits on Inspection (1891–1902)

Ratio per 1,000

Cause	1891	1892	1893	1894	1895	1896	1897	1898	1899	1900	1901	1902
Under chest measure	93	96	108	110	126	140	89	74	66	60	49	57
Defective vision	40	42	41	42	39	40	41	42	41	36	35	39
Underweight	32	27	39	39	36	35	45	34	33	28	25	21
Underheight	27	32	33	28	28	28	24	20	20	15	13	12
Imperfect constitution	18	10	9	5	3	4	4	5	6	5	3	4
Disease of veins	16	16	17	15	15	15	15	15	14	11	14	12
Disease of heart	16	18	17	19	20	18	17	17	15	13	16	17
Disease of lower extremities	15	17	14	17	18	18	18	17	13	10	16	12
Varicocele	13	12	13	14	12	13	13	12	11	11	14	12
Flat feet	11	9	12	14	13	17	16	12	12	9	11	12
Loss or decay of teeth	11	14	15	16	18	20	24	26	25	20	26	49

Table 5.2

never have they been so hungry as now. When they were little they used to get scraps of food, and now and again a good meal, and this was enough to allow them to live a free, careless life in the fields or alleys. But at last the school board officer got on their track. They were led into a big school, and obliged to read, write, sing, calculate."[2]

A study carried out in a poor district of Dundee in 1905 revealed that the children were significantly underweight and underheight compared to the national average.

"It may be fairly affirmed, after a dispassionate consideration of the facts disclosed by the Medical Reports, that there are in the Dundee schools a large number of children who should be under medical supervision, and whose future in life is imperilled for want of it; that many children, either from disease or lack of personal cleanliness, are a source of danger and serious discomfort to their companions; and that many derive little benefit from school attendance, because they cannot apply their minds to lessons while their stomachs are empty."[3]

The second category of arguments for better treatment of schoolchildren was concerned with the common belief at the turn of the century that the people of Britain were suffering a physical decline.

Only a concerted campaign of 'national efficiency' could restore the vitality of the nation and this had to start in the schools.

The poor physical condition of recruits during the Boer War (1899–1902) highlighted the problem. The minimum height requirement for entry into the army had to be dropped from 5 feet 6 inches in 1845 to 5 feet 2 inches before the Boer War. The leader of the Social Democratic Federation (SDF), Hyndman, claimed at the time that 50% of urban working-class recruits had been unfit for the war due to their poor physical condition.

Two reports appeared in the wake of the Boer War, both stimulated by the alarm over the 'physical deficiency' of the British people. The Royal Commission on Physical Training in Scotland (1903) set out to investigate the physical condition of children in Scotland. It did this by comparing children's height and weight in Aberdeen, Edinburgh, Boston (USA) and Britain as a whole. (See Table 5.3.)

Although Aberdeen seems to have been about average compared to the rest of Britain, Edinburgh children were significantly underweight and underheight*. The

Royal Commission recommended that "provision should be made for regular inspection of school children." It also came out in favour of education authorities providing school meals, working with the relevant voluntary bodies. In the following year, the Report of the Interdepartmental Committee on Physical Deterioration was published. It also recommended that

"... a systemised medical inspection of children at school should be imposed as a public duty on every school authority ... (and) ... that definite provision should be made by the various Local Authorities for dealing with the question of under-fed children ... ."

The Education (Provision of Meals) Act, 1906
Much of the credit for the school meals Bill lies outside the Liberal Party. There was widespread public concern created by the two reports and the new parliamentary presence of the Labour Party also pushed the Liberals into taking action. The Liberals had not campaigned on a platform of social welfare reform in the run-up to the General Election in December 1905 and there was little indication from their manifesto that Britain was about to experience a period of radical social reform.

---

*The findings of the Royal Commission stimulated another body, the Sanitary Institute, to produce its own Inquiry into the Physique of Glasgow School Children in 1904. Not surprisingly, it showed that Glasgow children were even more underweight than those in Edinburgh.

The stimulus for action came from a Labour backbencher, William Wilson, the Chairman of the Amalgamated Society of Carpenters and Joiners. He introduced the school meals proposal as a Private Member's Bill and because it was so well received in the House of Commons, the Liberals decided to give it government time. The outcome was the Education (Provision of Meals) Bill which became law in December 1906. It was a cautious measure, allowing authorities to "take such steps as they think fit for the provision of meals", either in conjunction with voluntary bodies or on their own. Parents were to be charged if they could afford it or else the local authority could put a halfpenny on the rates.

The number of school meals provided rose from three million in 1906 to nine million in 1910 and then to fourteen million in 1914. By that time, the voluntary agencies had become overwhelmed by the scale of the scheme and most of the provision was in the hands of the local authorities, who in turn were in receipt of a 50% grant from the Treasury. Within a short time, a publicly-funded welfare service, administered by the Board of Education, was beginning to replace a patchwork of local charitable efforts. There was still a long way to go, however, and by 1912 over half the local authorities had not set up a school meals service.

"This measure was important, first, because it was the first extension from the field of schooling into that of welfare of the principle that a publicly-financed benefit could be granted to those in need, free both of charge and of the disabilities associated with the Poor Law; second, it was a step towards recognition that parents were not necessarily culpable for the undernourishment of their children and that, with public support, needy children could be well cared for at home and did not require withdrawal into public or voluntary care."[4]

Education (Administrative Provisions) Act, 1907

School medical inspection "owed as much to administrative pressure as to Liberal initiative."[5]

The government was not at all enthusiastic about the proposal because it knew that inspection would inevitably reveal chronic health problems. This would lead to demands for publicly-funded medical treatment facilities which the Liberals felt they could not afford at that time. The administrative drive mentioned above came from Robert L Morant, the Permanent Secretary of the Education Board. During 1906, he had been persuaded about the need for school medical inspections through contact with Margaret Macmillan.

"I have for some time past come to feel that for the good of the children and the public, what subjects are taught and how much they are taught do not matter anything like so much nowadays as attention a) to the physical condition of the scholars and the teacher and b) to the physiological aspect of the school ... Between us we shall do something, I am sure, if we can avoid a public hubbub against our efforts ..."[6]

SCHOOL MEDICAL INSPECTIONS

"... the statutory medical inspection ... should take account of the following matters:

1 Previous disease including infectious diseases.

2 General condition and circumstances.
   a height and weight
   b nutrition (good, medium, bad)
   c cleanliness (including vermin of head and body)
   d clothing (sufficiency, cleanliness and footgear)

3 Throat, nose and articulation (mouth-breathing, snoring, stammering, tonsillar and glandular conditions, adenoids).

4 External eye disease and vision testing.

5 Ear disease and deafness.

6 Teeth and oral sepsis.

7 Mental capacity (normal, backward, defective).

8 Present disease or defect."

Comparisons of Height and Weight of British and American Schoolchildren

	British	Boston	Aberdeen	Edinburgh
Height (inches)				
Boys 6–9	45.7	46.2	46.0	44.5
Girls 6–9	44.6	45.9	45.4	44.5
Boys 9–12	51.7	52.1	51.2	50.2
Girls 9–12	50.9	51.7	50.1	49.9
Boys 12–15	57.1	53.3	57.3	55.3
Girls 12–15	57.7	58.7	57.4	55.7
Weight (pounds)				
Boys 6–9	49.6	49.6	51.1	46.1
Girls 6–9	47.1	48.2	47.9	45.6
Boys 9–12	66.6	66.3	64.0	59.5
Girls 9–12	61.8	63.9	60.9	57.8
Boys 12–15	83.7	89.1	84.5	74.0
Girls 12–15	86.7	90.9	83.3	78.4

Table 5.3

Morant's influential position as Permanent Secretary enabled him to get his own way whilst avoiding the "public hubbub". It was his job to draw up the fine details of the Education (Administrative Provisions) Bill. He managed to smuggle the school medical inspection provisions into this rather innocuous Bill, which was passed into law in 1907. Under the Act, medical inspection of all elementary school pupils was to take place. (See page 57.)

As predicted, inspection revealed the disturbing fact that children were going untreated because their parents were too poor to afford the doctors' bills. The government was soon under pressure to treat the problems revealed by its own inspectors. In 1912, the Board of Education started to give grants to local authorities for treatment and school clinics were set up for the first time.

In Scotland, the medical inspection of children was authorised under the *Education (Scotland) Act* of 1908. The Act also gave School Boards the power to take action against parents who allowed their children to come to school in a filthy or verminous condition. Inspection was made compulsory and Medical Officers or nurses were hired for the purpose. Perhaps not unexpectedly, the first report of the school medical inspection service for Glasgow exposed both the level of ill health amongst pupils and the lack of ongoing treatment for their ailments.

> "... it emerged that between 80% and 90% of the children examined had defective teeth; that about 9% suffered from rickets (due to inadequate diet); and that about 30% were verminous. It was found that 55% of children with defects had not had any form of treatment, while many of the others had not received the continuing treatment which they required."[7]

Children Act, 1908

Like the *Education (Scotland) Act*, the *Children Act* made it a legal offence for parents to neglect their children. The Act also brought together and organised into a proper system a mass of previous rulings. It became known as the 'Children's Charter'. Most of the provisions were for the protection of children.

- Children under sixteen were forbidden to smoke or drink and stiff penalties were brought in for shops selling alcohol or tobacco to children.

- Children were forbidden to beg.

- Young offenders were no longer to be tried in the ordinary courts but in new juvenile courts.

- Remand homes were set up to keep child offenders out of prison while waiting for trial.

- If convicted, children were to be sent to borstal (a corrective school) rather than to prison.

- Probation officers were appointed for the after-care of young offenders.

Lloyd George. This portrait was taken in 1912.

1908—A TURNING POINT IN THE PACE OF REFORM

The first two years of the Liberal government had seen only relatively minor reform measures, but between 1908 and 1911 several major social welfare reforms were passed. The turning point came in 1908 when Prime Minister Campbell-Bannerman was forced to resign due to ill health. His replacement, Asquith, brought into the Cabinet two key figures who were to play a significant role in the next few years—Lloyd George (Chancellor of the Exchequer) and Churchill (President of the Board of Trade). Both were strongly committed to social reform and they were mainly responsible for the welfare legislation which was passed over the following three years.

The Liberal Party itself was in the process of changing some of its fundamental values in line with 'New Liberal' thinking. Lloyd George outlined the broad principles now underlying the government's policy in a speech at Swansea in October, 1908.

> "It has not abandoned the traditional ambition of the Liberal Party to establish freedom and equality; but side by side with this effort it promotes measures for ameliorating the conditions of life of the multitude."[8]

Lloyd George himself was genuinely concerned for the welfare of the people because of his own background.

> "I am a man of the people, bred amongst them and it has been the greatest joy of my life to have had some part in fighting the battles of the class from whom I am proud to have sprung."

Apart from this concern for social justice for the underprivileged, the Liberals had other motives for wanting to put social reform at the head of their policy agenda. In particular, they recognised the growing threat to Liberalism posed by the Labour Party. Lloyd George, though, was confident that Labour would only oust the Liberals if they failed "to cope seriously with the social condition of the people, to remove the national degradation of slums and widespread poverty in a land glittering with wealth".[9]

Churchill was also keenly aware of the challenge from Labour. He saw social reform as a means of halting socialism. In his by-election campaign at Dundee in 1908, he pointed out that "Socialism wants to pull down wealth, Liberalism seeks to raise up poverty ... Socialism assails the maximum pre-eminence of the individual, Liberalism seeks to build up the minimum standard of the masses. Socialism attacks Capital, Liberalism attacks Monopoly".[10]

Finally, both Lloyd George and Churchill were influenced by the question of 'national efficiency'. Lloyd George was particularly impressed by the advances made in Germany as a result of Bismarck's social legislation. He was also struck by the emerging military might of Germany and the way in which its national strength was directly related to an enlightened welfare programme. Churchill echoed this concern and in December 1908 he informed Asquith that "There is a tremendous policy in social organisation. The need is urgent and the moment right. Germany with a harder climate and far less accumulated wealth has managed to establish tolerable basic conditions for her people."[11]

All of these factors came together during and after 1908 and resulted in major steps forward such as old age pensions and insurance against sickness and unemployment.

THE OLD

The *Old Age Pensions Act* of 1908 was the culmination of more than twenty years of debate and inquiry into the subject of poverty amongst the elderly. Leading figures such as Charles Booth and Joseph Chamberlain had taken up the cause of pensions in the 1890s. Both were members of the Royal Commission on the Aged Poor, set up in 1893 to consider "whether any alterations in the system of Poor Law relief are desirable, and the care of persons whose destitution is occasioned by incapacity for work resulting from old age". The Commission was dominated by advocates of laissez-faire and not surprisingly, the Majority Report (1895) came out against any major alteration of the current system. Chamberlain's contribution to the Minority Report contained cautious proposals—not for a universal system of old age pensions but "a tentative scheme which might develop into something much more complete, on a contributory basis, with sufficiently liberal help from the State to make the scheme attractive. The scheme provides for a State Pension Fund, to which Parliament would make an annual grant, supplemented from the Poor Rate which old age pensions would ultimately relieve."[12]

During his evidence, Chamberlain cited two difficult hurdles which would have to be overcome before progress with old age pensions could be made. Firstly, he argued that the cost of a state scheme would create opposition.

> "Mr Booth's scheme (ie. state pensions financed out of taxation) is logical and would do what it set out to do, but it would cost £20-£24 millions and the House of Commons would never provide the money."[13]

Secondly, he feared opposition from the Friendly Societies who gained a great deal of business from providing pensions for the working class.

> "I attach great importance to Friendly Societies. They are in touch with the thriftily minded section of the working class. Their criticism of any scheme would be very damaging: their opposition might be fatal. They have very great Parliamentary influence and I should myself think twice before attempting to proceed in the face of hostility from so important and dangerous a quarter."[14]

Chamberlain's words had a prophetic ring because these two issues were largely instrumental in delaying progress on pensions in Britain. In the meantime, Germany (1889), Denmark (1891) and New Zealand (1899) had all established their own systems of old age pensions before the coming of the twentieth century.

Problems of Cost

In August, 1899, the Conservative government set up a committee under Sir Edward Hamilton to look into the financial implications of an old age pension scheme. It is not clear how close the government was to making a commitment to pensions but the financial implications of the Boer War put a stop to such costly adventures. Bonar Law, writing in 1912 in defence of the Conservative government, claimed that the Boer War made "all schemes of social reform impossible" and even up to 1905, "... the finances of the country had been so disorganised that even then such a scheme was impossible."[15]

The Liberals also found that the cost of any proposed scheme was a significant factor. Asquith, the new Chancellor of the Exchequer, would only commit the government to the introduction of a Pensions Bill once the budget was in surplus. Inside government, the Treasury had an important part to play in the final outcome. For example, when the Treasury balked at the cost of setting up and administering a contributory pension scheme, Asquith decided upon a non-contributory scheme financed out of taxation. When it was calculated that the cost to the state of pensions at sixty five would be £17 million a year, the Treasury set an upper limit of £7 million.

Asquith decided to opt for the less generous starting age of seventy, against his better judgment. Even then, the Treasury persuaded the government to add in more exemptions to the final scheme in order to get the cost down further.

Payment of old age-pensions began in 1909. This engraving was taken from *The Graphic*.

Friendly Society Opposition

The Friendly Societies were opposed to the state intervening to take over pensions because this would directly threaten their own vested interests. The friendly societies were simply reflecting the anti-state attitudes of their clientele—the 'better-off' working class.

The Foresters was one of the largest friendly societies. The following quotation from their own journal is fairly representative of the views of most friendly societies towards state pensions. Notice also how the passage emphasises the ennobling virtue of working-class mutual self-help.

"The aim of the working class ought to be to bring about economic conditions in which there should be no need for distribution of state alms. The establishment of a great scheme of state pensions would legalise and stamp as a permanent feature of our social life the chronic poverty of the age. The desire of the best reformers is to remove the conditions that make that poverty so that every citizen shall have a fair chance not only of earning a decent wage for today but such a wage as shall enable him to provide for the future ... Employers have presented carefully organised barriers to the workmen getting more wages ... We have always held that the only object of (reform) was to transfer the burdens from employer to labour ...

PENSION COSTS

Cost to government if pensionable age fixed at:

	65	70	75
1901	£10.3m	£5.9m	£2.9m
1911	£12.6m	£7.4m	£3.7m
1921	£15.6m	£9.5m	£4.9m

Table 5.4

Man is a responsible being. To rob him of his responsibility is to degrade him. The working class should rise to the occasion and insist upon being capable of using their own wages to their own advantage."[16]

However, public opinion began to shift unrelentingly in the direction of publicly financed pensions and by 1903 the trade unions and the cooperative movement had come to the conclusion that this was desirable. The friendly societies had also come to accept that old age pensions were going to be brought in soon and they reluctantly came down in favour of a non-contributory scheme.

The Old Age Pensions Act, 1908

As with the children's legislation, the Liberals had not campaigned specifically for old age pensions during the election campaign in 1906. Nevertheless, there was growing public and pressure group demand for action. For example, the National Committee of Organised Labour for Old Age Pensions (NCOL) had been gaining support outside Parliament for pensions at sixty five financed out of taxation. In the Commons, one of the Liberals' own backbenchers, the philanthropist soap manufacturer, WL Lever, attempted to force the pace by introducing a Private Member's Bill on pensions. Although the Bill failed, there was widespread support for the principle in the House.

The NCOL pensions campaign and Liberal inaction together appeared to be benefiting Labour—at least

the government seems to have interpreted its two by-election defeats to Labour in 1907 (at Jarrow and Colne Valley—previously safe 'Old Liberal' seats) in this way. It was a timely warning that action was necessary.

It was the task of Lloyd George, the new Chancellor of the Exchequer from April 1908, to get the Liberal Old Age Pensions Bill through the Commons. He had maintained an interest in this area for a long time, having been a member of the Chaplin Committee on Pensions in 1899. That committee had looked in great detail at the New Zealand and Danish schemes, but Lloyd George appeared to be more interested in the German scheme. The following passage shows how impressed he was, not only with the pensions scheme but with the whole system of national insurance.

"I never realised before on what a gigantic scale the German pension system is conducted. Nor had I any idea how successfully it works. I had read much about it, but no amount of study at home ... can convey to the mind a clear idea of all that state insurance means to Germany ... It touches the great mass of German people in well-nigh every walk of life. Old age pensions form but a part of the system. Does the German worker fall ill? State insurance comes to his aid. Is he permanently invalided from work? Again he gets a regular grant whether he has reached the pension age or not."[17]

Lloyd George successfully steered the Bill through the House of Commons and there was very little opposition, except on detail. In the Lords, there was more evidence of hostility to the principle. The following extract from the Earl of Wemyss's speech gives us a flavour of the laissez-faire response to proposals for social welfare legislation.

"The State invites us every day to lean upon it. The strongest man, if encouraged, may soon accustom himself to the methods of an invalid. He may train himself to tot-

ter, or to be fed with a spoon. Every day the area for initiative is being narrowed, every day the standing ground for self-reliance is being undermined: every day the public impinges—with the best intentions, no doubt—on the individual; the nation is being taken into custody by the State ... It was self-reliance that built the Empire; it is by self-reliance ... that it must be welded and continued."[18]

The Bill passed all its stages and became law in August 1908, with effect from January 1909. It entitled people over seventy with an annual income of between £21 and £31 to between 1 shilling (5p) and 5 shillings (25p) a week of a pension. The government was honest enough to admit that these payments were not meant to be a complete solution to the problem of poverty in old age. The maximum pension of 5 shillings a week was still 2 shillings (10p) short of what Rowntree considered to be the minimum necessary for an individual to remain above the 'poverty line'. Also, there were exemptions. Any seventy-year-old was entitled to the pension provided:

- they were British and had been resident in the UK for the previous twenty years;
- they had avoided imprisonment in the previous ten years;
- they had not habitually avoided work;
- they had avoided detention under the *Inebriates Act* in the previous ten years.

The government miscalculated how many people would come forward for the pension. They estimated 500,000—in fact 650,000 applied. A significant number of 'pensioners' had no birth certificates, and it was difficult to prove that they were not over seventy years of age. By 1914, the number had increased to nearly a million. The government very quickly became aware of the level of poverty amongst the old. These were people who had worked all their lives and, as Lloyd George said were

"... too proud to wear the badge of pauperism".[19]

Just how grateful many old people were for the meagre pension is vividly portrayed in Flora Thompson's book *Lark Rise*.

"When the Old Age Pensions began, life was transformed for such aged cottagers. They were relieved of anxiety. They were suddenly rich. Independent for life! At first when they went to the Post Office to draw it, tears of gratitude would run down the cheeks of some, and they would say as they picked up the money, 'God bless that Lord George!' (for they could not believe one so powerful and munificent could be a plain 'Mr') 'and God bless you, miss!', and there were flowers from their gardens and apples from their trees for the girl who merely handed them the money."[20]

THE SICK

"The aged we have dealt with ... we are still confronted with the more gigantic task of dealing with the rest—the sick, the infirm, the unemployed, the widows and orphans."
(Lloyd George, speaking in Swansea on his return from Germany, 1908)

Lloyd George was in no doubt that Britain needed a more comprehensive system and he was determined this time not to be bullied by outside pressures. Instead, the government would construct its own policy on sickness and invalidity. He immediately instructed his civil servants to set out detailed proposals for a scheme similar to the German one. However, yet again, he was to come up against the resistance of powerful vested interests such as the friendly societies and the doctors and he had to modify his original scheme accordingly. As Chancellor of the Exchequer, Lloyd George was also acutely aware of the cost implications of national insurance and he had to provide for that in the 1909 Budget.

THE DAWN OF HOPE.

Mr. LLOYD GEORGE'S National Health Insurance Bill provides for the insurance of the Worker in case of Sickness.

Support the Liberal Government
in their policy of
SOCIAL REFORM.

Published by the LIBERAL PUBLICATION DEPARTMENT (in connection with the National Liberal Federation and the Liberal Central Association), 42, Parliament Street, Westminster, S.W., and Printed by the National Press Agency Limited, Whitefriars House, London, E.C.
[Leaflet No. 2383.]   28/6/11.   [Price 5s. per 1000.

'The Dawn of Hope.' Leaflet published in support of Liberal social reforms.

The People's Budget, 1909

"The wealth of this country is enormous. It is not merely great, but it is growing at a gigantic pace, and I do not think it is too much to expect the more favoured part of the community who have got riches so great that they have really to spend a good part of their time in thinking how to spend them, to make a substantial contribution to improve the lot of the poorer members of the same community to which they belong, because it is in their interest after all that they should not belong to a country where there is so much poverty and distress side by side with gigantic wealth."[21]

With these words in the House of Commons, Lloyd George signalled his intent to bring in a redistributive tax on the rich in order to finance the national insurance scheme which was in the pipeline. Income tax was made more progressive—the more you earned, the higher the tax rate.

£ Income tax would start at 9d (4p) and go up to 1s 2d (6p) in the pound for average earners.

£ The very rich earning over £5,000 would have to pay an extra supertax of 2d (1p) in the pound.

£ Much more controversial was the proposed 20% capital gains tax on the sale of land and even land which was unused was to be taxed.

Lloyd George justified these radical proposals in his budget speech.

"This is a War Budget. It is for raising money to wage implacable warfare against poverty and squalidness. I cannot help hoping and believing that before this generation has passed away we shall have advanced a great step towards that good time when poverty and wretchedness and human degradation which always follow in its camp will be as remote to the people of this country as the wolves which once infested its forests."[22]

The 1909 Budget was rejected by the House of Lords and a major constitutional crisis ensued, culminating in the *Parliament Act* (1911) which curbed the powers of the House of Lords. The People's Budget was passed in 1910. The government now had the revenue to implement its social welfare programme.

The health insurance scheme was contained in Part I of the *National Insurance Act* (1911).

Lloyd George admitted that the final scheme was a compromise and that more would have to be done for the disadvantaged in society. The following is a note to his private secretary, RC Hawtree, written on 7 March, 1911.

"Insurance necessarily temporary expedient. At no distant date hope State will acknowledge a full responsibility in the matter of making provision for sickness, breakdown and unemployment. It really does so now, through the Poor Law; but conditions under which this system had hitherto worked have been so harsh and humiliating that working-class pride revolts against accepting so degrading and doubtful a boon. Gradually the obligation of the State to find labour or sustenance will be realised and honourably interpreted."[23]

In his famous speech in the House of Commons (10 June, 1911), Lloyd George used the metaphor of the ambulance wagon to make this same point.

"This year, this session ... I am in the ambulance corps. I am engaged to drive a wagon through the twistings and turnings and ruts of the parliamentary road. There are men who tell me I have overloaded that wagon. I have taken three years to pack it carefully, I cannot spare a single parcel, for the suffering is great. There are those who say my wagon is half empty; I say it is as much as I can carry. "[24]

Opposition of the Friendly Societies, Trade Unions & Industrial Insurance Companies

Lloyd George realised very quickly that his idea of a contributory scheme would be seen by the friendly societies as encroaching on their business and, consequently, he decided to administer the system through the societies. Those trade unions which gave sick pay would also have to be included.

However, the real problem arose with the Industrial Insurance Companies (IICs). They were in business for profit and they objected to Lloyd George's proposal to include widows' and orphans' benefits. The IICs were a very important part of the existing insurance set-up, with large companies, such as the Prudential, involved. There were also about 80,000 door-to-door collectors throughout the country. In the weeks running up to the 1910 Election, the IICs waged a successful political campaign to secure pledges from candidates to back their claims and on 1 December Lloyd George was forced to back down and exclude the two 'funeral' benefits.

The commercial interests had won this particular battle. They, along with the friendly societies, were designated 'approved societies' by the *National Insurance Act,* thereby enhancing their status with the public when conducting their other commercial business.

The Doctors

When Lloyd George brought out his proposals, the British Medical Association immediately put up

NATIONAL INSURANCE ACT (1911)

Provision of Part II

 CONTRIBUTIONS
Workers 2¹/₂d per week.
Employers 2¹/₂d per week.
The State 3d per week.

 TRADES INVOLVED
Shipbuilding, mechanical engineering, building, construction, iron founding and sawmilling, (the scheme was compulsory for these trades because of the cyclical/ seasonal pattern of unemployment).

 ENTITLEMENT
After a week of unemployment, the insured worker would get 7 shillings (35p) a week for up to 15 weeks in any one year.

 PAYMENT
The insured worker had to register as unemployed at the Labour Exchange and he would get paid at the Exchange.

 CONDITIONS
If a worker was dismissed for his conduct, then he would not be entitled to benefit.

objections. They were concerned that the government was simply going to reproduce, on a national scale, the existing unsatisfactory arrangement between the friendly societies and the doctors, whereby the doctors felt that they were being paid a pittance for treating the societies' working-class clients. They also wished the medical side of the insurance scheme to be run by the profession and to be free from friendly society domination.

Lloyd George met with the doctors and told them frankly that the so-

MAJORITY REPORT WANTED	MINORITY REPORT WANTED
● *National labour exchanges*	● *National labour exchanges coordinated by new Ministry of Labour*
● *Unemployment insurance*	● *Non-contributory benefits (not compulsory)*
● *Training for the unemployed*	● *Training for the unemployed*
● *Better technical education*	● *Better technical education*
● *Temporary public works to be set up, designed to eliminate economic depressions*	● *Ten year programme of public works only during times of very high unemployment*
● *Juvenile labour to be reduced, introducing part-time education and raising the school leaving age*	● *Juvenile labour to be reduced introducing part-time education and raising the school leaving age*
● *Labour colonies for the idle*	● *Labour colonies for the idle*

cieties were too powerful for him to resist, but that he was offering the doctors a higher contract fee of 4 shillings (20p) per patient and 2 shillings (10p) to cover drug costs. This was more than the friendly societies had been willing to concede. When the Act was passed, there was a rush by the poorer doctors to join the new 'panel' system. Many of them were able to double their income at a stroke.

The House of Commons also came down on the side of the doctors when it voted for an amendment putting the administration of medical benefit in the hands of Local Health Committees, later called Insurance Committees. All in all, the 1911 Act was so favourable to the doctors' case that it acquired the alternative title of 'the General Practitioners' Act'.

THE UNEMPLOYED

Up until the turn of the century, unemployment was still seen partly as a moral problem caused by individual idleness and partly as a cyclical or seasonal problem for certain industries such as construction and shipbuilding. Few were willing to accept that unemployment might be due to structural factors outwith the control of individual workers.

Thinking about the causes of unemployment was blinkered by the Victorian belief in 'self-help', based on thrift and hard work, which went unchallenged for a long time because of a lack of accurate information about the scale of the problem. Nevertheless, attitudes were changing. The Chamberlain Circular (1886), encouraging local authorities to provide public works schemes, was a first step towards the state taking action on unemployment. TH Green argued powerfully that the state had a moral duty to intervene positively to help the weakest members of society.

The unemployed, though, were not as impotent as they had been

previously. They now had the vote which compelled the established parties to take notice of their demands. Hunger marches and unemployment demonstrations took place during the trade depression between 1903 and 1905. The working class also aquired growing organisational strength with the establishment of the Labour Party in 1900.

The Liberal Party came to power in 1906 with no policy on unemployment. The outgoing Conservative government had passed the *Unemployed Workmen's Act* before it left office, but it was 1909 before a clear statement of intent emerged from the Liberals. They had preferred to set up the wide-ranging Royal Commission on the Poor Laws (1905) and were content to wait for its conclusions.

However, the members of the Commission could not agree and two documents were published, the Majority and the Minority Reports. (See opposite.) Lloyd George laid out the government's plan for unemployment insurance during the important Budget speech of 1909. It steered a middle course between the 'voluntarism' of the Majority Report and the 'socialism' of the Minority Report.

The government had taken five years to finalise its unemployment policy which was enshrined in Part II of the *National Insurance Act*. (See page 63.)

The Unemployed Workmen's Act, 1905

The Liberals inherited the *Unemployed Workmen's Act* from the previous Conservative administration. It was designed to provide help for unemployed workmen by setting up Distress Committees in boroughs with a population of more than 50,000 (and equivalent burghs and counties in Scotland). The Committees had the discretion to assist 'proper cases', namely unemployed workmen who had proved themselves previously to be thrifty, of good character and

THE RIGHT TICKET FOR YOU!
YOU ARE TRAVELLING
ON A SAFE LINE

1913
GOVERNMENT LINE
MALE WORKER PAYS 4ᴰ
EMPLOYER PAYS 3ᴰ
STATE PAYS 2ᴰ

YOUR RETURN
DURING ILLNESS
10/- Per Week
FOR 26 WEEKS
5/- AFTERWARDS (TILL 70)
WHILE INCAPABLE OF WORK
FREE DOCTOR & MEDICINE
30/- Maternity Grant
SANATORIUM BENEFIT

AND ARE ASSURED
A SAFE RETURN

A Liberal Party election poster of 1913 concerning health insurance.

who had not received poor relief in the previous year. They could then set up public works schemes and give financial help for families to emigrate or to find work elsewhere in the country. Some also bought up land to organise farm and labour colonies. For example, the Glasgow Distress Committee acquired 591 acres of land for this purpose in 1907 and for the next three years sent two hundred men by train every day to the colony at Palacerigg. The Aberdeen Committee organised stone-breaking for one hundred and twenty men at Dancing Cairns Quarry.

Nationally, the scheme was to be funded by voluntary donations and from the rates. A sum of £153,000 was raised through an appeal by Queen Alexandra, but the money soon ran out. A report by the London committees in 1907–8 concluded that "it is impossible to deal adequately with unemployment by local authorities and (we are) therefore of the opinion that in future

legislation the question should be dealt with nationally".[25]

As the Queen's fund had been used up by the time the Liberals came to power, it was decided to grant a further £200,000 from the Treasury coffers. Depending on how one interprets this decision, it was either a paltry gesture or a historic decision by the state to use national funds for the first time to deal with the problem of unemployment. In the short term, the temporary work schemes to 'tide people over' failed to get to the root of the problem. In the longer term, though, the government had set a precedent by taking some responsibility for the welfare of those out of work.

Labour Exchanges
In February 1909, two reports and a book were published, all advocating the establishment of Labour Exchanges throughout Britain. The two reports were the Majority and Minority Reports of the Royal

Commission on the Poor Laws and the book was William Beveridge's *Unemployment—A Problem of Industry*. Beveridge argued that the current arrangement, which involved men standing outside factories in the morning waiting to be chosen for casual work, was very inefficient. A Labour Exchange would enable employer and employee to register their requirements at one central location and their separate needs could then be met. The Exchange would also benefit from having detailed information about job vacancies.

Churchill had heard about Beveridge's ideas in advance of the publication of his book and had managed to persuade him to join the Board of Trade team in July 1908. Beveridge's remit was to lay out detailed plans for a Labour Exchanges Bill. These were ready in a few months and the Bill had passed all its stages by September 1909. By the following February, eighty three Labour Exchanges

An unemployed workman at home with his family, 1908.

had been set up; by 1913 there were four hundred and thirty Exchanges throughout Britain. Despite wariness from both employers and employees, about 3,000 people were being fixed up with work every day by 1914.

Unemployment Insurance
Churchill envisaged Labour Exchanges as having two roles—firstly to allow the unemployed to register for and find work and secondly to pay out unemployment benefit to those who were insured. It was to insurance that Churchill now turned. The final scheme for unemployment insurance was worked out by Llewellyn Smith, Permanent Secretary at the Board of Trade, and Beveridge. Since there were no vested interests involved (like the doctors and friendly societies were with health insurance), Part II of the National Insurance Bill had a relatively easy passage through Parliament.

Churchill was not able to supervise the transition of the Bill into law as he was made Home Secretary in February 1910. His successor at the Board of Trade, Sidney Buxton, remarked during the debate in the Commons: "... if the Bill had been introduced ten years ago it would not have found ... a single supporter from either of the front benches." It was certainly true that the climate of opinion had changed. Charity and self-help were no longer seen to be adequate remedies for the evils of unemployment. Now the state was going to intervene to help the most vulnerable workers to insure themselves.

The Unemployment Insurance scheme got under way in July 1912 but benefits were not payable until January 1913. Within two years, 2.3 million workers were insured. Although this was still a small proportion of the total working

population, both Churchill and Lloyd George saw it as the beginning of a much more comprehensive system for dealing with the problem of unemployment.

THE EMPLOYED
The Liberal government also passed four laws which sought to improve workers' conditions, providing:

● compensation for injuries sustained at work;

● shorter hours to compensate for the dangerous and difficult job done underground by coal miners;

● minimum wages for exploited female labour in 'sweated trades';

● a half-day off each week for shop assistants who were mostly non-unionised.

Taken together, these measures constituted a significant improvement for millions of workers, many of whom had no one to speak up for them.

1 *The Workmen's Compensation Act* (1906) built on the previous Acts of 1897 and 1900 which had made employers in a few specified trades liable to pay compensation for injuries sustained as a result of conditions at the workplace. The 1906 Act extended this to cover nearly all employees. Employers were now also liable to pay compensation for the contracting of industrial diseases by their workforce.

2 *The Coal Mines Act* (1908) gave miners an eight-hour day, for which they had been campaigning for forty years.

3 *The Trade Boards Act* (1909) set up Boards to negotiate minimum wage levels for the notoriously badly paid and non-unionised 'sweated trades' which usually employed women working long hours in four trades—box, lace and chain making and tailoring. A total of 200,000 workers were involved in these trades. However, no attempt was made to define what a 'minimum' wage was.

4 *The Shops Act* (1911) stated that shop assistants were entitled to a weekly half-day off and a reasonable break for meals.

AN ASSESSMENT OF THE LIBERAL REFORMS, 1906–1914

Between 1906 and 1914, the Liberals introduced old age pensions, unemployment and sickness insurance, labour exchanges, school meals and medical inspections for schoolchildren, the eight-hour day for miners, minimum wages for 'sweated trades', and a half-day off each week for shop assistants. Taken together, this formidable list of social reform measures adds up to a significant shift away from minimum government in the laissez-faire tradition.

There is general agreement among historians over the extent to which the Liberals broke with the past: welfare benefits being given as of right, removing the moral element of the Poor Law; providing welfare benefits out of general taxation; interfering with the 'laws' of the market economy by setting up Labour Exchanges and negotiating minimum wage levels in certain trades.

As we have seen, the Liberals came into power with few definite plans for social reform, although many Liberal candidates had stressed the need for social welfare reform in their election campaigns. Because of this, the new government seems to have been much more open to influence from outside bodies and individuals than previous administrations. Organisations like the BMA and the friendly societies, and individuals like Beveridge, Morant and the Webbs, were able to put pressure on Ministers and get their ideas enshrined in law. Especially in the complex areas of pensions and national insurance, the 'experts' and top civil service officials played a very important role in determining the final outcome of these Bills.

The key reforming Ministers, like Lloyd George and Churchill, had to rely on a mixture of expert advice and acute political judgment. After all, there were both political costs and benefits involved in every measure of social reform. These 'New' Liberals understood the dangers of excessive public expenditure and how that could alienate the 'Old' wing of the Party. Even after such a modest step as old age pensions for the over seventies, Lord Rosebery, the former Liberal Prime Minister, condemned the scheme as "so prodigal of expenditure as likely to undermine the whole fabric of the Empire".

Liberal Ministers were keenly aware of the potential threat from the new Labour Party and in some ways they considered their social reform programme to be a political antidote to socialism. Nevertheless, the working class were not wholeheartedly in favour of the efforts made on their behalf by the Liberals. Some saw the new insurance schemes and their attendant bureaucracy as little more than middle-class interference.

At the same time, the real threat to Liberal power was the Conservative Party. It could be said that the Liberals hoped to introduce social reforms as they knew that the next Conservative government could introduce similar reforms and reap the benefits in terms of votes. Lloyd George introduced a 'Free Trade' Budget in 1909, based on raising taxes not tariffs, to hit back at the government's critics, and also to pay for the reforms.

Some historians go further and argue that we can see the origins of the 'Welfare State' in the Liberal reforms, 1906–1914. They justify this claim by saying that old age pensions and safeguards against unemployment and ill health, which the Liberals brought in for the first time, are cornerstones of the modern social welfare system. Other historians disagree with this interpretation. They argue that the Liberal reforms were very limited in scope and failed to deal adequately with such important welfare issues as education and housing.

Clearly, the significance of the Liberal welfare reforms will continue to be debated. Certainly, by the standards of the time, they were considered to be radical measures of social reform. On the other hand, looking back from the perspective of modern 'Welfare State' Britain, the Liberal reforms appear to be very limited. However, it is important to realise that both Lloyd George and Churchill saw their reforms as first steps, which were brought to a halt by the outbreak of the Great War.

6

The National Governments of the 1930s

THE SOCIAL and economic problems facing the National Governments of the 1930s had their origins in the 1920s and before. We will therefore need to look at the preceding period before we can make any assessment of the governments of the 1930s.

THE IMPACT OF THE GREAT DEPRESSION

The Origins of Britain's Economic Problems: 1900–29

Between 1900 and the outbreak of the Great War, there were clear signs that Britain was no longer the pre-eminent industrial power it had been. As the USA and several European countries developed and industrialised, so they imported fewer manufactured goods from Britain, in fact becoming keen competitors with Britain for international trade.

There were both encouraging and depressing lessons to be learned from Britain's trade performance with the rest of the world. For example, Britain's share of world export trade fell from 20% to 14% between 1880 and 1914. However, it is important to note that the country's total output was still rising at a decent 2% per annum. Coal still seemed to be doing well. Output was up from 223 million tons in 1900 to 287 million tons in 1913. On the other hand, the coal industry was overmanned, with more than one million men working in the pits before the First World War. Cotton output was increasing and exports were improving, but how long could British markets in the Far East be secure when Japan, India and China were all building their own mills?

Overall, Britain's place in the international league of industrial nations may have been slipping, but the UK was still a major economic force in the 1920s, despite the failure of many British industrialists to respond to changing international circumstances. However, to stand still while other countries

were emerging as serious competitors was shortsighted. Britain's comparative economic decline was also compounded by the unprecedented worldwide economic crisis which originated in the USA at the end of the decade.

The Wall Street Crash, 1929

The Great Depression originated in America with the 'Wall Street Crash' of October 1929. The panic selling of shares on the New York Stock Exchange led to a catastrophic financial collapse throughout the USA. Banks folded, people's life savings were lost and businesses went bankrupt. Very quickly, the economic shock waves from America began to affect the employment situation in Britain. Demand for British goods in America dried up and workers had to be laid off.

Unemployment had increased dramatically from 1 million to 2.5 million by December 1930. How to tackle the problem was a grave test for the Labour government. However, since neither of the other parties was in very good shape, and neither of them had viable alternative policies, the government's position was not threatened. What did put the government at risk was the banking crisis precipitated by the Wall Street Crash.

Ramsay MacDonald became Prime Minister, for the second time, in May 1929. As in 1924, the Labour government did not have an overall majority of seats in Parliament, so it had to rely on the Liberals for survival. To make matters worse, MacDonald's term of office coincided with the onset of a worldwide economic depression. As unemployment figures doubled, the Labour government came to grief over a financial crisis in August 1931. The performance of the second Labour government has been criticised by historians ever since, but given the circumstances, few parties could have succeeded in dealing with the problems which that government faced.

NATIONAL GOVERNMENTS 1931–39
Prime Ministers and Chancellors of the Exchequer

Prime Minister	Chancellor of the Exchequer
Ramsay MacDonald (Lab) August 1931–June 1935	Philip Snowden (Lab) August 1931–November 1932
Stanley Baldwin (Con) June 1935–May 1937	Neville Chamberlain (Con) November 1932–May 1937
Neville Chamberlain (Con) May 1937–May 1940	Sir John Simon (Con) May 1937–October 1940

Banking Crisis 1930–31

The fate of most of the European economies was intricately tied up with the financial health or otherwise of the USA. Germany, for example, was dependent on loans from America under the Dawes Plan. Without these loans, German industry would not have been able to recover after the inflationary collapse of 1923. Germany's economic revival enabled it to pay reparations to France and Britain. The latter needed the reparations payments to pay back American war debts. In this way, the economies of Europe and America were tied up in a circle of loans and repayments of debts. One break in the circle would affect everyone.

American loans had been keeping the German economy afloat since 1924, and when these eventually dried up in 1931, the German unemployment figure had reached four million. However, it was the collapse of the German banks that began to affect Britain. In March 1931, the main Austrian bank collapsed, followed soon after by the German Danat and Dresdner Banks. The German government immediately froze all foreign assets, including £90 million from London. Pressure transferred to the Bank of England in mid-July. Foreign creditors began to withdraw their assets from London at the rate of £4 million in gold per day. As the Bank had relatively small reserves of gold, it was forced to seek loans of £50 million from France and the USA.

The Second Labour Government 1929–31

Governments, on coming to power, rarely have a free hand to do as they wish. Ramsay MacDonald, as Leader of the Labour Party, became Prime Minister in May 1929. However, although the Labour Party had 'won' the General Election, due to the quirks of the 'first-past-the-post' electoral system it had secured 300,000 fewer votes than the Conservatives. The distribution of seats was Labour 288, Conservatives 260 and Liberals 59. Given the fact that 14 million out of the 22.5 million electors had rejected the Labour manifesto at the polls, MacDonald felt, honourably, that he could not carry out the Labour pledges. In his opening speech as Prime Minister in the House of Commons he said,

> "I wonder how far it is possible, without in any way abandoning any of our party positions ... to consider ourselves more as a Council of State and less as arrayed regiments facing each other in battle."[1]

Some historians see this statement as evidence that MacDonald had been contemplating forming a National Government in 1929. A more likely explanation is that it hints at his insecurity over the government's weak position. One supporter advised him simply to "keep things going". Hoping for cooperation from the other parties was another blind alley. The Liberals and the Conservatives, clearly in disarray, had internal leadership quarrels based on policy differences. As

a result, the options available to MacDonald were few and far between. He felt he could not carry out Labour's preferred programme. Economic orthodoxy, in the form of balanced budgets and strict economies, were the order of the day.

The May Committee Report

The Banking Crisis of 1931 coincided with the publication of the gloomy findings of the May Committee. This Committee, under the chairmanship of Sir George May, was set up in February 1931 to explore ways of reducing government expenditure after it became known that the unemployment insurance fund had a debt of £90 million, due to the rising levels of payouts of unemployment benefit. All three political parties were represented on the Committee. The May Committee predicted that by April 1932, the government would be in deficit to the sum of about £120 million and recommended some stern orthodox measures in the form of cutbacks to remedy the situation.

- They proposed to raise only £24 million by taxation and the rest, £97 million, was to be found, or more accurately lost, by reductions in government spending. (The two Labour members of the Committee disagreed with the majority findings. They advocated increased taxation.)

- Of that £97 million, £30 million was to come from cuts in the pay of the police, the armed forces and teachers (the latter to suffer a 20% decrease).

- The remaining £67 million was to come from a 20% reduction in unemployment benefit.

The Report, and its timing, was a further blow to international confidence in the pound. What made matters worse was the fact that MacDonald made no statement on the May Report and promptly left London on holiday, allowing the crisis to linger on. In the meantime, fears that Britain was heading for financial collapse led foreign investors to withdraw gold, which only added to the problem. MacDonald was forced to cut short his holiday, and a meeting of the Cabinet Economic Committee was held. A £30 million cut in salaries was agreed to, but the committee refused to take the distasteful step of cutting the standard rate of unemployment benefit.

Since the measures to be taken would need some degree of support from the other parties, MacDonald met with the Opposition leaders, Samuel and Baldwin, who rejected the Cabinet proposals as inadequate. On 21 August, the Cabinet met again and a final figure of £56 million of cuts was reluctantly agreed. MacDonald knew that this was as far as his colleagues were prepared to go. Unfortunately, the financial crisis had taken a turn for the worse. The Deputy Governor of the Bank of England, Sir Ernest Harvey, informed MacDonald that immediate loans would have to be sought from the US Federal Reserve Bank to maintain the value of the pound. These loans would only be granted if MacDonald could guarantee further tough cuts in government expenditure.

The fate of the Labour government lay in the hands of the American Federal Reserve Bank. The Cabinet, without committing themselves, asked MacDonald to find out if a further £20 million cut in government spending (involving a 10% cut in the standard rate of unemployment benefit) would be sufficient to release the necessary loan from the Federal Reserve. It was. MacDonald had to persuade his Cabinet colleagues to commit themselves to carry out these cuts which, he said, were, "… the negation of everything that the Labour Party stood for".[2] He went on to say that these vile measures were in the national interest and would help to rescue the country from the brink of collapse.

Twenty Cabinet Ministers were present at the meeting. Eleven voted for the cuts, nine against. There was no way that the government could now carry on, and MacDonald left the meeting to hand in the resignation of the government to the King. Earlier that day, MacDonald had held a secret meeting with the King, to discuss the next steps, in the event of a Cabinet split. The King had then seen the two Opposition leaders. They agreed that if the government were to collapse, a 'National Government' should be formed with MacDonald as Prime Minister. The next day, Monday 24 August, MacDonald saw the King again and agreed to head a National Government.

An Assessment of the Economic Performance of the Labour Government, 1929–1931

It might have been expected that a Labour government would have made efforts to get the jobless back to work, and would have attempted to improve and extend

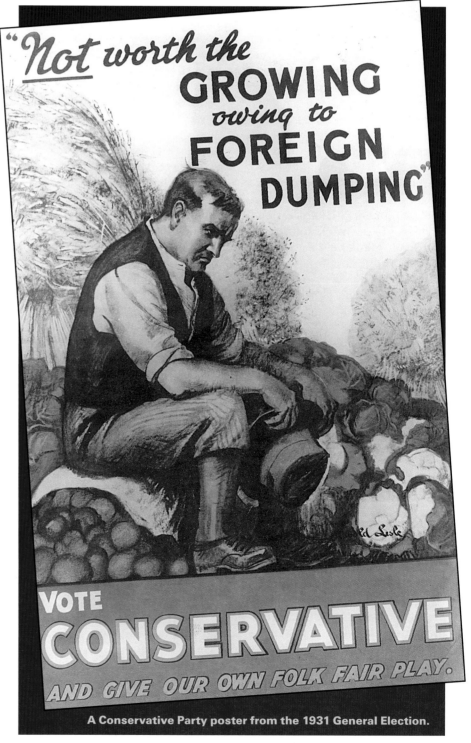

A Conservative Party poster from the 1931 General Election.

A Labour Party poster from the 1931 General Election.

In August 1931, MacDonald's Cabinet appeared to be indecisive when it came to framing new economic policy. As a result, the Bank of England, financial investors and foreign banks lost confidence in the Labour government. This point was made by representatives of the Bank of England who said that, "the cause of the trouble was not financial but political, and lay in the complete want of confidence in His Majesty's Government among foreigners".[3]

Skidelsky is more critical of the government. He argues that the August 1931 crisis was largely self-inflicted. Labour had been given two years to carry out practical policies to remedy some of the economic problems facing the country, but it had failed because its "commitment to a nebulous Socialism made it regard the work of the 'economic radicals' such as Keynes as mere 'tinkering', when in fact it was they who were providing the real choice".[4]

THE NATIONAL GOVERNMENTS

Formed in August 1931, the new National Government contained members of each of the three main parties, although the majority of Labour Ministers and MPs refused to support it. The government's most pressing task was to restore international confidence by a policy of strict economy and a balanced budget. When the bankers were convinced that this would materialise, the promised loan of £80 million was raised in Paris and New York and the run on the pound stopped (for a few days).

unemployment benefit. On neither count did the Labour government perform well. Certainly, the huge rise in unemployment during the period 1929–31 cannot be blamed on the government. There were deeper causes relating to the poor state of British industry and the worldwide economic depression sparked off by the Wall Street Crash. However, by sticking rigidly to a laissez-faire policy, the government offered no hope to the unemployed.

It has been estimated that, at best, the government found work for about 60,000 men—a paltry effort given the enormity of the problem. On the positive side, the government passed the *Unemployment Insurance Act* in 1930. Those claiming benefit no longer had to prove that they were 'genuinely seeking work' and the number of people who could claim benefits was extended. Any good done here, though, was more than wiped out by the last act of the government in voting for cuts in unemployment benefit.

Composition of Government August 1931

Prime Minister	MacDonald (Lab)
Lord President	Baldwin (Con)
Chancellor	Snowden (Lab)
Home Secretary	Samuel (Lib)
Foreign Secretary	Issacs (Lib)
Health Secretary	Chamberlain (Con)

On 10 September 1931, Snowden produced his balanced budget. Some of the main provisions were:

➤ income tax raised from 4s 6d (22.5p) to 5s (25p) in the pound

➤ salaries of civil servants and members of the armed forces cut by 10%

➤ teachers' salaries cut by 15%

➤ unemployment benefit cut by 10%

➤ a 'means test' introduced to assess the income and circumstances of households applying for assistance

Just how insecure Britain's financial position was can be seen in the events of the week following the budget. On 15 September, sailors of the Atlantic Fleet based at Inver-gordon refused to fall in for duty in protest at the 10% cut in pay. News of a 'mutiny' in the Royal Navy spread panic amongst foreign investors. There was an immediate rush to withdraw gold from London. By 19 September, government stocks were down to only £130 million.

In order to stem the flood, the government was forced to come off the Gold Standard. Economic experts predicted dire consequences, but they failed to materialise. The value of the pound, compared to the US dollar, fell from $4.86 to $3.40. Incredibly the government, which had been put into power to maintain the Gold Standard only a few days previously, was forced to abandon it by 12,000 sailors, in what seems to have been "the politest possible form of mutiny".[5]

"A few days before, a managed currency had seemed as wicked as family planning. Now, like contraception, it became a commonplace. This was the end of an age."[6]

The government had, "... unwittingly stumbled upon an important remedy: the consequent devaluation of the pound assisted exports, and the mild bout of inflation fostered economic expansion."[7]

One of the many posters from the 1931 General Election.

The General Election, October 1931

The Labour Party was now irretrievably split. MacDonald and those who went along with him to form the National Government were expelled from the Party and branded as traitors. Similarly in the Liberal Party divisions had emerged—Lloyd George refused to have anything to do with the government, or the Liberals in it.

MacDonald appealed to the country for a 'doctor's mandate'. In other words, the power to heal the ailing economy. The election campaign turned out to be very bitter and also very confusing for the voters, as each of the parties fighting under the 'National' banner brought out their own manifestos. Nevertheless, the public gave the National Government a huge vote of confidence. As the figures in

1931 General Election Result

National Government		Opposition	
Conservatives	473	Labour	52
National Liberals	68	Lloyd George Liberals	4
National Labour	13	Others	5

Table 6.1

Table 6.1 show, the real winners were the Tories, and the clear losers were Labour, who in the space of a month had gone from being the governing party to having a rump of fifty two Opposition MPs.

"... MacDonald asked for 'a doctor's mandate' ... In those days, before the development of modern remedies, all a doctor could prescribe for most ailments was rest, while natural recovery took its course, and this was much what the National Government did in the end."[8]

The National Government was Conservative in everything but name:

➤ 473 out of 554 MPs were Conservative

➤ 67% of voters supported the National Government out of a 76% turnout: 55% Conservatives; 10% National Liberals; 1.6% National Labour

➤ Henderson, who led Labour opposition to MacDonald, lost his parliamentary seat.

Ramsay MacDonald gave up his position as Prime Minister in 1935, due to ill health and failing eyesight. He was replaced by the Conservative leader, Stanley Baldwin. This change at the top did little to alter the balance of power in the Cabinet, because Baldwin had been very much in control in the latter stages of MacDonald's Premiership. Another key Labour figure, Snowden, retired as Chancellor of the Exchequer in 1932, and he was replaced by another Conservative, Neville Chamberlain. Chamberlain would succeed Baldwin as Prime Minister in 1937.

How would the National Government deal with the Economic Crisis?

The second Labour government's policies between 1929 and 1931 could hardly have been defined as 'socialist'—they were virtually indistinguishable from those of their Tory and Liberal predecessors. No significant government action was taken to help or protect industry, or the growing ranks of the unemployed. Voters might have expected to see more of the same orthodox economic policies. Instead there was a significant trend away from laissez-faire towards limited state intervention in certain areas.

The National Governments of the 1930s began to take a more 'hands on' approach to economic matters. However, the move from laissez-faire to state intervention would follow a more definite pattern only after World War II and Labour's victory in the 1945 General Election. The National Governments straddled the old orthodoxies of laissez-faire, and the interventionist consensus of the post-1945 Welfare State era.

The Treasury view was dominated by the theory of supply and demand:

£ the free market would regulate production levels and the demand for labour;

£ balance was necessary between imports and exports, production and consumption, borrowing and lending;

£ equilibrium could be achieved through a combination of balanced budgets, Free Trade and low levels of public expenditure and taxation;

£ it was necessary to maintain the value of the currency through fixed exchange rates, and by linking sterling to the Gold Standard.

The most influential alternative view was based on the ideas of JM Keynes who argued for increased government expenditure and investment to prepare the country for economic recovery. "In particular, the government should undertake massive schemes of investment in order to revive industry and cut unemployment."[9]

In marked contrast to the Five Year Plans of the Soviet Union, and America's New Deal, Britain's National Governments continued to believe that there was nothing much that they could do to promote recovery. Orthodox policies of economy and restraint were the conventional wisdom of the day, although we begin to see certain laissez-faire beliefs abandoned, as concessions to 'Keynesianism'. In particular, the Gold Standard and Free Trade were abandoned. Government subsidy and regulation of agriculture and industry, albeit in limited form, paved the way for the more radical departures of the Labour government between 1945 and 1951.

1935 General Election Result

National Government		Opposition	
Conservatives*	432	Labour	154
(* including small number of National Liberals and National Labour)		Liberals	21
		Others	9

Table 6.2

ECONOMIC RECOVERY

There is a general consensus among historians that Britain's economic recovery from 1934 onwards took place largely in spite of, rather than because of National Government policies. Unlike many European states, rearmament played little part in Britain's economic recovery. The main sources of economic growth up to 1938 were:

➤ building (new houses),

➤ transport (new roads and public transport, particularly in the south-east of England),

➤ new industries, such as car manufacturing and electrical goods (whose growth was encouraged by the introduction of 'hire purchase' or buying on credit).

"... the Conservative-controlled National Government was ... from the autumn of 1932 onwards, in uninterrupted command of the nation's affairs until the spring of 1940. The 1935 election, although it increased Labour's strength in the Commons to 154 seats, did not materially alter the situation."[10]

"... the government naturally took the credit for this recovery. Probably the claim was unjustified. World trade generally recovered somewhat in 1933 for no apparent reason."[11]

"In general economic activity, Britain's position in the thirties does contrast very favourably with that of such other countries as the United States and France. For this, the National Government can take at least some credit, though in the main its policies were fortuitous, or just irrelevant. Fundamental to British recovery (was) ... the general picking up of world trade."[12]

"How much (the government policies) contributed to the prosperity of the economy is anyone's guess. If they did, it was by accident rather than by design."[13]

Circumstances beyond the government's control helped Britain back on the road to recovery. World prices of primary products (especially foodstuff) began to fall and this lowered industry's costs and generally lowered the cost of living. Those in work saw their standard of living increase as a result. (See Table 6.6.) Feeling better off

encouraged people to buy more and this helped to stimulate the new industries in particular. The government added to consumer spending in a limited way by restoring unemployment benefit cuts in 1934 and lowering income tax from 5s.(25p) to 4s.6d (22.5p)in the pound. On the whole, the government continued orthodox policies of thrift and economy. For example, in 1932 it lowered interest rates from 6% to 2% with the intention of reducing its own debt charges. It saved £80 million on its War Loan. However, the effect of low interest rates was the reverse of what the government wanted. Industry was encouraged to start new projects with cheap loans and cheap mortgages stimulated a private housing boom.

For AJP Taylor, "the building boom was the outstanding cause for the recovery of the thirties." [14] Nevertheless, rather than encouraging the building industry, the government's orthodox remedy was to economise. In 1932, Wheatley's *Housing Act*, which had provided £9 million in state subsidies for the

The Dundee contingent of hunger marchers at Euston Station prior to their departure from London. November 1932.

building of council houses, was revoked. However, cheap private houses, combined with low mortgage rates and greater general affluence, more than cancelled out the government's policy.

During the 1930s, individuals built three million private houses. This benefited construction and some of the new industries. Houses now had electricity installed (there were nine million users by 1938) and this in turn stimulated the electrical appliances sector (cookers, radios, vacuum cleaners etc).

GOVERNMENT SUPPORT FOR AGRICULTURE AND INDUSTRY

Throughout the 1930s, the National Governments began to introduce a series of measures which, though limited in scope and only partially successful, added up to a marked shift in policy, away from laissez-faire, towards interventionism.

Agriculture

Free trade had hit British farmers badly during the 1880s with the influx of cheap grain from America and refrigerated dairy produce from New Zealand. The Tory-dominated government was determined to help its traditional constituency, the farmers, by passing the *Wheat Act* in 1932 which guaranteed the price of the home product. This was followed by a variety of measures, including direct subsidies and help to market farm produce.

* *Agricultural Marketing Act* (1933) set up marketing boards to buy up, market and sell milk, potatoes and bacon.
* *Cattle Industry Act* (1934) provided subsidies for cattle.
* *Sugar Industry Act* (1936) provided subsidies for sugar.

Although these protectionist measures helped farmers to increase output during the 1930s, they failed to stem the number of labourers leaving the industry—about 100,000 every year in the thirties. The government's policy

also cost the country dearly. By 1939, it was spending £100 million to grow home-produced food which could have been imported more cheaply.

During the 1920s, coal mining had been in a very weak position, suffering the effects of foreign competition and overmanning. Subsidies were ruled out as being against good business practice, market forces having to be given free rein. However, when farming faced similar problems, the old arguments were quietly forgotten.

Industry

Government intervention in industry was more limited than in agriculture but again it signalled a changed attitude. The government concentrated on the 'old' industries. These were to be 'rationalised'—the smaller, inefficient units were to be shut down or amalgamated to produce factories better able to deal with foreign competition.

* The British Iron and Steel Federation, the National Shipbuilders Security and the Lancashire Cotton Corporation rationalised their respective industries.

* A £9.5 million loan was given to help the building of ships for the North Atlantic Fleet.

* The *Special Areas Act* (1934) provided £2 million and two commissioners to help attract new industries to the depressed industrial areas such as Clydeside, South Wales, West Cumberland and Tyneside. Rate, rent and income tax relief was given to employers starting up factories in these districts. However, even in spite of the government increasing its support to £5 million, its policy generally did not succeed. By 1938, fewer than 15,000 jobs had been created under this scheme, and this hardly scratched the surface of the problem. This lack of success was more marked in Scotland

where over 20% of insured workers in the Scottish Special Areas were unemployed, which was twice as high as the figure for England as a whole.

Free Trade Abandoned

As the economic depression began to bite, countries throughout the world put up tariff barriers to protect their own products. Britain joined in, with the passing of the *Abnormal Importations Act* of 1931. This put 50% import duties on woollen and cotton goods for the following six months.

However, the real break with the policy of free trade came with the appointment of Neville Chamberlain as Chancellor in 1932. Chamberlain was a confirmed protectionist, following in the footsteps of his father Joseph, who had campaigned unsuccessfully with his Tariff Reform League in 1903. Britain's adherence to the doctrine of Free Trade, established in the 1840s and '50s by Peel and Gladstone, was ended at a stroke with the passage of Chamberlain's *Import Duties Act* in February 1932. Duties of between 10% and 20% were imposed on about half the goods imported into Britain, with the exception of food and raw materials. Goods coming in from the Empire were exempted pending the outcome of the Ottawa Imperial Conference.

The Ottawa Conference took place in July and August 1932 and attempted to revive the idea of imperial preference (again a favourite idea of Joseph Chamberlain at the turn of the century). Under this, it was hoped to organise a self-contained economic unit consisting of Britain along with its Dominions and Colonies. Britain would guarantee to buy primary products from the Empire and in return the colonies would provide an unrestricted market for British manufactured goods. Such a system failed to materialise at Ottawa.

This kind of paternalistic trading relationship might have been possible a century previously, but was inappropriate in the 1930s. Canada, for example, was developing its own industries and wanted to protect them against British imports. Furthermore, it was inevitably developing a strong trading relationship with its powerful neighbour, America. Limited agreements were signed, but fell far short of imperial preference. Nevertheless, trade with the Empire did grow over the next decade. The abandonment of free trade by Britain was probably an inevitable reaction to the protectionist measures imposed by the other major trading nations. If British markets had not been protected the ranks of the unemployed would only have increased.

"Although the abandonment of the Gold Standard and the establishment of protection had come as a shock to some, these moves were largely an immediate response to what appeared to be the dictate of economic expediency. They did not point to a new adventurous radicalism in facing the crisis of the depression."[15]

"... the whole affair was topsy-turvy. Protection was carried by the Conservatives who claimed to believe in free enterprise. It was opposed by Labour, whose programme demanded a planned economy."[16]

SOCIAL AND ECONOMIC ISSUES IN THE 1930s
In this section, we will look at the success or otherwise of the National Governments in handling the following four social and economic issues:

● Unemployment

● Standards of Living

● Health

● Housing

UNEMPLOYMENT
As we saw earlier in the chapter, there were international as well as domestic causes of unemployment in the 1930s. On the international side, economic historians had observed that for many years Britain had experienced cyclical unemployment in line with the up-

swings and downturns of world trade. What compounded the problem in the thirties was the extra dimension of structural unemployment—persistently high levels of unemployment in the 'old' or 'staple' industries. In boom or slump, the old industries had higher rates of unemployment compared to the average.

The decline in the number of workers involved in these industries was also part of a larger and longer-term process of technological change. As the British economy became more advanced and more scientifically based, so it shed unskilled manual workers and took on more white-collar, non-manual workers. This disruptive period, when people's skills became redundant, was particularly marked in the 1920s and 1930s (as it was in the 1980s).

Throughout the 1930s, the number of unemployed did not fall below 1,400,000 and, in 1932, peaked at almost 3,000,000, or 22% of the registered labour force. As late as 1938, the unemployment rate stood at 13.8%. There were unemployment 'black spots' (eg. South Wales, Central Scotland, Northwest and North-east England—centres of the 'old industries') while other areas enjoyed relative prosperity (eg. South-east England). (See Table 6.5)

Government Measures
As we have seen, the government was not inclined to take radical action against the evils of mass unemployment. Like large sections of the population, including the victims themselves, they felt that the slump was a natural phenomenon and all they could do was to 'sit it out' and wait for the recovery. Apart from the *Special Areas Act* and the restoration of the 1931 benefit cuts, little was done for the unemployed. On the negative side was the *Anomalies Act* of 1931, which tightened the regulations on who was allowed to claim benefit. Under it, over 130,000 married women lost their right to benefit.

Most hated of all measures, though, was the 'Means Test'.

The Unemployment Assistance Board, with a staff of 60,000, was set up to administer unemployment relief, or the 'dole', on a national basis. Those on unemployment benefit could claim it for only twenty six weeks. After that, they were transferred onto 'transitional payments'. To get this, the claimant had to undergo a 'household means test'. An official would visit the home to investigate the income and circumstances of the person. He would also look into other money coming into the household, savings and other available assets—all with a view to saving the government as much as possible in payouts. These officials did their job well, saving £24 million in 1931–2 alone.

"The Means Test was specifically feared and hated by every unemployed worker. The regulations insisted that any member of a household who was working was responsible for the household—that is, he or she had to support the rest of the family. If anyone in a house was working—including uncles, aunts, cousins and even lodgers sometimes—then unemployment benefit wasn't paid to the other people in that house.

It broke up families. Sons and daughters went to live away from home; fathers in work became bitter towards their children. Cases were reported in the newspapers where worry over the Means Test had actually led to suicide. It produced despair—and also the most massive demonstrations by the unemployed all over the country."[17]

"One little collier boy fifteen years of age went home to his parents the other day and proudly announced that he had an increase of 3 shillings (15p) a week. The following week, the Board reduced the allowance of his unemployed father."[18]

"The most cruel and evil effect of the Means Test is the way in which it breaks up families. Old people, sometimes bedridden, are driven out of their homes by it. An old age pensioner, for instance, if a widower,

"Charles Mark Palmer started Jarrow as a shipbuilding centre without considering the needs of his workers. They crowded into a small colliery village which was hurriedly extended to receive them. They packed into insanitary houses. They lived without any social amenities. They paid with their lives for the absence of any preparation for the growth of such a town. And in 1933 another group of capitalists decided the fate of Jarrow without reference to the workers. A society in which the decisive decisions are invariably taken by one group, and in which those decisions are reached only by considerations of their own welfare, is not a just society."

(E Wilkinson *The Town that was Murdered* page 171)

would normally live with one or other of his children; his weekly ten shillings goes towards the household expenses, and probably he is not badly cared for. Under the Means Test, however, he counts as a 'lodger' and if he stays at home his children's dole will be docked. So, perhaps at seventy or seventy five years of age, he has to turn out into lodgings, handing his pension over to the lodging-house keeper and existing on the verge of starvation. I have seen several cases of this myself. It is happening all over England at this moment, thanks to the Means Test."[19]

James Maxton, ILP leader and Labour MP for Glasgow Bridgeton, led a well-orchestrated campaign against the Means Test. He clearly showed how various households in Glasgow would be seriously affected, thus causing further financial hardship for the poor.

In December 1932 Maxton continued his attack on the Means Test in a debate on BBC Radio with the Conservative MP, Harold MacMillan. The latter defended means testing on the grounds that the payments were not tied to insurance contributions and in the present economic conditions there were limits to what the state could afford. Maxton could not accept the Tory argument.

"He could understand a state which said, 'our total resources are very limited: it is impossible to allow anyone to have a very high income.' But he could not understand the state which said, 'our resources are limited: we must drive down the income of the whole working class to one dead level of poverty while other classes are left in affluence.'"[20]

Regional Variations in Unemployment

At the height of the Industrial Revolution, the 'boom areas' of low unemployment were the north and west of England and southern Scotland, based on the location of the coalfields. During the 1930s, we began to see a reversal of the geography of affluence. The new industries, fuelled by electricity, were located in the south and east where the markets were and the old industrial areas went into almost permanent decline.

In the worst affected regions, there were also marked localised variations in fortunes. Hardest hit was Jarrow with 67% of the workforce 'idle' following the closure of Palmer's shipyard. 'Jarrow' has since come to symbolise the darkest days of the Depression through the evocative images of the hunger march to London and the desperate

UNEMPLOYMENT 1929–39	
YEAR	UNEMPLOYED
1929	1.2 (MILLIONS)
1930	1.9
1931	2.7
1932	2.8
1933	2.5
1934	2.1
1935	2.0
1936	1.7
1937	1.4
1938	1.9
1939	1.3

Table 6.3
Source: P King *Twentieth Century History Made Simple* page 128.

plight of the people highlighted in Ellen Wilkinson's book *The Town that was Murdered*. (See above.)

Towns like Jarrow, which were dependent on single industries, were the worst hit. For instance, Merthyr relied on the coalfield and had 62% out of work in 1934; Manchester, on the other hand, had a variety of different industries and consequently fared much better. Halifax was doing very well with its machine-tool industries in contrast to the depressed woollen mill towns in the vicinity.

77

Unemployment in Staple Industries (%)

INDUSTRY	1929	1932	1936	1938
Coal	18.2	41.2	25.0	22.0
Cotton	14.5	31.1	15.1	27.7
Shipbuilding	23.2	59.5	30.6	21.4
Iron & Steel	19.9	48.5	29.5	24.8
Average for all industries	9.9	22.9	12.5	13.3

Table 6.4

Source: J Stevenson *British Society 1914–45* page 270.

Writers like George Orwell and JB Priestley described the degradation and misery of life on the dole.

"When I first saw unemployed men at close quarters, the thing that horrified and amazed me was to find that many of them were ashamed of being unemployed ... The middle classes were still talking about 'lazy idle loafers on the dole' and saying that 'these men could all find work if they wanted to' ... I remember the shock of astonishment it gave me, when I first mingled with tramps and beggars, to find that a fair proportion, perhaps a quarter, of these beings whom I had been taught to regard as cynical parasites, were decent young miners and cotton-workers gazing at their destiny with the same sort of dumb amazement as an animal in a trap. They simply could not understand what was happening to them ..."[21]

"There is no escape anywhere in Jarrow from its prevailing misery, for it is entirely a working-class town. One little street may be more wretched than another, but to the outsider they all look alike. One out of every two shops appeared to be permanently closed. Wherever we went there were men hanging about, not scores of them but hundreds and thousands of them ... The men wore the drawn masks of prisoners of war. A stranger from a distant civilisation, observing the condition of the place and its people, would have arrived at once at the conclusion that Jarrow had deeply offended some celestial emperor of the island and was now being punished. He would never believe us if we told him that in theory this town was as good as any other and that its inhabitants were not criminals but citizens with votes."[22]

STANDARDS OF LIVING

We can judge whether the standard of living was rising by looking at two areas of evidence.

- The 'real' incomes of people ie. what they could buy with their income compared to previous years.

- Evidence of increased spending on goods, services and increased saving and investment.

Table 6.6 provides fairly clear evidence that living standards for most people were rising during the 1930s. Further evidence of rising living standards is given in the statistics below:

£ Working-class families on average spent 76% of their income on food, rent and rates in 1914; in 1938, they were only spending 44% of their income on these items.

£ One thousand million tickets to the cinema were sold in Britain in 1938.

£ Savings in building societies rose from £82 million in 1920 to £717 million in 1938.

£ Between 1935 and 1939, 350,000 houses were being built every year, on average.

£ The number of building society mortgages taken out increased from 0.55 million in 1928 to 1.39 million in 1937.

£ In 1931, 1.5 million cars were bought in Britain; in 1939, 2 million were bought.

£ Spending on food went up from £835 million in 1920 to £1,177 million in 1939. Consumption of fruit went up by 88%, vegetables by 64%, butter and margarine by 50% and eggs by 40%.

£ In 1930, 3.5 million radio licences were taken out, but 9 million were taken out in 1938.

£ The sale of vacuum cleaners doubled from 200,000 in 1930 to 400,000 in 1938.

£ Twenty million British people were taking a holiday by the sea by the late 1930s.

The British capitalist system had always contained stark contrasts between the rich and the poor. The lives of the poor were harsh and perhaps were made bearable only by the knowledge that they were not suffering alone. However, those unaffected by the scourge of unemployment had the completely different experience of a steadily rising standard of living. In the 1930s, those in employment enjoyed an increase in 'real wages' of up to 30%, as prices fell or remained relatively stable.

As poverty continued to be a problem for many families throughout the thirties, those unaffected by it were shocked, because it existed alongside their growing affluence. Also, social investigators were revealing to the general public the true extent and depth of the problem. A study of London in 1934 found that 10% of the population were living in poverty. Even in booming Bristol, Herbert Tout concluded that 19% had "insufficient income" and 10% were in poverty.

In 1936, Rowntree decided to survey the extent of poverty in York for a second time. His team of investigators used the same definition of the 'poverty line' as was

REGIONAL *Unemployment (%)*

Region	1929	1932	1937
London & SE England	5.6	13.7	6.4
SW England	8.1	17.1	7.8
Midlands	9.3	20.1	7.2
Northern England	13.5	27.1	13.8
Wales	19.3	36.5	22.3
Scotland	12.1	27.7	15.9
Northern Ireland	15.1	27.2	23.6

Table 6.5
Source: J Stevenson *British Society 1914–45* page 270.

used in his 1899 survey of the town. The results showed that there had been a considerable improvement in the people's standard of living during these thirty seven years. (See Table 6.7.)

However, there were still some black spots. For example, Rowntree found that half of working-class children were living in poverty. There were also some tragic cases of individual hardship.

"One family of five, all out of work, was found to be living on bread and margarine alone for more than half of each week. This was in spite of unemployment assistance and a widow's pension ... An old lady of seventy two, living alone, had no bed and had to sleep on an old sofa. After paying her rent and buying a bag of coal, she had 3s 3d (16p) a week for all her other needs."[23]

Clearly, a safety net of welfare provisions to prevent the poor from falling below minimum standards of living still had to be created. For too many of the unemployed, the elderly and the young, the thirties was the hungry decade.

HEALTH
Evidence of improving health is given in the statistics below.

+ Life expectancy for those born between 1901 and 1912 was 51.5 (men) and 55.4 (women). Those born in 1930–2 could expect to live to 58.7 (men) and 62.9 (women).

+ In 1911, there were 6.2 doctors for every 10,000 of population; in 1941, there were 7.5.

+ Infant mortality rates went down from 67 per 1,000 live births in 1930 to 61 in 1940.

+ Tuberculosis (TB) killed 51,000 in 1910; 27,000 in 1940.

+ Two-thirds of prospective soldiers were declared unfit for service in the First World War; only one-third were rejected during the Second World War.

+ Deaths from measles went down from 389 per million of population in 1921–30 to 217 per million in 1931–9.

The government did play a limited role in helping the statistics along. A slum clearance programme was carried out in the interwar years which undoubtedly took people out of an insanitary and overcrowded environment. One and a half million families were cleared from the slums between 1919 and 1939.

The Public Health Act (1936) continued and extended the previous work done by local authorities in improving the water supply and

sewage systems. By 1935, 80% of the population of England and Wales was supplied with water by their local councils. By 1936, the National Health Insurance Scheme, introduced in 1911, had been extended to nineteen million wage earners who had free access to doctors and medical treatment. School milk, either free or subsidised, was being given to three million children by 1937. 4% of children were now receiving free school meals.

Much needed to be done though. The persistence of unemployment and poverty hindered overall progress in the health field. The following incident was witnessed by Frank Cousins. He encountered a young couple with a child who were walking from South Shields to London to find work.

"They came into the cafe and sat down, and they fetched a baby's feeding bottle out, and it had water in it. They fed the baby with water, and then lifted the kiddy's dress up—it was a small baby—and it had a newspaper nappy on. They took this off, and wiped the baby's bottom with it and then they picked up another newspaper and put that on for a fresh nappy."[24]

The middle class lived significantly longer than the working class. Poor areas had higher death rates than average. Merthyr, for example, had a 52% higher death rate than the average for the region; Jarrow was 30% higher. The infant death rate for England and Wales was 58 per 1,000 live births; less affluent Scotland had a rate of 80 per 1,000; Glasgow had 104 infant deaths per 1,000 live births.

Poverty, then, was a key factor affecting the health of the nation. If you were unfortunate enough to be working class or unemployed and living in the poorer north of the country, you were likely to have a below average health record and inadequate access to health care. Britain still lacked both a national health service and comprehensive free medical treatment.

HOUSING

Private Housing

As we have seen, the 1930s saw an unprecedented house-building boom which contributed significantly to Britain's economic recovery. The bulk of building was in the private sector. Three million houses were built in the thirties, of which more than two-thirds were private. Owner-occupation grew from 10% to 31% of the population between the wars. Private semi-detached houses were on sale for as little as £400 (the equivalent of two year's wages for many people), and low mortgage rates were also on offer. Despite this fact, it was only the middle class and the very top end of the working class who could afford to buy them.

Council Housing

The *Housing Act* obliged local authorities to clear slums, and deal with overcrowding. After 1935, many local authorities began to make a start on council house building. Between 1931 and 1939, 700,000 council houses were built. By 1939, 14% of the population rented council houses compared to 1% in 1919. Building standards in the new council housing estates were good and vastly better than the inner city dwellings many people had been used to.

Houses were built with electricity installed, a piped-in water supply giving hot and cold running water, inside toilets, and gardens. Unfortunately, only the better-off skilled and semi-skilled manual workers and their families could afford to pay the rents charged by the local authorities. Many councils were unable to subsidise rents sufficiently to meet the needs of the poorest and worst-housed members of their community.

Housing the Poor

The poor lived in private rented accommodation which was frequently damp, ill-ventilated, lacking in basic amenities and overcrowded. Here, George Orwell describes some of the housing conditions he found in Barnsley.

"1. House in Wortley Street. Two up, one down. Living-room 12ft by 10ft. Sink and copper in living-room, coal-hole under stairs. Sink worn almost flat and constantly overflowing. Walls not too sound. Penny in slot gas-light. House very dark and gas-light estimated 4d (1.5p) a day. Upstairs rooms are really one large room partitioned into two. Walls very bad— walls of back room cracked right through. Window-frames coming to pieces and have to be stuffed with wood. Rain comes through in several places. Sewer runs under house and stinks in summer but Corporation 'says they can't do nowt'. Six people in house, two adults and four children, the eldest aged fifteen. Youngest but one attending hospital —tuberculosis suspected. House infested by bugs. Rent 5s 3d (26p), including rates.

2. House in Peel Street. Back to back, two up, two down and large cellar. Living-room 10 ft square with copper and sink. The other downstairs room the same size, probably intended as parlour but used as bedroom. Upstairs rooms the same size as those below. Living-room very dark. Gaslight estimated at 4$\frac{1}{2}$d (2p) a day. Distance to lavatory, 70 yards. Four beds in house for eight people—two old parents, two adult girls ... one young man, and three children. Parents have one bed, eldest son another, and remaining five people share the other two."[25]

The government did take steps to deal with these problems. By 1939, 350,000 slum houses had been cleared, but the local authorities estimated that 600,000 slums were still standing. The problem was concentrated in the old industrial areas, with Scotland again breaking all records with ease. A survey of Scottish housing in 1936 found that 22% of the stock was overcrowded (defined as more than two people per room). Glasgow had 200,000 families living more than three people to a room.

Clearly, problems such as these would not be solved by market forces. The government believed that houses vacated by the lower middle class, who were buying new houses, would be taken up by people further down the economic ladder. It did not happen because the poor could not afford the increased rent. Despite the record number of houses being built, demand still outstripped supply by 800,000 houses. The need was for cheap, affordable rented accommodation and it was not being supplied in sufficient quantities by the government and local authorities.

"Whatever the shortcomings of the new developments, there had been greater progress by the end of the thirties in providing an adequate solution to the housing conditions of the working class than in any previous decade."[26]

There is no doubt that the working class were better housed than in

Wages, Prices & Real Earnings 1930-38

Year	Weekly Wage Rates	Retail Prices	Average Annual Real Wage Earnings
1930	100.0	100.0	100.0
1931	98.9	93.4	105.1
1932	97.9	93.4	105.7
1933	95.7	88.6	107.6
1934	95.7	89.2	108.1
1935	96.8	90.5	108.3
1936	98.9	93.0	107.7
1937	103.2	97.5	105.4
1938	106.4	98.7	107.7

Table 6.6

Source: Adapted from DH Aldcroft *The Inter-War Economy: Britain, 1919–1939* pages 352 & 364.

previous decades. There is also no doubt that the government could have done a lot more to help those in areas of multiple deprivation. Whether they should have done so, or were capable doing so, is a matter of debate.

AN ASSESSMENT OF THE ECONOMIC PERFORMANCE OF THE NATIONAL GOVERNMENTS

For historians who have grown up in Welfare State Britain where comprehensive care 'from the cradle to the grave' is taken for granted, the record of the National Governments must fall short of the standards of the post-war era.

By ideological inclination, the National Governments were loathe to spend money on social and economic problems. In fact, during the depths of the Depression, we have seen that unemployment benefit was cut. The prevailing belief, stemming from laissez-faire doctrine, was that people should fend for themselves and that the government's role was to curb its spending and tax people as little as possible. The welfare of the citizens would then be conditional on their own efforts and on the success of the economy as a whole, where wealth would trickle from the rich downwards.

The above belief helps to explain the persistence of high unemployment in the depressed, 'black spot' areas. It has been said that "in spite of plenty of available advice, the government failed to produce any positive strategy for curing long-term unemployment in those areas, largely because it refused to accept that the problem could be

January 1934. Unemployed from Scotland set off on their march to London.

Changing Britain 1850–1979

solved."[27] Faced with the massive problems of decline of the traditional staple industries in the depressed areas, one historian has said that there was virtually nothing that the government could have done to make these old industries competitive.

It is argued that the economic problems of the interwar years were of such magnitude that politicians in each of the three major political parties struggled to come up with practical solutions.

> "Liberals, Conservatives and Labour politicians all fudged and fumbled in a situation essentially new to them."[28]

As a result the National Governments' policies were generally orthodox, linked to budgetary controls and avoided substantial investment, although they "did seek increasingly to create a more favourable climate for recovery ... Coming off the Gold Standard in

POVERTY

	1899	1936
Nº. in poverty	7,320	3,767
Total population in poverty (%)	9.9	3.9

Table 6.7
Source: RJ Cootes *The Making of the Welfare State.*

1931 effectively devalued the pound by about 30% and made possible a reduction in interest rates from 6% to 2%".[29]

However, the Treasury feared that increased government expenditure and investment to stimulate economic recovery ('Keynesianism') could lead to a disastrous short-term economic boom.

> "Chamberlain and the Treasury demonstrated great reluctance to rearm in case it slowed economic recovery.

The Treasury argument was that spending on armaments could not be increased because if rearmament was financed by more borrowing, this could risk added inflation, while if it was financed by increased taxes this might slow the steady rise in average living standards in Britain, since 1932."[30]

Stephen Lee, in *Aspects of British Political History 1914–1995*, goes so far as to say that government policy played a marginal part in rather than being crucial for economic recovery during the 1930s. More important were factors such as the fall in prices which led to an overall increase in buying power. Indeed, according to Peter Catterall in *Britain 1918–51* only when the consumer-based recovery began to slow in 1938 did rearmament give further life to the flagging economy, allied to the revival of the world economy. At that point the rearmament programme produced new jobs, and even put pressure on scarce resources.

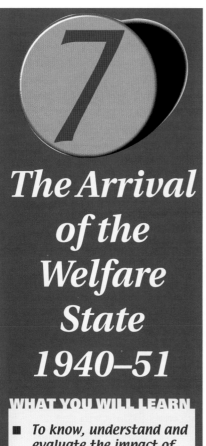

The Arrival of the Welfare State 1940–51

WHAT YOU WILL LEARN

- *To know, understand and evaluate the impact of World War II in paving the way for the post-1945 Welfare State.*

- *To know, understand and assess the significance of the Beveridge Report.*

- *To be able to compare the reactions of both major parties to the Beveridge Report.*

- *To be able to compare and contrast the election manifestos of the two main parties in 1945.*

- *To describe and evaluate the measures taken by the Labour government to tackle Beveridge's 'Five Giants': 'Want'–National Insurance; 'Disease'–Health Service; 'Idleness'–Employment; 'Ignorance'–Education; 'Squalor'–Housing.*

- *To be aware of different views of historians on the significance of Labour's reforms, 1945-1951.*

WE HAVE SEEN that the state began to take on more responsibility for the welfare of the people from the 1870s onwards. Now we will argue that the Welfare State which was fully in place by 1951 was not the exclusive creation of the 1945 Labour Government. Its arrival has to be seen in the broader context of the total experience of the Second World War. Part of that experience involved Labour politicians pushing forward progressive ideas and plans. However, there was also a broad consensus among all three parties about what postwar Britain should be like.

The war itself created a powerful unity of purpose in the country. Wartime leaders began to realise that, in a lengthy war, the British people needed an ideal to fight for as well as an ideology to fight against. If warfare was the weapon to conquer the evil of Hitler, welfare could provide the healing medicine to treat the backlog of ills persisting from the 1930s. The wartime Coalition Government mobilised the nation's resources and intervened in so many areas of people's lives that it would have been difficult for any post-war government to have disengaged rapidly from such commitments. The Labour government of 1945–51 completed the modern state welfare structure with a flurry of legislation carried out with great enthusiasm, but had the Conservatives won the General Election in 1945, a very similar social services system may have been put in place.

THE SOCIAL IMPACT OF WORLD WAR TWO

Evacuation

There had been a growing awareness of poverty as far back as the social investigations of Booth and Rowntree in the last decade of the nineteenth century. These were followed up, in the inter-war period, with studies by Tout and the Bristol Trust. However, there is a difference between knowing the facts and seeing examples of social deprivation with your own eyes. It was the latter experience which stirred the conscience of many middle-class families. When war broke out in September 1939, the government put its evacuation plan into operation. About 1.5 million people, mostly children, were moved from the major cities to smaller towns and the countryside. These children were mainly from poor inner-city families who could not afford to make their own arrangements to protect their families. The depth and extent of poverty in urban Britain was revealed. About 20% of the children evacuated from cities such as Liverpool were infested with lice. Many were clothed in little more than rags, were filthy, and had very primitive sanitary habits.

> "Evacuation was part of the process by which British society came to know itself, as the unkempt, ill-clothed, undernourished and often incontinent children of bombed cities acted as messengers carrying the evidence of the deprivation of urban working-class life into rural homes."[1]

> "... country people, and to a certain extent even the wealthy, learnt for the first time how the city poor lived. English people became more mixed up than before ... The Luftwaffe was a powerful missionary for the Welfare State."[2]

Neville Chamberlain, who was the Prime Minister at the start of the war and who had been Minister of Health between 1924 and 1929, was shocked by what he experienced and admitted in a private letter that, "I never knew that such conditions existed, and I feel ashamed of having been so ignorant of my neighbours. For the rest of my life, I mean to try to make amends by helping such people to live cleaner and healthier lives."[3]

Equality of Sacrifice

Two long-term effects of laissez-faire ideology and capitalism were to produce great inequalities in society, and a reluctance by the ruling class to interfere with the outcomes of the market system.

However, the war required great sacrifices from rich and poor alike and these common experiences brought about a change in the social attitudes of the country's elite. It produced a more egalitarian consensus which enabled people on both the left and the right of the political spectrum to come to similar conclusions about the need for a more caring and interventionist state.

Both the rich and the poor suffered during the Blitz. Hitler's bombers had no respect for class distinction. Four million homes were damaged or destroyed, and over 61,000 civilians were killed. Even some of the better-off, who had extolled the virtues of hard work and self-help, were forced to rely on the benevolence of the state after their properties had been reduced to rubble. Rationing too had a levelling effect on society, and there was popular support for it because it ensured fair shares for all. Everyone was reduced to the same basic level. Even the Royal Family entered into the spirit of sacrifice by eating tins of spam.

War Socialism
The free market, based on supply and demand, was no longer adequate in wartime conditions. The government had to abandon laissez-faire to an even greater extent and intervene to control the distribution and price of food and clothing. More generally, the economy had to be managed and planned from the centre. A form of 'war socialism' developed out of necessity. Production was coordinated, women were directed once more into the factories and onto the farms and full employment was maintained. A whole new government bureaucracy had to be established to bring these changes about. Ministries of Supply, Home Security, Economic Welfare, Information, Food, Shipping and Aircraft Production were added to the existing administrative machinery. This indeed was a total war effort and out of it grew a popular belief that if the burdens were to fall equally on all, then peacetime Britain in turn ought to distribute resources more equally to all.

Changing Attitudes to Social Security
In one sense, there is an in-built conflict between capitalism and the Welfare State, since the former tends to distribute resources in the form of rewards, whereas the latter distributes resources according to need. However, as we have seen, the workings of pure capitalism had to be modified during the war. At the same time, the needs of the whole nation had to be taken into account, if the war was going to be fought efficiently. A healthy, well-fed workforce had to be supported. This meant that access to the nation's resources had to be open to all, not just to those who could afford to pay for them. During the war, the framework of a modern social welfare system was set up by popular demand.

"In hotels, camps, factory canteens, hostels, railway trains, bars, restaurants, I listened and talked and argued. Topic Number One was probably the state of the war at the particular time; but Topic Number Two, running Number One very close, was always the New World after the war. What could we do to bring our economic and social system nearer to justice and security and decency? That was the great question ..."[4]

"The overall impact of the war was to increase the dependence of many even among the better-off on state services, and once this occurred, the remnants of the poor law and workhouse traditions that still underlay some of these services could not long survive."[5]

"From assistance only to those most in need through poverty, the responsibility of the community had been extended, without discrimination, to all who needed its help; from marginal provision to the destitute and helpless, it had developed into a pooling of national resources to see all its members through any of the ills that social care could relieve."[6]

Government Action 1940–1942
Churchill's Coalition Government took over in May 1940 during Britain's 'darkest hour'. The country was now fighting alone against Hitler. Several historians see this period as a turning point in the advance towards a Welfare State.

"The resolution and uplifting of hearts that came with Dunkirk and all that it stood for brought also a mood of unity in sacrifice that was to colour the whole nation's attitude to social problems and ensure that things would never again be as they had been."[7]

"Dunkirk, and all that the name evokes, was an important event in the wartime history of the social services. It summoned forth a note of self-criticism, of national self-criticism, of national introspection, and it set in motion ideas and talk of principles and plans."[8]

Adding substance to this 'Dunkirk spirit' was the presence of the key Labour leaders in the government—Attlee, Bevin, Cripps, Morrison, Greenwood, Dalton and Alexander. They were very prominent in the development of social and economic policy on the Home Front. Several initiatives soon arose.

National Milk Scheme
This was set up the week after the evacuation at Dunkirk. The scheme granted nursing and expectant mothers and under-fives half-price milk. By 1944, 95% of those eligible were participating in the scheme. 30% of mothers got free milk as their income was below £2 per week. The scheme was extended in 1941 to include the provision of vitamins, cod-liver oil and orange juice.

Provision of School Milk and Meals
Before the war, school meals were provided for the poor, but the system was tainted with the stigma of the old Poor Law and charity. Now, the Cabinet was determined to supply a service for all.

"There is a danger of deficiencies occurring in the quality and quantity

Sir William Beveridge in his study at University College, Oxford where he compiled the 'Beveridge Report', November 1942.

of children's diets ... there is no question of capacity to pay: we may find the children of well-to-do parents and the children of the poor suffering alike from an inability to get the food they need."[9]

Thanks to government subsidies, the number of children taking school meals rose from 130,000 daily in 1940 to 1,650,000 in 1945 and school milk uptake increased from 19% to 46% during the war.

Immunisation
This was provided free from 1941 onwards and an intensive publicity campaign was launched by the government. Child deaths from diphtheria dropped from 3,000 before the war to 818 in 1945.

State Nurseries
These were set up during the war to enable mothers to return to war work.

Old Age and Widows' Pension Act, 1940
This provided supplementary pensions for three-quarters of a million old people in need.

Determination of Needs Act, 1941
Under the hated household Means Test, husbands, parents, grandparents and children were legally bound to support those in need. Now, the dislocation of the war rendered this measure unworkable. The new Act provided a narrower, more humane form of Means Test.

The cumulative effect of these measures was to move the emphasis of the social security system away from selective benefits based on the old Poor Law towards universal benefits based on need. It can be argued that the foundations of the modern Welfare State were being laid during World War

The Beveridge Report, 1942
More than any other person, William Beveridge is associated with the establishment of the 'blueprint' for the postwar welfare state. Beveridge's *Report on Social Insurance and Allied Services* was published in December 1942. It created a great deal of public interest at the time and conditioned many to expect that the recommendations would be carried out, if not immediately, then directly after the war. Incredibly, this rather dry report broke all records for sales of government publications, selling 635,000 copies. The main principles behind the Beveridge Report were that the social security system would be:

✔ *Comprehensive:* It would meet all the social problems faced by people from the cradle to the grave.

✔ *Universal:* It would be open to everyone by right regardless of means.

✔ *Insurance-based:* People would contribute weekly payments to finance future benefits.

✔ *Compulsory:* People in work would have to be in the scheme.

✔ *Integrated:* It would bring together all the individual schemes, to be covered by one payment.

✔ *Flat-rate:* Everyone would pay the same contributions regardless of income.

✔ *Able to provide subsistence:* It would provide the minimum benefit necessary for food, clothing and shelter.

✔ *Non-means tested:* Benefits would no longer be stopped or reduced depending on a person's financial means.

In essence, Beveridge advocated that all people in work would pay a single weekly flat-rate contribution into the state insurance fund. This would cover all possible contingencies that people might face throughout their lives. In return for their contributions, a new Ministry of Social Security would provide people with subsistence in the form of sickness, medical, maternity, old age, unemployment, widow's, orphan's, industrial injury and funeral benefits.

Beveridge talked about the need to tackle the Five Giants—Want, Disease, Idleness, Ignorance and Squalor. His Report only dealt with Want. The other problems still had to be conquered:

➤ *Disease* by the establishment of a new health service;

➤ *Idleness* by the state aiming for full employment;

➤ *Ignorance* by reform of the educational system;

➤ *Squalor* by a new house-building and slum-clearance programme.

Beveridge also took for granted that the government would introduce Family Allowances.

In a sense, it is understandable that Churchill should have been cool towards the Beveridge Report and the interest it had generated in the country. He was preoccupied with winning the war, whose outcome was by no means certain in late 1942. However, there is little doubt that Churchill misunderstood the public feeling or that his handling of the issue was inept. In December 1942, a pamphlet explaining the Beveridge Report was issued to army units for discussion in 'current affairs hour', but soon after they were issued, orders were put out to return the pamphlets. The strong impression given was that the government was embarrassed by the Beveridge Plan and wished to shelve it.

At home, six by-elections took place in February 1943—a 'mini general election'. Despite a wartime truce between the major parties, the Conservative vote against Independent candidates went down in four of the seats, sending a clear signal to the government.

Churchill then attempted to allay public fears by speaking to the nation on the radio in March. Again he blundered. On the one hand, he did commit a postwar Conservative government to "national compulsory insurance for all classes for all purposes from the cradle to the grave".[10] However, nowhere did he mention Beveridge, nor did he convey great enthusiasm for the measures. The moment was lost. Churchill had passed up the opportunity to champion a universally popular idea.

The public quickly perceived that Labour was more likely to put Beveridge's vision into practice. After Labour's House of Commons motion in favour of the immediate implementation of the Beveridge Report had been defeated in February 1943, James Griffiths accurately predicted that "this makes the return of the Labour Party to power at the next election an absolute certainty".[11]

Views on the BEVERIDGE REPORT

THE AUTHOR

"The scheme here is in some ways a revolution but in more ways it is a natural development of the past. (Beveridge)

THE HISTORIANS

A country whose history has been so much concerned with freedom, the freedom to speak, to write, to vote, was now being given a new lesson in liberty, that true freedom lay in freedom from want, from disease, from ignorance, from squalor and from idleness. Here, in the totality of the vision, was the revolutionary element of the Beveridge Report.
(D Fraser *Evolution of the British Welfare State 4th Edition* page 216.)

All this amounted to no revolutionary proposal. The Beveridge Plan ... rounded off and carried to their logical conclusion all the established services, but made no extravagant demands on the State. In fact, it deplored the already accepted government responsibility for the long-term unemployed.
(M Bruce *The Coming of the Welfare State* page 307.)

THE POLITICIANS

A dangerous optimism is growing up about the conditions it will be possible to establish here after the war ... The question steals across the mind whether we are not committing our forty five million people to tasks beyond their compass ... Ministers should, in my view, be careful not to raise false hopes, as was done last time by speeches about 'homes fit for heroes' etc.
(Winston Churchill, Conservative Prime Minister. Cabinet notes from 12 January 1943 from Churchill *The Second World War* pages 861–2.)

Believe me, it is by acceptance or rejection of the plan that we shall be judged by this nation ... It is because we are convinced that the nation wants this plan and that the nation ought to get it, and that we can afford it, that we have put down this Amendment.
(James Griffiths (Labour)—speech in the House of Commons on 18 February 1943 proposing the immediate implementation of the Beveridge Report—amendment defeated—quoted in RC Birch *The Shaping of the Welfare State* page 113.)"

GOVERNMENT RESPONSES 1944-45

Beveridge, like the general public, believed that the government would quietly drop his proposals. However, Churchill came to the conclusion in late 1943 that detailed plans would have to be drawn up for peacetime Britain. Under the direction of Lord Woolton, the Minister for Reconstruction, White Papers on Health, Employment and Social Insurance were drafted, and an *Education Act* was passed in 1944—all clearly influenced by the Beveridge Report.

White Papers 1943-4

● *Educational Reconstruction* (July 1943) provided the basis for the *Education Act* in 1944.

● *A National Health Service* (February 1944) proposed a comprehensive system of health provision which would be 'free' ie. financed out of taxation and available to all who wanted to use it. Discussions on the White Paper had to be suspended because of the war and were taken up by the new Labour government.

● *Employment Policy* (May 1944) committed the government to the maintenance of a "high and stable level of employment" after the war. For the first time, the state was admitting that it had a responsibility to intervene in order to avoid the sort of mass unemployment experienced after the First World War. If depression appeared to be approaching, the government would use public expenditure to stimulate the economy—in other words, it would use classic Keynesian methods.

● *Social Insurance* (September 1944) was based largely on the Beveridge Report and proposed a comprehensive insurance scheme. Unlike Beveridge, however, benefits would not be based on the subsistence principle. The White Paper, with

A 'Beveridge Report' meeting outside a factory.

a few modifications, became the *National Insurance Act* of 1946.

During the war, the Beveridge Report and the various White Papers laid down the principles and much of the legislative detail out of which emerged the postwar Welfare State. Before the end of the war, two pieces of social legislation were enacted—the *Education Act* and the *Family Allowances Act*.

Education Act 1944

This was the major legislative achievement of the wartime Coalition Government in the area of social welfare. The Bill was skilfully steered through Parliament by the progressive Conservative RA Butler, then President of the Board of Education. The Butler Act, as it became known, set out the following provisions for England and Wales:

1 School leaving age to be raised to fifteen by 1947 and sixteen as soon as was practicable.

2 The school system to have three stages—nursery schools (attendance voluntary), primary schools (five–eleven-year-olds) and secondary schools (eleven years and over.)

3 Attendance at primary and

secondary school to be compulsory. (Until the Butler Act, parents had only been required to ensure their children's attendance for "efficient elementary instruction in reading, writing and arithmetic".)

4 Although not in the Act, it was recommended that secondary schools be divided into grammar, secondary modern and secondary technical schools, based on pupils' abilities and aptitudes. These would be tested at the end of primary school by an 'eleven-plus' exam.

5 Provision of school meals and milk to be compulsory.

6 A school medical service to be developed.

A parallel *Education (Scotland) Act* was passed in 1946. After the 'eleven-plus', pupils would go either to a senior secondary for an academic education or a junior secondary for a practical/technical education. Although the Act stated that there was supposed to be 'parity of esteem' between the different types of school, it was clear that a first-rate and a second-rate structure were being put in place, very much reflecting the persistence of social class divisions in society as a whole.

Family Allowances Act 1945

During the time between the break-up of the Coalition Government and the election of the Labour government, Churchill presided over a 'caretaker' government which brought in family allowances.

It provided five shillings (25p) a week for each child after the first. Although Beveridge had included family allowances in his Report as one of the three 'assumptions', the origins of the idea lay in a memorandum by an all-party group of MPs to the Chancellor of the Exchequer in 1941. It called for family allowances "to prevent the spread of discontent between the richer and poorer classes".[12] Employers in particular wanted to keep wage claims down after the war and saw family allowances as a way of doing this. The memorandum also advocated family allowances "to prevent a fall in the birth rate".[13] A decline in the birth rate had been predicted by demographers in the 1930s. However, the amount of the allowance was very

small, even by 1945 standards, and therefore was likely to have only a marginal impact on family finances.

The motives of the MPs could hardly be described as high-minded and certainly had very little to do with the welfare of the poorest families. There was one enlightened aspect of the scheme though. Family allowances were to be the legal entitlement of the wife, not the husband. This provision was added as a result of a campaign by the feminist MP Eleanor Rathbone who argued that if the male bread-winner squandered the weekly wage on beer,

cigarettes and gambling, the wife would at least have control over the family allowance.

THE 1945 GENERAL ELECTION

Five years of coexistence and co-operation in the wartime government produced a remarkable degree of convergence between the two major parties on social welfare issues, as can be seen by comparing their respective manifestos. (See page 89.)

Although there was nothing to choose between the parties on social policy, the public saw Labour as being more committed to the creation of a welfare state immedi-

Clement Attlee PM with his Ministers and senior civil servants at the back of 10 Downing Street, 1945.

Changing Britain 1850–1979

MANIFESTOS COMPARED

CONSERVATIVE MANIFESTO 1945

National Insurance
One of our most important tasks will be to pass into law and bring into action as soon as we can a nationwide and compulsory scheme of National Insurance based on the plan announced by the Government of all Parties in 1944.

Health
The health service of the country will be made available to all citizens ... We propose to create a comprehensive health service covering the whole range of medical treatment from the general practitioner to the specialist ...

Education
The Education Act set forth in the 'Four Years' Plan' has already been piloted through Parliament by Mr Butler. Our task in the coming years will be to remodel our educational system to the new law ...

LABOUR MANIFESTO 1945

Social Insurance Against the Rainy Day
The Labour Party has played a leading part in the long campaign for proper social security for all ... A Labour government will press on rapidly with legislation extending social insurance over the necessary wide field to all.

Health of the Nation and its Children
Money must no longer be the passport to the best treatment. In the new National Health Service there shall be health centres where the people may get the best that modern science can offer, more and better hospitals ...

Education and Recreation
An important step forward has been taken by the passing of the recent Education Act. Labour will put that Act not merely into legal force but into practical effect ...

ately after the war. One historian has written of Labour alone being able to understand and project the new mood of the British people. This impression was confirmed by Labour's election campaign which concentrated on postwar domestic issues. Its manifesto, appropriately called *Let Us Face the Future*, contrasted with the Conservatives' document *Mr Churchill's Declaration of Policy to the Electors,* which relied too heavily on their leader's wartime reputation. There was a negative side to Churchill's war image, particularly his mishandling of the Beveridge Report. He was to do the Conservative Party further damage in the Election campaign, when he launched a bitter attack on the Labour Party:

"There can be no doubt that socialism is inseparably interwoven with totalitarianism and the abject worship of the State ... Socialism is in its essence an attack not only upon British enterprise, but upon the right of an ordinary man or woman to breathe freely without having a harsh, clumsy tyrannical hand clasped across their mouth and nostrils ... (The Socialists) ... would have to fall back on some form of Gestapo, no doubt very humanely directed in the first instance."[14]

This sort of vindictive rhetoric was out of tune with the spirit of unity and consensus at the end of the war and it backfired on the Conservatives. However, it is unlikely that either the broadcast or the Conservative handling of the campaign had a decisive impact on the final outcome of the Election. Opinion polls conducted by Mass Observation showed a consistent Labour lead from 1942 onwards.

THE LABOUR GOVERNMENTS 1945–51
With an overall majority in Parliament, the new Labour government was able to carry out its social and economic policies to the full. Labour's priorities were economic reconstruction and the establishment of a Welfare State. The spirit of excitement at the beginning of the Labour era was captured in a House of Commons debate when

Clement Attlee re-elected as MP for Limehouse, London, July 1945.

the Attorney-General, Sir Hartley Shawcross, stated "We are the masters at the moment, and not only at the moment, but for a very long time."[15]

We will now attempt to describe and evaluate the measures which the new 'masters' of Westminster and Whitehall took in order to tackle Beveridge's Five Giants—Social Security, Health, Education, Housing and Employment.

Social Security

National Insurance (Industrial Injuries) Act, July 1946

Labour inherited this Bill from the Coalition Government, which in turn had based its proposals on the Beveridge Report. Accidents at work were no longer to be a private matter between employer and employee, but the responsibility of society as a whole. Universality and compulsion were built into the scheme—all workers and employers would have to contribute payments. In return, the state would provide insurance against industrial injury. Benefits were set at a higher rate (45 shillings (£2.25) per week) than those for ordinary sickness.

National Insurance Act, August 1946

Like Industrial Injuries, the *National Insurance Act* was based on the 1944 White Paper. In a wartime radio broadcast, Churchill had promised compulsory national insurance for all classes for all purposes from the 'cradle to the grave'. The insured population would be entitled to unemployment, sickness, maternity and widow's benefit, guardian's allowance, retirement pension and a death grant for funeral expenses. Benefits were set at the rate of 26 shillings (£1.30) for a single adult and 42 shillings (£2.10) for a couple.

Sickness benefits could only be claimed after one hundred and fifty six contributions and unemployment benefit could only be given for a period of between one hundred and eighty and four hundred and ninety two days.

National Assistance Act, 1948

The aim of the Act was to "make further provision for the welfare of disabled, sick, aged and other persons, and for regulating homes for disabled and aged persons ... out of moneys provided by Parliament". In other words, national assistance was supposed to be a 'safety net' to meet the needs of those whose circumstances were not adequately catered for by the National Insurance scheme. The Act set up a National Assistance Board (replacing the Unemployment Assistance Board of the 1930s) to carry out these duties.

Criticisms of the Social Security System

In theory, National Insurance was supposed to be comprehensive and the payments sufficient to meet the people's needs. National Assistance was therefore designed only to provide a residual, back-up role to National Insurance. In practice, it did not work out like that. The government calculated and decided on benefit levels in 1946. These were to be fixed for the next five years, after which they would be reassessed. However, by the time the scheme came into operation on the 'Appointed Day' (5 July, 1948), prices of goods had increased significantly, thus reducing the purchasing power of the benefits. One historian has calculated that welfare benefits in 1948 were only 19% of the average industrial wage and therefore well below subsistence level. Because of this, many more people than expected, particularly the elderly, were forced into applying for National Assistance. In 1949, 48% of all National Assistance went to supplement retirement pensions. That figure had risen to 68% by the late 1950s. The problem here was that National Assistance was 'means tested' and many old people were reluctant to apply for it, fearing the stigma attached to the hated Means Test of the 1930s.

"This dependency of many recipients of National Insurance benefits on means-tested assistance—even if these needs tests cannot be compared with the notorious household means test—constituted a major inroad into the principle of universality and of benefits paid as of right as a consequence of the insurance principle."[16]

Compared to the social security provision of the past, the system put in place by 1948 was a marked improvement, but looking back from the present, it is equally clear that there was still a long way to go before the problems of poverty and deprivation were to be adequately addressed.

Health

The National Health Service Bill was piloted through Parliament by the Health Minister, Aneurin Bevan, becoming law in November 1946. During the debate in the House of Commons, Bevan spoke about the deficiencies of the existing setup and the benefits of the new health service.

General Election RESULT 5 July 1945

Parties	Total Votes	MPs	% of Votes
Conservatives*	9,988,306	213	39.8
Labour	11,995,152	393	47.8
Liberal	2,248,226	12	9.0
Others	854,294	22	2.8
Total	25,085,978	640	100.0

*Includes Liberal Nationalists

Table 7.1
Source: C Cook & J Stevenson *British Modern History 1714–1987* page 78.

"The first reason why a health scheme of this sort is necessary at all is because it has been the firm conclusion of all parties that money ought not to be permitted to stand in the way of obtaining an efficient health service. Although it is true that the health insurance system provides a general practitioner service and caters for something like twenty one million of the population, the rest of the population have to pay whenever they desire the services of a doctor ... and therefore tend to postpone consultation as long as possible (while) there is the financial anxiety caused by having to pay doctors' bills ... In the second place, the national health insurance scheme does not provide for the self-employed, nor, of course, for the families of dependants ... One of the first merits of this Bill is that it provides a universal health service without any insurance qualifications of any sort. It is available to the whole population and ... it is intended that there shall be no limitation on the kind of assistance given in the general practitioner service, the specialist, the hospitals, eye treatment, spectacles, dental treatment, hearing facilities, all these are to be made available free."[17]

The *NHS Act,* like the other social services, was scheduled to come into operation in July 1948. Almost right up to the 'Appointed Day' though, the doctors campaigned vigorously for changes to the proposed health service. In a survey of British Medical Association (BMA) members early in 1948, 40,814 doctors voted against the *NHS Act* and only 4,734 voted for it. Clearly, without their cooperation the NHS would not work. In the end, Bevan bought the doctors off, starting at the top with the consultants. Much to the dismay of the Labour backbenchers in the Commons, Bevan announced in February 1948 that consultants would be allowed to continue their private practices on a part-time basis as well as having their own lucrative pay-beds for private patients in NHS hospitals.

The ordinary doctors had two chief complaints. Firstly, they objected to the fact that the sale of private practices was prohibited under the Act. Bevan sugared that

particular pill by setting aside £66 million to compensate the doctors for the loss of their private practices. The other main complaint was against the NHS becoming a completely salaried medical service. Bevan eventually agreed that GPs would be paid on the basis of a capitation fee for each patient on the doctor's list. With a fee of 15 shillings (75p) per patient, this would guarantee doctors an income of between £1,000 and £2,500. Doctors in 'unfashionable' practices would get an extra payment of £300. With all these concessions and sweeteners, doctors' reservations dwindled, and by the 'Appointed Day', 90% of doctors had agreed to enter the NHS.

If many of the doctors joined up with some reluctance, ordinary people celebrated the arrival of the NHS. The following colourful extracts come from Paul Addison's book *Now the War is Over.*

Mrs Bond of Leeds recalled how her family reacted.

"When the National Health Service started, oh it was fantastic. My mother and dad had been having problems with their teeth for ages, and I think they were the first at the dentist, as soon as he opened, they were there for an appointment. And instead of having just a few teeth out, they had the complete set out. And free dentures. You know? Thought it was wonderful ..."

Mrs Law of Manchester described her mother's reaction to the inauguration of the NHS.

"I can remember this particular day, everything was in the radius of a few minutes' walk and she went to the optician's, obviously she'd got a prescription from the doctor, she went and she got tested for new glasses, then she went further down the road ... for the chiropodist, she had her feet done, then she went back to the doctor's because she'd been having trouble with her ears and the doctor said ... he would fix her up with a hearing aid ..."[18]

Stories like this were by no means uncommon and they highlighted

the backlog of untreated problems which the NHS faced. Doctors, dentists and opticians were inundated with patients queuing up for treatment. Prescriptions rose from 7 million per month before the NHS to 13.5 million per month in September 1948. In the first year of the health service, five million pairs of spectacles were dispensed and eight million dental patients were treated.

The enormous expense of the NHS came as a shock. From the beginning, the government accepted that National Insurance funds would be inadequate to meet the needs of the nation's health and that most of the money would have to come out of general taxation. In fact, National Insurance only contributed 9% of NHS funding in 1949. By 1950, the NHS was costing £358 million a year, and the Labour government was forced to backtrack on the principle of a free service by introducing charges for spectacles and dental treatment. The government, of course, was constrained by the economy, which was still recovering from the war. Plans for new hospitals and health centres had to be shelved. Nevertheless, despite the criticisms, the compromises and the constraints, the NHS was arguably "the greatest single achievement in the story of the welfare state".[19]

Education
The Labour government inherited the *Education Act* from the Coalition Government and had to put it into effect. The most immediate problem was the shortage and poor condition of school buildings. About 20% of existing school stock had been destroyed or damaged during the war. Due to the scale of the problem and the economic constraints of the postwar period, Attlee was forced to concentrate on the replacement of schools bombed during the war and on the building of new primary schools to accommodate the children resulting from the 'baby boom' of 1942–7. By 1950, 1,176 new schools had been built or

were under construction, 928 of which were primaries. At the secondary level, very few technical schools were built. Consequently, the proposed tripartite structure of secondary education in reality boiled down to a dual system of grammar schools and secondary modern schools.

> "There were grammar school places for about 20% of children and technical places for no more than 5%, so most children were classified as non-academic and allocated to the residual category of modern school."[20]

Children were to be allocated to the three types of school after an 'intelligence' test at 'eleven-plus'. This was supposed to be an objective and fair means of selecting pupils irrespective of their social class background. What it turned out to be was a socially divisive and highly contentious selection procedure for the limited number of prestige places at the grammar schools.

> "From the outset ... (secondary modern schools) suffered from the crippling disadvantage that the grammar schools alone were geared, by tradition, organisation and staff, to the task of preparing their pupils for public examinations; therefore, only by going to a grammar school could a child be sure of obtaining access either to a university or to one of the professions. This made secondary modern schools inferior to the grammar school in that they offered their children fewer opportunities."[21]

Why, then, did the Labour government do so little to enhance the opportunities for working-class children, most of whom left school at fourteen (fifteen after 1947) with no paper qualifications? Several historians put this down to the educational background of the Labour leaders. On the one hand, Attlee, Cripps and Dalton had all been educated at public (independent or private in Scotland) schools, and had little understanding of the state system. Others like Bevin, Morrison and Shinwell had received little formal education.

Tomlinson, who became Education Minister in 1947, had left school at the age of twelve.

Compared to the equality of opportunity and provision being carried out in the areas of social security and health, the Labour government did little for the educational welfare of the working-class. It was 1964 before the idea of comprehensive schools for all abilities and social backgrounds became Labour Party policy.

Housing

The chronic housing shortage at the end of the war was the most pressing problem facing the government. There had already been a serious shortage before the war and this was compounded by the destruction of 700,000 houses by Hitler's bombers and rockets. In 1945, one-third of all houses in Britain were in serious need of repair and renovation. At the end of the war, the government's housing policy was hindered by the lack of building workers and the shortage and high cost of building materials. Timber had to be imported from Sweden and America. In 1947, the housing programme had to be cut back on Treasury insistence because of the effect of raw material imports on Britain's Balance of Payments.

The responsibility for Britain's housing problems fell to Bevan at the Health Ministry. (Labour failed to create a Housing Ministry as promised.) His policy was to help those most in need ie. the working class. Most of the scarce building materials were allocated to the local authorities to build council houses for rent. Between 1945 and 1951, four council houses were built for every private house built. Also, Bevan insisted that council homes were to be built to a high standard, with an average floor area of 1,000 square feet compared to 800 square feet in the 1930s.

The government also continued into peacetime the production of

prefabricated houses as a temporary stop-gap to meet the crisis. Between 1945 and 1948, 157,000 'prefabs' were assembled. Despite all these efforts, there were still chronic shortages. Many desperate families, out of sheer frustration, took to squatting on disused army camps in the summer of 1946. The government wisely decided not to prosecute them and, realising that this would help to reduce waiting lists, instructed the local authorities to provide basic services and amenities for these people.

The Labour government's record on house-building does not compare well with prewar levels or with the achievements of the Conservatives in the 1950s. Poor housing and homelessness were still serious problems at the end of the Labour period. The 1951 census revealed that there were 750,000 fewer houses than there were households in Britain. This was roughly the same level of homelessness as in 1931. However, given the scale of social and economic problems facing the government in 1945, historians have tended to judge Labour less harshly than the voters did in 1951.

Employment

The 1944 White Paper on Employment Policy had committed the government to "the maintenance of a high and stable level of employment after the war". Beveridge had reckoned that unemployment could not be brought down below 3%, but by 1946 the figure was running at only 2.5%. Dalton, the first postwar Labour Chancellor of the Exchequer, claimed that full employment was "the greatest revolution brought about by the Labour Government."[22] What is less certain is whether the government's economic policies or a mixture of postwar boom and Marshall Aid from America brought this about.

The postwar economy was not without its difficulties. Between 1945 and 1951, Britain experienced bread and potato rationing,

HOUSES *built in England & Wales* 1935-54

Year	Local Authority	Private	Total
1935–39	346,840	1,269,912	1,616,752
1940–44	—	—	151,000
1945–49	432,098	126,317	588,415
1950–54	912,805	228,616	1,141,421

Table 7.2
Source: Cook & Stevenson *Modern British History* page 129.

fuel shortages during the winter of 1947, a 30% devaluation of the pound, inflation, and Balance of Payments problems. Perhaps it is to the credit of the Labour governments that they completed the Welfare State structure, and maintained full employment under the shadow of such serious economic problems.

AN ASSESSMENT OF THE LABOUR REFORMS 1945–51

Hostile Viewpoints

It is important to remember that there was still a great deal to do. In the austere world of postwar Britain adequate houses, schools and hospitals were in short supply. Labour had not ushered in a socialist utopia as many had expected. Deprivation and poverty had been reduced but not eliminated. The capitalist system, with all its attendant inequalities, continued much as before, despite the nationalisation of the 'commanding heights' of the economy. The Welfare State, it is argued, was applying a bandage instead of carrying out the radical surgery needed to treat the ailing British patient. At best, some have said that "Labour's achievement was more one of modernising, improving and greatly extending an existing structure than of building an entirely new edifice."[23]

While universal benefits were good for everyone, in theory, the middle-class were "more adept at claiming their rights than the poor." Equality of opportunity favoured the middle class more than the working class. Grammar

school fees were abolished, and government spending on grammar schools raced ahead of expenditure on secondary moderns and junior secondaries.

Although the National Health Service has been seen as the most effective expression of the Labour ideal, it has been said that Bevan made too many compromises in order to meet the demands of the BMA. The NHS did not eliminate private health care. Bevan allowed private patients, in 'pay beds', in NHS hospitals. Charles Webster, the official historian of the NHS, is very critical:

"The NHS failed to improve the general medical service available to the bulk of the population. The middle class benefited to some extent, but the lower classes continued to experience a humiliating standard of care. The middle classes were liberated from doctors' fees and they enjoyed the services of better practitioners, while the lower classes, especially after the introduction of the prescription charge in 1952, continued to receive an inferior service, but for a higher level of payment through taxes and direct charges."[24]

From another point of view, Labour's contribution can be challenged if we look at the development of the Welfare State over the long term, from its origins in the 1870s until 1948. During much of the time, Conservative and Liberal governments were in power. Therefore, it can be argued that Labour simply completed the Welfare State originated by others, namely Lloyd George (Liberal), Churchill (Liberal and latterly Conservative), Beveridge (Liberal) and Butler (Conservative). As well as the roles of individuals and parties we must not forget the forces which shaped the growth of the Welfare State, especially the social impact of mass unemployment followed by war in the 1930s and 1940s. The two principal historians of the Welfare State agree that the war was extremely important.

"The decisive event in the evolution of the Welfare State was the Second World War."[25]

"The war was to have a decisive influence in producing a common experience and universal treatment for it."[26]

What the war helped to create for the first time was a popular and also political consensus about how Britain's social problems should be treated and the role of the state in this process. In 1945, Labour, the Liberals and the Conservatives all came out with remarkably similar welfare proposals. In fact, it could be argued that if Churchill had become the first postwar Prime Minister instead of Attlee, the historic achievement of the completion of

UNEMPLOYMENT *levels* 1931-51
(thousands)

1931	2,630	**1938**	1,791	**1945**	137
1932	2,745	**1939**	1,514	**1946**	374
1933	2,521	**1940**	963	**1947**	480
1934	2,159	**1941**	350	**1948**	310
1935	2,036	**1942**	123	**1949**	308
1936	1,755	**1943**	82	**1950**	314
1937	1,484	**1944**	75	**1951**	253

Table 7.3
Source: Cook & Stevenson *Modern British History* page 217.

the Welfare State might have been attributed to the Conservatives rather than to Labour.

Right-wing critics of the Welfare State claim that "Britain took the wrong fork in 1945 and Attlee's Labour administration bears much of the responsibility. The country needed new homes and hospitals, but these should only have been provided (as in Germany) after the re-creation of an efficient industrial base."[27]

Friendly Viewpoints

Labour's social security legislation and the creation of the National Health Service went a long way towards completing the social welfare system which had been developing since the abandonment of Victorian 'laissez-faire' attitudes. By 1948, the 'Five Giants' of 'want', 'disease', 'idleness', 'ignorance' and 'squalor' were under attack. The state was now providing a 'safety net' which protected people of all classes 'from the cradle to the grave'. When Rowntree investigated conditions in York in 1950, he found that primary poverty had gone down to 2% compared to 36% in 1936.

A monumental task faced a Labour Cabinet which lacked experience of peacetime government, and which was hemmed in by serious economic problems in the immediate postwar years. Britain had lost almost one-quarter of its national wealth during World War II. Added to this decline, Britain had lost overseas assets and markets, and was faced with a severe shortage of raw materials while trying to deal. with the legacy of pre-war industrial decline which had been masked by the short-term demands of a wartime economy. Labour's achievement was to complete the structure of the modern welfare state in a flurry of legislation between 1945 and 1948.

Some have argued that Beveridge provided a 'blueprint' for the post-war 'Welfare State' and Labour merely followed his instructions, but that is not the case. Although Labour's legislative achievements owed a great deal to Beveridge, his report did not provide Attlee's Ministers with a reform programme which was ready to be implemented. Bevan had to "draw up plans for a comprehensive health service virtually from scratch".[28]

Apart from a disappointing record on housing, Labour carried out its manifesto promises. By 1951, Britain had a comprehensive system of social security, unified health and education services, and full employment. Above all, Labour was firmly identified with the Welfare state. We need to remember the immediate benefits enjoyed by millions.

"One woman later recalled how, on the evening before the Health Service came into operation, she was delivered of her baby shortly before midnight. The next morning, she was presented with a bill for £6 by the doctor; had the baby been born fifteen minutes later, there would have been no charge. This was what most Labour supporters understood by socialism in practice."[29]

It is important to consider the reality of the so-called postwar political consensus.

"For Conservative social observers, (evacuation) confirmed the view that the bulk of the problems were caused by an incorrigible underclass of personally-inadequate 'cultural orphans' for whom a Welfare State could do little. Evacuation thus shows us that the ideological consensus of wartime ... was something of a myth."[30]

Many doubt whether the Conservatives would have completed the social welfare system had they won the Election in 1945.

"The Conservatives were always inclined to return to a more limited Welfare State of means-tested benefits. Labour, on the other hand, viewed the Welfare State as a bridgehead of social equality from which further advances could be made."[31]

While Attlee's reforms have been criticised for not being radical enough, they could be seen as being pragmatic. He wanted his government's reforms to last, and not be swept aside by the Conservatives the next time they got into power. In this he was successful, for the Conservatives largely accepted the Welfare State brought in by Labour.

The Growth of Political Nationalism in Scotland 1880–1979

WHAT YOU WILL LEARN

- **Understand the main reasons for dissatisfaction with the existing political arrangements in Scotland in the 1880s.**

- **Know what measures of administrative devolution were put in place in the 1880s.**

- **Explain why demands for legislative devolution persisted into the post-World War I period.**

- **Know the main organisations striving for legislative devolution and how and why they came together to form the National Party of Scotland (NPS) in 1928.**

- **Understand why the NPS and its successor, the Scottish National Party (SNP) were weak and divided in the early years.**

- **Explain in detail how and why the SNP achieved spectacular growth / success in the late 1960s/early 1970s.**

ANY ATTEMPT to explain the origins of modern Scottish nationalism must take as a starting point the Treaty of Union of 1707 whereby Scotland was incorporated, with England, into the new state of Great Britain. Scottish institutions such as the Church of Scotland and the law were guaranteed a continuing, distinct identity under the Treaty, a provision which has largely been observed. Other institutions such as the banks also retained a distinctive identity. Consequently, a Scottish national identity survived after 1707 and has evolved ever since. This sense of who the Scots are, both as a people and in relation to the other British nations, continues to influence the Scottish political agenda right up to the present.

A Scottish Identity?

For much of its history, Scotland was a divided country. The Jacobite rebellion after the Union was as much a Scottish as a British civil war, pitting 'backward' Catholic/Episcopalian, Gaelic-speaking Highlanders against the 'modern' Presbyterian Lowlanders. The triumph of the latter over the former was followed by the systematic eradication of all things Celtic (removal of powers of clan chiefs, disarming of the clans, the banning of the wearing of the kilt). Scotland after the '45 had thus become a more 'united' country thanks to the suppression of the old political order in the Highlands and with it, in due course, much of the Gaelic culture.

Curiously, although the victory of the Hanoverian forces at Culloden meant that Scotland became more 'Lowland' in culture, between 1746 and the 1850s the Scots began to prefer to see their country in terms of 'Highland' symbols—the kilt, bagpipes, whisky, the clan. These images, popularised by Sir Walter Scott, helped to differentiate the Scots from the English much more than the anglicised culture of the Lowlands would allow. Out of this grew the myth that the Scots had a common heritage (Wallace, Bruce, Culloden, Burns)—a shared history which was both distinctive and heroic. In other words, by the middle of the nineteenth century, the Scots had forged (or more accurately) invented, for themselves a national identity. The royal seal of approval was granted to the 'tartan' image of Scotland when Queen Victoria took up summer residence at Balmoral from the 1840s.

Did this identity conflict with the reality that Scotland was part of the British state? The answer is that most Scots were quite able to live with a dual identity. After all, many Scots benefited from the Union. The entrepreneurial middle classes in particular were in the forefront of managing the Empire, providing engineers, administrators and soldiers. They were proud of the achievements of the British Empire and proud to be called British. Some were even content to refer to Scotland as 'North Britain'.

However, Scots were at ease with being both Scottish and British only as long as the Empire continued to work in Scotland's favour and as long as Scotland received favourable treatment within the Union relationship. As soon as these conditions appeared to go against Scotland in the 1920s, a new phenomenon—modern nationalism—began to arise.

Scotland in the 1880s

The Scottish economy, and especially industry, was at its peak in the last two decades of the nineteenth century. The heavy industries were all doing well—coal, iron, steel, engineering and shipbuilding. At this time, half of all the men employed in shipbuilding in Britain were working on the Clyde. The economy had been growing rapidly and the wealth of the nation had nearly doubled in the previous thirty years. The economic advantages of the Union were clear to most Scots. In fact, one historian, HJ Hanham, has gone as far as to say that "... during the Victorian age, Scotland enjoyed a prosperity so great by comparison with that of the past that unionist sentiment seemed likely to destroy Scottish national self-consciousness altogether".[1]

While it is true that Scotland as a whole had never had it so good, there were areas of the country (for example, the Highlands during the Clearances) which did not reap the benefits of the Union. Many of the working-class people in Scotland's cities did not experience a sense of progress and material improvement—health and housing conditions were worse in Glasgow, the 'second city of the Empire', than anywhere south of the border. However, the working class were politically insignificant in the 1880s since the vast majority of male unskilled workers would only be enfranchised in 1918.

While Hanham in the quote above is undoubtedly correct to suggest that Scotland's favourable position in the Union did help to keep the Scots 'British', there were other factors (cultural and political) which tended to run counter to this and helped to raise Scottish national consciousness.

One such factor was the growth of government intervention. Industrialisation was now compelling governments to abandon laissez-faire and deal with the social and economic problems which affected Britain's cities—poor housing, public health, conditions in factories. Scots, hitherto "among the least governed people in Europe"[2], now began to experience the uniform hand of central government. There was a feeling that Scotland's distinctiveness in the Union was being eroded and hence there was a need to reassert Scottish identity.

Another factor which evoked a 'nationalist' reaction in Scotland was the coming of nationwide transport and communication facilities. Railways, the telegraph and national newspapers all served to undermine local/national differences within the UK. Although the vast majority of people welcomed these triumphs of modern technology, there were those in Scotland who saw the dangers. Lord Rosebery feared for the survival of Scottish traditions and character:

"Much of this character has been taken away from us by the swift amalgamating power of railways, by the centralisation of anglicising empire, by the compassionate sneer of the higher civilisation."[3]

The 1880s' variant of nationalism was mainly the preserve of the middle class who were concerned with raising Scotland's cultural profile above the level of tartan and bagpipes. The historian Michael Lynch considers that "there was ... a real sense in the 1880s and 1890s of a renewed national consciousness".[4]

Lynch cites the founding of the Scottish National Portrait Gallery (1889), the Scottish History Society (1887) and the Scottish Text Society (1884) as examples of this re-awakened national identity which "depended not so much on official institutions as on various agencies within civil society, ranging from friendly or temperance societies to the Boys' Brigade".[5]

This view is supported by other historians who assert that "this was a period when Scottish culture became more Scottish ... the buildings announced themselves as Scottish with their thistles, crow-stepped gables and baronial turrets".[6]

"... the middle class were wearing Highland dress on Sundays; the use of words like Scotch or North Britain instead of Scots or Scottish, or England instead of Britain, was incurring authoritative disapproval."[7]

If, then, we wish to use the term 'the growth of nationalism' for the 1880s, we are referring to a very moderate phenomenon compared to the post-1918 version. Late Victorian nationalism was based on a desire for Scotland's history, language and culture to be preserved in the face of anglicising tendencies. Another strand to nationalism was the call for Scotland to be better managed and represented within the context of the UK. This latter strand—called 'Home Rule'—came to the fore in the 1880s.

ADMINISTRATIVE DEVOLUTION IN THE 1880s

To understand why dissatisfaction arose about Scotland's administrative arrangements, we again need to refer back to the Union of 1707. The Union of Parliaments did not mean that Scotland was completely submerged into a British state. A good deal of administrative devolution was built into the settlement. For example, Scotland retained its own Minister in the government, the Secretary of State for Scotland. However, in the aftermath of the Jacobite Rising, the post of Secretary of State was abolished. From 1746 until 1782, Scotland was run by the Northern Department and from then until the 1880s by the Home Office in London, with the chief Scottish law officer, the Lord Advocate, becoming business manager for Scotland. During that time, Scottish affairs were neglected by the government. There was no one at Cabinet level fighting for the interests of Scotland.

By the 1880s, both Liberal and Tory MPs were agreed that something must be done about the neglect of Scottish affairs. This was an issue which had been smouldering for thirty years. As far back as 1853, the National Association for the Vindication of Scottish Rights had called for the restoration of the post of Secretary of State. In 1869, a majority of MPs wrote a letter to Gladstone (then Prime Minister) pointing out the need for a Scottish Minister. Gladstone duly set up a Royal Commission of Inquiry to look into the matter. The Commissioners recommended what the MPs had been advocating. However, neither Gladstone nor Disraeli, when he became Prime

Minister in 1874, acted on this recommendation.

The issue did not disappear and political pressure was reapplied in 1881. The key figure again was the Earl of Rosebery, a young Liberal politician who had the advantage of being a good friend of Gladstone. Rosebery spoke in the House of Lords about the need for a Minister of Scottish affairs, warning that "The words Home Rule have begun to be distinctly and loudly mentioned in Scotland".[8]

Gladstone, already preoccupied by Irish demands for Home Rule, reacted by appointing Rosebery as Parliamentary Undersecretary of State at the Home Office with the remit of reorganising Scottish administration. Here Rosebery met with considerable opposition from both the Home Office and the Treasury. They maintained that since there was hardly any Scottish business transacted through their Departments, the effort and expense required to set up a separate Scottish Office would outweigh any advantages gained. Rosebery tried to persuade the Home Office that this was an unsatisfactory way to treat Scottish matters, but to no avail. His campaign for an independent Scottish Office and a Scottish Secretary with a seat in the Cabinet seemed to have failed, so he resigned in May 1883. In his letter of resignation, he said:

> "From the day of the first meeting of the new Parliament until the present day of its third session ... not one minute of Government time has been allotted to Scotland or Scottish affairs. Can you be surprised that the people of Scotland complain?"[9]

The government finally conceded that there was a need for a Scottish Office. The *Secretary for Scotland Act* was passed in August 1885 by the new Conservative government headed by Lord Salisbury. The post of Scottish Secretary fell to the Duke of Richmond and Gordon who, up until this time, had been firmly opposed to the idea. Replying to Salisbury's offer of the post,

he wrote "You know my opinion on the office, and that it is quite unnecessary, but the Country and Parliament think otherwise—and the office has been created and someone must fill it. Under these circumstances, I am quite ready to take it and will do my best to make it a success (if that is possible!)."[10]

The powers of the new Secretary for Scotland and his department, the Scottish Office, were decided over the next two years. Here again, the Whitehall bureaucracy was reluctant to let go of power. The Treasury and the Home Office in particular fought a rearguard action to retain as much power as possible at the centre. Most contentious of all was the transfer of education and law and order to the Scottish Office. However, both of these areas, along with local government, were successfully transferred from the Home Office to the Scottish Office (whose headquarters were at Dover House in London with only a token presence in Edinburgh). By 1887, the Scottish Office was "the unchallenged agency of the central government for 'purely Scottish affairs', and the Scottish Secretary was regarded as 'Scotland's Minister'".[11]

Scotland, then, had gained its first measure of administrative devolution by the creation of the Scottish Office and the position of Scottish Secretary. How had this been achieved? In 1853, the National Association for the Vindication of Scottish Rights began campaigning for the restoration of the post of Scottish Secretary. From the 1860s onwards, there was a growing consensus among Scottish Tory and Liberal MPs that something needed to be done to remedy the inefficiency of the Scottish administrative system. Resistance in both the House of Lords and the House of Commons had eventually broken down by 1885.

However, it should not be thought that this was a radical change in the government of Scotland nor

that it was a victory for 'nationalism'. Firstly, the Liberal and Tory MPs who were pushing for these modest measures of devolution were doing so in order to strengthen the Union and to secure 'good government'. Secondly, the post of Scottish Secretary was not exactly high-powered—it did not come with Cabinet status and was "largely ceremonial and an ability to stir up apathy was one of the main talents it demanded".[12] Thirdly, the Scottish Office only had a staff of four to administer all the affairs of Scotland!

THE DEMAND FOR LEGISLATIVE DEVOLUTION IN THE 1880s

The first mention of legislative devolution came in a Commons debate in 1877 when the Liberal MP Sir George Campbell warned that Home Rule might be the only remedy for Scotland's problems. Scottish MPs were continually frustrated by the lack of time available at Westminster for Scottish legislation. The Scottish local authorities and the business community complained bitterly about the cost of getting private Bills put through Parliament. However, the political will to bring about such a major change to the Constitution was not there until 1885.

It was Gladstone who brought Home Rule to the forefront of politics. At this time, UK politics was dominated by the Irish problem. In the summer of 1885, Gladstone unexpectedly did a U-turn and came out in favour of Home Rule for Ireland. This immediately gave hope that concessions might also be made to demands for Scottish Home Rule. What was good for Ireland must also be good for Scotland. 1886 saw the founding of the Scottish Home Rule Association (SHRA). This was mainly a Liberal organisation, although it became the recruiting ground for future Labour and Nationalist leaders. Ramsay MacDonald (first Labour Prime Minister) and Keir Hardie (founder of the Scottish Labour Party) were both involved with the SHRA as was RB Cunninghame

Graham, the first President of the National Party of Scotland. Further progress was made when, in 1888, the Scottish Liberal Association came out in favour of granting Home Rule to Scotland so that "the Scottish people could have the sole control and management of their own national affairs".[13]

Although the issue of 'Home Rule for Scotland' did gain a political foothold in the 1880s, it was far from secure. For example, the SHRA failed to persuade Scottish public opinion of the validity of its cause. At the national level, the political impetus collapsed with the defeat of the Irish Home Rule Bill in 1886. The Liberal Party also split over the issue. Unlike the Irish, the Scots had no real economic grievances to fuel full-blown nationalism. On the contrary, it seemed that the voters were content at this stage with the concessions already granted—an increase to seventy in the number of Scottish MPs at Westminster, and a Scottish Office with its own Minister. The historian Michael Fry gives another reason for the Scots' coolness towards legislative devolution —their "devotion to imperial ideals". Scottish pride was involved in the contribution of its people to the success of the Empire and "here nationalistic feeling may actually have led away from a desire for national self-determination".[14] The 1880s had seen a reawakening of the Scots, but not to the extent of destabilising the Union.

HOME RULE FRUSTRATED 1890s–1918

Although Scotland had made gains in the 1880s (establishment of the Scottish Office and the post of Secretary for Scotland), the demands for more administrative devolution and more effective representation continued up to and beyond the Great War. Very few concessions were granted.

The new Scottish Office was a disappointment. We saw earlier how unenthusiastic the Duke of Richmond was about his new post of Scottish Secretary. Most of the early Scottish Secretaries were also peers (members of the House of Lords). They tended to see the post as ceremonial rather than as a position of power and influence.

"They kept out of the major Scottish controversies and ... spent much time merely travelling the country reassuring people that Westminster had not forgotten them."[15]

A further weakness of the early Scottish Secretaries was that since they were peers, they could not steer Scottish legislation through the House of Commons. This had to be done by the Lord Advocate. Some people complained that the Scottish Office had its headquarters at Dover House in London.

Being part of the Whitehall structure and being so remote from Scotland were unlikely to promote a distinctively 'Scottish' Office. Another shortcoming of the Scottish Office was that much of the day-to-day running of Scottish business was carried out by administrative boards. These boards more or less ran their own affairs unchecked—the Scottish Office had no power to oversee their workings.

Two marginal improvements were made in reaction to criticism of the inadequacy of the Secretary for Scotland's position and the weakness of the Scottish Office. After 1892, all Scottish Secretaries were, in practice, made members of the Cabinet, although it was 1926 before the post was officially up-

KEY POINTS
Scotland in the 1880s

☑ Most Scots were doing very well in the 1880s and saw the Union as a good thing.

☑ However, Scotland was becoming less distinct as a nation within the UK because of the impact of the Industrial Revolution and the increasing powers of central government.

☑ Scots reacted by setting up their own distinctive national institutions and societies. There was evidence of a cultural renaissance in the 1880s.

☑ Scots began to complain about the way Scottish affairs were dealt with at Westminster and Whitehall. The first campaign for Home Rule began in this decade.

☑ The government response was to create the Scottish Office and the new post of Scottish Secretary. This was a typical Unionist reaction to Scottish demands—to be repeated many times in the next century.

☑ Scottish 'nationalism' in the 1880s was a very moderate affair. In fact, it is misleading to call it this because most of those who were advocating change wanted to strengthen Scotland's position in the Union.

☑ A nationalist political party was not to be established for another fifty years.

Scottish Home Rule Bills and Motions 1889–1914

Date	Motion or Bill	Proposer	Result
1889	Scottish Home Rule Motion	Dr Clark	Defeated by 200 to 79
1891	Federal Home Rule Motion	Dr Clark	Counted Out
1892	Federal Home Rule Motion	Dr Clark	Defeated by 74 to 54
1893	Scottish Home Rule Motion	Dr Clark	Defeated by 168 to 150
1894	Scottish Home Rule Motion	Sir Henry Dalziel	Carried by 180 to 170
1895	Federal Home Rule Motion	Sir Henry Dalziel	Carried by 128 to 102
1899	Scottish Home Rule Bill	DV Pirie	Defeated at First Reading
1908	Government of Scotland Bill	DV Pirie	1st Reading carried 257 to 102
1911	Scottish Home Rule Bill	Sir Henry Dalziel	1st Reading carried 172 to 73
1913	Scottish Home Rule Bill	Sir WH Cowan	2nd Reading carried 204 to 159
1914	Scottish Home Rule Billl	I Macpherson	Adjourned at 2nd Reading

graded to Secretary of State for Scotland with automatic Cabinet status. Secondly, in 1914 the government set up a Royal Commission to look into the workings of the administrative boards. It recommended that the functions of the boards should be transferred to the Scottish Office. However, this was not put into practice until 1928.

Many Scottish politicians still believed that Home Rule was the only answer to Scotland's unsatisfactory position within the UK. When Rosebery became Prime Minister in 1894, he tried to appease his critics by setting up a Scottish Grand Committee in the House of Commons. Scottish MPs would now be able to discuss Scottish affairs without being a permanent minority in the Commons. However, the Committee could not pass or reject legislation—its only function was to look at the details of Bills at the Committee stage. The Scottish Grand Committee only lasted for a year before it was abandoned.

A similar story of frustration bedevilled the campaign for Home Rule in Parliament. Between 1889 and 1914, the issue of Scottish Home Rule was debated in Parliament fifteen times. Four of these occasions involved the discussion of fully-fledged Scottish Home Rule Bills. However, none of these attempts made any headway because the majority of English MPs who would have had to vote in favour of the Bills were either hostile towards them or else apathetic. In contrast, all of the Scottish Home Rule Bills were supported by a majority of Scottish MPs. One of the Bills (1913) would have given Scotland a Parliament of one hundred and forty MPs legislating on those areas then supervised by the Scottish Office. It even passed its second reading in August 1914 but had to be abandoned due to the onset of the war.

In the period 1890–1906, the Scottish Home Rule cause was hindered by a variety of circumstances. At the UK level, the Conservatives were the dominant party (1886–92, 1895–1906) and they were firmly unionist in outlook. On the Home Rule front, Ireland was the big issue, pushing Scotland into the shade. Irish militancy on the Home Rule question also tended to have a negative effect on Scottish support for a Scottish Parliament. The dilemma for Scottish Home Rule activists was "if they escalated their activism beyond accepted political norms, they alienated potential support, and if they agitated along established channels their cause was treated as a secondary problem".[16]

Despite this, there was a new enthusiasm for Home Rule within the ranks of the Scottish Liberals. In 1908, they had officially adopted Home Rule as party policy. This was part of a larger 'New Liberal' drive for social reform. It was argued that Home Rule would be necessary in order to get specifically Scottish laws onto the statute books. Experience had shown with the *Children Act* (1908) that Parliament was unable to come up with an effective Scottish version of the law within the time limits set down. Only six hours of parliamentary time were allocated to Scottish Bills, and this was thought to be completely inadequate. Another commonly held belief among Scottish Liberals was that there had been a demand for social reform in Scotland for many years, but that the English Conservative majority had stifled and delayed the passing of much-needed social legislation. This could only be remedied by the setting up of a Scottish Parliament to deal with Scotland's unique social problems.

As already stated, the First World War intervened to put a stop to the Home Rule bandwagon. Between 1890 and 1918, the only concession granted was the setting up of the Scottish Grand Committee. After its demise in 1895, the Committee was resurrected in 1907, its remit being to discuss the details and amendments to Scottish legislation. This clearly fell far short of the aims of the Home Rulers. The administration of Scotland by the Scottish Office improved marginally during this period, and there was no change here. The administrative boards were still outwith the democratic supervision of the Scottish Office, except that they had to submit an annual report to the Scottish Secretary. Complaints continued about the inadequacy of the post of Scottish Secretary:

"His daily round was in the minutiae of government, dealing with complaints and injustices and guiding through Parliament minor amending measures or Scottish clauses tacked on to English bills."[17]

FACTORIES OPENED IN DEPRESSED AREAS

DATE	SCOTLAND	UK
1933	3	467
1934	5	520
1935	2	514
1936	6	551

Table 8.1

THE INTERWAR YEARS– OPTIMISM DASHED

There was considerable optimism about the prospects for Scottish Home Rule in nationalist circles at the end of the First World War. The war itself seemed to demonstrate that national self-determination was the way forward for international peace. Empires had caused the war, and so they should now be broken up into nation states.

On the home front, Labour temporarily emerged from the war as a major force in Scottish politics. Indeed at the 1922 General Election, Labour was the largest party in Scotland with twenty nine seats despite Conservative triumph in Britain as a whole. This was good news for Home Rule because Labour appeared to be taking over the mantle as the Home Rule party from the Liberals who were sinking into irreversible decline. The Scottish Labour Party's 1918 election manifesto pledged to set up a Scottish Parliament.

The hopes of the home rulers, however, were to be cruelly dashed in the interwar years. Labour was in power twice during this time but only as a minority government. By the time of the first Labour government in 1924, the Labour leaders were beginning to lose interest in Home Rule. Those in nationalist circles who had pinned their faith on

Labour became increasingly disillusioned and frustrated and out of this arose a number of Home Rule/nationalist organisations to fill the gap. The Scottish Home Rule Association was re-formed in 1918, followed by the Scots National League in 1920, the Scottish National Movement in 1926, the National Party of Scotland in 1928, the Scottish Party in 1932 and finally the Scottish National Party in 1934.

On the surface, this impressive list of organisations would seem to suggest that nationalism was on the rise. As we will see, this was not necessarily the case. A Scottish Parliament was further away in 1939 than it had been in 1914 and from the point of view of UK politics, the SNP was an irrelevance.

THE IMPACT OF WAR AND DEPRESSION ON SCOTLAND'S IDENTITY

For many Scots, their attachment to the Union was based as much on practical advantage as it was on emotional commitment. In the thirty years before the Great War, most Scots were proud of their country's achievements. The Scottish economy was strong (shipbuilding, heavy engineering) and Scots were heavily involved in the running of the great British Empire. Being part of the United Kingdom had done Scotland more

good than harm and consequently Scots were comfortable with their dual identity—both Scottish and British.

Gradually, the balance of economic advantage swung away from Scotland. At the turn of the century, Scotland had 12.5% of British industrial production; by 1924, it had 10.5% and by 1930, this had shrunk to 9.5%. The Scottish economy was too dependent on the old heavy industries. Scottish industrialists were slow to respond to the deep-seated problems of the economy. Very little was done to diversify into the new industries which gravitated towards the south of England. Government help was not forthcoming. Scotland's economic crisis was compounded by the worldwide economic depression in the 1930s. Unemployment soared. In the 1930s, Scotland's unemployment rate was 50% higher than England's. Phrases like 'the southward drift of industry' and 'that distressed area: north Britain' and 'the slum problem' were commonly used to describe and explain Scotland's social and economic decline in the interwar years.

Scotland's relatively poor economic performance compared to England forced many Scots to re-

Cartoon from *The Scots Independent* Vol VIII No. 90 April 1934.

assess their attitude to the union. Nationalist writers in particular began to highlight the downward spiral of the Scottish economy. Table 8.1 shows quite clearly how unfavourable Scotland's economic prospects were.

Such gloomy figures over a period of years began to eat away at the confidence of the Scots. Economic decline, it was said, was symptomatic of a larger national decline. Scots were losing control of their industries to the English, with even traditional industries like farming and fishing doing badly. Scotland was being 'invaded' by Catholics from Ireland. Scots were unhealthier than the English and housing conditions were still far worse than those south of the border. Some commentators at the time started referring to the Scots as a 'dying race' and cited as evidence the falling birth rate and a net decline in population due to emigration.

Attempts were made by the Scottish literary establishment to re-

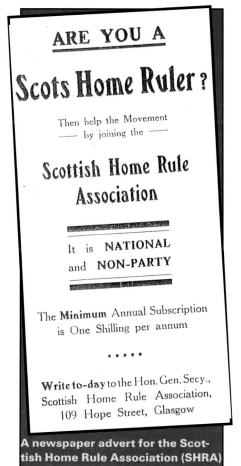

A newspaper advert for the Scottish Home Rule Association (SHRA)

vive traditional Scots language and dialects, but these were met with much scepticism outside their own small circle. The *Scots Magazine* in August 1926 commented "To hark back artificially to older things or to dredge the dictionary for archaic Scottish words is to achieve nothing new."

This feeling that the past and the present were unworthy percolated down to school level where the teaching of Scottish history was given a low priority by the Scottish Education Department.

Scots on the whole had a low or negative image of their country during the 1920s and '30s. The dislocation and decline associated with the war and the Depression had robbed many people of their confidence about their culture, identity and even the future existence of Scotland as a nation. The *Daily Record*, in its review of 1929, summed up the mood of the nation perfectly:

"In certain respects the year which closes today will remain memorable to Scotland as a nation. Certainly no year within memory of any living Scot has witnessed so much heart-searching. Never before has there been so much airing of the question: what is wrong with Scotland?"[18]

Nationalists had a simple and powerful answer to what was wrong with Scotland. It was the unfair and unequal treatment of Scotland which could only be remedied by a Scottish Parliament or complete independence. The interwar years provided fertile ground for nationalist propaganda—a nation in terminal decline, its people deserting the homeland for brighter prospects overseas, combined with a government unconcerned with the particular problems facing the country. Whereas in the 1880s Scotland lacked the economic grievances which fed Irish nationalism, the postwar years gave Scottish nationalists all the ammunition they needed to make the case for Home Rule.

THE GROWTH OF NATIONALIST ORGANISATIONS

On the political front, there was considerable optimism over the prospects for Home Rule at the end of the war. It was unclear at this stage that the Liberals were about to sink into irreversible decline. They continued to advocate Home Rule. The Scottish Labour Party also flagged a Scottish Parliament as one of its key election manifesto pledges in 1918. The Scottish economy briefly boomed in the wake of the war and this helped the Home Rule cause.

"Many socialists and Liberals thought that the creation of a powerful Scottish parliament to harness the powerful Scottish economy would be essential in order to clear slums and raise wages: Home Rule was a sign of economic confidence, not pessimism."[19]

However, as we have seen, the Scottish economy went into severe recession, the Liberals disintegrated into insignificance and Labour gradually shied away from Home Rule, looking instead for centrally-planned, UK-based solutions to the economic problems of the 1920s and '30s. There were two attempts to get Home Rule Bills passed in Parliament (1924 and 1927), but both failed. Nationalists who hoped that a Scottish Parliament was in sight were in turn disappointed, then betrayed by Labour, then galvanised into action. The failure of the 1927 Home Rule Bill led directly to the setting up of the first independent political party with Home Rule as its main aim. This was the National Party of Scotland in 1928. What follows is a brief outline of the various Home Rule organisations inhabiting the Scottish political landscape from 1918 until the birth of the modern SNP in 1934.

The Scottish Home Rule Association

This was re-formed in 1918 by RE Muirhead, a wealthy businessman who provided the funds. The SHRA was intended to be a cross-party

General Election RESULTS (Scotland) 1929 & 1931

Party	Vote(%)	MPs
1929		
Conservative	35.9	20
Labour	42.4	36
Liberals	18.1	13
NPS	0.1	0
Others	2.5	2
1931		
Coalition	63.9	64
Labour	32.6	7
NPS	1.0	0

Table 8.2

pressure group ie. you could be a member of any political party as long as you believed in Home Rule for Scotland. The idea was to keep the issue alive by canvassing prospective parliamentary candidates and extracting a pledge from them in favour of Home Rule—those who agreed would get the backing of the SHRA at the election. The SHRA's aim was for a Scottish Parliament, but for Scotland to remain within Britain and the British Empire. By 1920, the SHRA had 1,150 individual members and 138 affiliated organisations, most of which were also affiliated to the Labour Party.

Most SHRA support came from the Labour Party and by the mid-1920s Labour had virtual control of the organisation. Muirhead became disillusioned because his ideal of cross-party cooperation to force Home Rule onto the legislative agenda had failed. The SHRA's hopes were briefly raised in 1924 by the election of a minority Labour government, the coming to power of Ramsay MacDonald, an old SHRA campaigner and the presentation to Parliament of a Private Member's Bill on Home Rule for Scotland by the Labour MP, George Buchanan. These hopes were dashed by the dismal failure of the Bill on first reading and by MacDonald's lack of commitment to pass future legislation.

The final straw came in 1927, by which time Labour had all but dropped Home Rule as a practical proposal. Another Labour MP, the Rev. James Barr, won the ballot for a Private Member's Bill. He chose to promote a new Home Rule Bill. Again it failed after only forty five minutes of discussion in the Commons. SHRA activists blamed the 'London-controlled' Labour Party. Calls were now made for the setting up of a National Party independent of Labour, with Home Rule as its central policy. Muirhead joined the new National Party of Scotland (NPS) in 1928 along with many individual members of the SHRA. The SHRA collapsed the following year.

The Scots National League

The SNL was founded in 1920 by Gaelic-speaking, London-based nationalists. In the early days, it had a 'cranky' image—it was mainly interested in cultural matters eg. it wanted to revive the Gaelic language and the Highland way of life. This was unlikely to win much support from Lowland Scots in the cities. Not surprisingly, the SNL had few members and little money. In 1924, Tom Gibson joined the SNL in disgust at the failure of the Buchanan Home Rule Bill. Under Gibson's influence, the SNL was transformed—the organisation was made more efficient and branches were set up. The SNL had its own newspaper, the *Scots Independent*, to air its policies. The new-style SNL tried to show that its policies were in tune with the social, economic and political problems facing Scotland. The SNL stood for complete independence for Scotland ie. Scotland would break the link with the UK and run all of its own affairs—only then would Scotland's economic problems be solved. Following the failure of the Barr Home Rule Bill in 1927, the SNL called for the creation of an independent National Party. The hope was that the SHRA and other sympathisers would join forces to fight elections against the 'London-based' parties.

The National Party of Scotland

The NPS was formed in February 1928 from members of the SHRA, the SNL and two other less important organisations. These were the Scottish National Movement (a small faction which had broken away from the SNL in 1926 under the leadership of the poet Lewis Spense) and the Glasgow University Student Nationalist Association formed in 1927 by John MacCormick. The GUSNA convened the meeting which founded the NPS.

The NPS was divided from the start. The moderate majority (ex-SHRA) wanted Home Rule within the UK whereas the 'fundamentalists' (ex-SNL) demanded complete separation from England. The wording of the NPS's central aim was a compromise between the two wings: "self-government for Scotland with independent national status within the British group of nations". The NPS failed to make the breakthrough at the polls—the Party only contested two seats at the 1929 General Election (both deposits lost) and five seats at the 1931 General Election, losing its deposit in two of them. (See Table 8.2.)

Disappointing electoral results brought the Celtic fundamentalists out into the open. Erskine of Marr began writing about the need to establish a kind of Celtic communism in Scotland; Hugh MacDiarmid, the leading Scottish writer and poet of his day started advocating a form of Scottish Fascism! The moderate leadership were worried that the cranks were losing the NPS credibility. Consequently, many of the 'fundamentalists' were expelled in 1933. The expulsions were brought to a head after the establishment in 1932 of a rival Home Rule movement, the Scottish Party (with a moderate, right-of-centre profile).

The Scottish Party (SP) had well-known leaders (Sir Alexander MacEwen and the Duke of Montrose) and a respectable im-

R E Muirhead, Chairman NPS. This photograph appeared in *The Scots Independent* Vol VIII No. 90, April 1934.

age. It also had the backing of the *Daily Express* and the *Daily Record* both of which were promoting a moderate Home Rule stance to gain extra readership at this time. These were the only credentials the Scottish Party had. It was "little more than a collection of notables who had nothing more in common than the fact that they believed something was wrong with Scotland. The Scottish Party had no coherent electoral strategy, no specific economic and social policies and ... no party organisation."[20]

John MacCormick, the real leader of the NPS, decided to press for a merger with the Scottish Party now that the extremists in his own party had been thrown out. He arranged for a joint candidate to contest the Kilmarnock by-election in 1933. The candidate was the Scottish Party's Sir Alexander MacEwen. He polled 17%, the highest yet for a nationalist candidate. This seemed to show that a moderate policy could reap electoral benefits. The Kilmarnock 'success' also paved the way for the merger of the two parties. The Scottish National Party, as it was known, came into being in April 1934.

The Scottish National Party (1934–9)

In the first few months of the SNP's existence, optimism flourished yet again. Supporters of nationalism had finally been united into one political party. In such an atmosphere, there was a willingness among the different tendencies in the new party to cooperate. For the time being, the SNP stood for a self-governing Scotland within the British Empire. The central aim of the Party was left deliberately vague in the meantime, a wise move given the potential for conflict between the separatists and the Home Rulers. During 1934–5, new branches were opened, there was an increase in party membership and the first full-time Party officials were appointed. Morale in the SNP was understandably high.

However, the euphoria associated with the launch of the SNP soon vanished. The reality was that the new party had incorporated people from the left, right and centre of the political spectrum. Some were for and others against cooperation with the UK parties; some wanted complete separation for Scotland, others did not. These differences were papered over in the first few months of the SNP's life, but gradually the cracks began to appear. The first sign of trouble came when a former Scottish Party leader, J Kevan McDowall, made known his views in the press that keeping the British Empire intact was more important than achieving Scottish Home Rule. Not surprisingly, this caused anger among the left-wing hardliners, especially because it highlighted differences which were better left private at this early stage in the Party's life. Under pressure, McDowall resigned from the SNP.

The united facade was given a further jolt when the SNP President, the Duke of Montrose, published an article in the *Glasgow Herald* in May 1935 advocating a merger with the Scottish Liberals. As if this was not bad enough, he also announced that he had been a mem-

ber and active supporter of the Conservative Party, but that he was going to resign his Conservative whip in the House of Lords in favour of the Liberals! Not only did the Duke open himself up to public ridicule, but he showed an embarrassing ignorance of SNP policy, namely that dual membership of parties was not allowed. This was the worst sort of publicity for the SNP, especially as the Montrose affair surfaced just before the General Election of November 1935.

The SNP fought eight seats. The result was a disaster. The newly amalgamated SNP gained fewer votes in the five seats which had previously been contested by its predecessor, the NPS. In total, the eight SNP candidates received only 29,515 votes. SNP activists were demoralised by their poor showing at the polls, by splits emerging within their ranks and by the image developing in the public mind of a disunited party. The *Scots Independent* blamed the merger of the right-wing Scottish Party with the left-wing NPS for weakening the enthusiasm of its core members and for the expulsion of dedicated nationalists. The influx of very moderate and dubious Scottish Party members like the Duke of Montrose had also damaged the Party.

Between 1936 and the war, the divisions in the Party grew wider. The watering down of the nationalist message and the resultant poor showing at the general election seemed to vindicate the hardline nationalists, who now gained the upper hand. Fundamentalists who had been expelled from the NPS in 1932 began to drift back into the SNP. At the same time, former Scottish Party members gave up and left. As a result, the radicals were able to push through their own agenda—there was to be no cooperation with the other political parties; fighting elections was to be the main strategy; the middle-class image of the Party was to go and new policies, designed to appeal to the working class, were to be formulated.

The remaining moderates in the SNP reacted to the leftward drift of the Party by simply going their own way. Their interpretation of events was that the SNP was no longer credible as an independent force in Scottish politics and that the best way forward was in seeking cross-party cooperation with the Liberals and sympathetic members of the Scottish Labour Party. For example, John MacCormick, the National Secretary, spent much energy in the next two years trying to set up a National Convention. This was more or less a reheated version of the old SHRA approach of trying to persuade the mainstream parties to adopt Home Rule as policy. The fact that MacCormick was able to pursue this policy in contradiction of the Party's stated aim of remaining an independent party shows how far discipline had broken down. According to one historian:

"The SNP was collapsing under the strain of its own contradictions. The Party contained disparate factions, each of which pursued its own agenda and so long as there was no interference from others, this state of affairs was allowed to continue."[21]

By the late 1930s, the SNP was at a low ebb—rejected by the public, dismissed by the mainstream parties, divided over policy and strategy, incapable of fighting more than a handful of seats and riven with personality feuds, resignations and dismissals. Even according to the expectations of its own leaders and supporters, the SNP's brief existence from 1934 until the onset of the Second World War must go down as a resounding failure.

HOW DID INTERWAR GOVERNMENTS RESPOND TO THE GROWTH OF NATIONALISM?

Governments in the interwar years were unconcerned about the growth of nationalism because it posed no electoral threat. As a result, Home Rule was not considered. Instead, some mild measures of administrative devolution were offered along with a few gestures designed to show that the government had not forgotten the Scottish people.

1919–21 In Parliament, a Speaker's Conference was organised to take up the issue of Home Rule where it had left off in 1914. The Conference recommended a Parliament for Scotland, but the Lloyd George government shelved the proposals.

1926 The office of Secretary for Scotland was elevated to Secretary of State for Scotland with automatic Cabinet status.

1928 The Scottish Boards of Agriculture and Health and the Prison Commission for Scotland were absorbed into the Scottish Office.

1937 The Gilmour Report reorganised the Scottish Office into four large Departments. Historians disagree about this measure of administrative devolution. Richard Finlay calls the Gilmour Report "a twin strategy designed to appeal to Scottish sentiment, while at the same time counteract demands for Scottish home rule"[22] whereas James Kellas says it was "not marked by any nationalism ... its theme is sober practicality."[23]

In the absence of decisive action to remedy the economic problems of the 1930s, the government came up with a series of gestures to appease Scottish national sentiment. The Scottish Office was relocated from London to Edinburgh in 1932. Royal visits to Scotland were to be increased and Holyrood Palace was to be occupied by a royal representative for three months of the year. Improvement grants were to be given to the National Library and the Scottish Records Office. Records removed by Edward I in the thirteenth century were to be returned to Scotland. The Empire Exhibition was to be held in Glasgow in 1938.

R B Cunninghame Graham, Honorary President of the Scottish National Party. Photograph appeared in *The Scots Independent* No. 9 Vol I, May 1936.

Comments on the Growth of Nationalism in the Interwar Years

It is easy to overestimate the growth of nationalism in the interwar period. Several nationalist organisations sprang up—the Scottish Home Rule Association, the Scots National League, the Scottish National Movement, the National Party of Scotland, the Scottish Party and the Scottish National Party. How effective were they? Did the Home Rule pressure groups succeed in persuading the mainstream UK parties to set up a Scottish Parliament? No. Did the NPS or the SNP have any success in electing MPs? No.

The very failure of the mainstream nationalist organisations promoted the growth of 'fringe' organisations, some with militant tendencies—Democratic Scottish Self-Government Organisation, Scottish Self-Government Federation and Scottish Watch, to name but a few. Some members of the SNP even dabbled in civil disobedience. For instance,

"in 1936 the Cumberland Stone at Culloden was defaced, in 1937 the

Wallace Sword was removed from the Stirling Monument on Abbey Craig and hidden under Bothwell Bridge and there were various episodes where Union flags were hauled down from various castles and Saltires hoisted in their place."[24]

Such activities reflected the weakness, frustration and immaturity of the SNP during the interwar period.

The SNP got off to a bad start. In hindsight, the merger of the NPS and the SP was a mistake. The SP had no more than one hundred members, yet their Dukes and Sirs gave them undue positions of prominence in the new party. The public perceived the SNP as being divided between left and right, extremists and moderates. They were right. The SNP had simply incorporated the old factions into the new party and failed to resolve the divisions one way or the other. The voters do not trust divided parties and they abandoned the SNP. This was a wasted opportunity because, for the first time since the 1880s, Scotland had economic grievances in the 1920s and '30s.

Conditions were extremely favourable for the growth of nationalism. There was a general sense of injustice about Scotland's position, and the National Government was worried that this discontent could favour the nationalists—hence the use of symbolic gestures like moving the Scottish Office to Edinburgh as a sop to Home Rulers. Unionist politicians took the nationalist threat much more seriously than before. Scots were repeatedly warned of the impending economic ruin which would come in the wake of a Scottish parliament. Whereas before the First World War unionists emphasised the positive benefits for Scotland of being a partner in the Union, during the 1930s unionism was on the defensive and concentrating on scare tactics—Scotland was now dependent on England for its economic survival. However, despite the favourable economic and political climate, the Nationalists

were unable to form a united front in order to capitalise on the mood of the times. Consequently, Scotland was further away from gaining a Parliament in 1939 than it had been in 1914.

By 1939, the SNP was an irrelevance in UK terms.

"Having campaigned and failed badly ... the nationalists exposed the inability of the home rule cause to mobilise the electorate, and thus allowed the major parties to take even less notice of it."[25]

Even more scathing of the SNP is Richard Finlay who says, "the Party failed to produce a clear political strategy and it failed to produce a distinctive political identity".[26]

On the other hand, there is a danger of being too critical and too ambitious for the nationalist movement at this early stage. Time was needed to build up an effective political organisation and to prepare the voters to accept that Scotland's overriding need at a time of great uncertainty was for a 'leap in the dark' into self-government.

N.G. (7) General

Scottish "Prosperity"
Under the "National" Government

"Encouraging" New Scottish Industries:

(1932) 20 Factories Opened	37 CLOSED	(that is, 17 fewer)
(1933) 15 Opened	31 CLOSED	(that is, 16 fewer)
(1934) 18 Opened	21 CLOSED	(that is, 3 fewer)
		... What a RECORD!

"Encouraging" Scottish Agriculture:

ENGLAND GETS SUBSIDY ON 375,000 ACRES OF BEET
SCOTLAND GETS SUBSIDY ON 7000 ACRES

In other words the Scottish tax-payer pays £1 and gets back 5/-

"CURING" Scottish Unemployment:

SCOTTISH UNEMPLOYMENT has increased so much under the "NATIONAL" GOVERNMENT that whereas the cost of maintaining able-bodied unemployed in Scotland in 1930–1931 was £743,000, in 1935–36 the cost rose to £1,200,000

Shipping Tonnage REGISTERED AT ENGLISH PORTS ROSE BETWEEN 1913–1932 : BUT AT SCOTTISH PORTS IT FELL BY WELL OVER A MILLION TONS!!

No country can long survive such Scandalous Neglect

Only the SCOTS NATIONALIST PARTY has a Policy for Scotland

Vote Scots Nationalist

Published by the SCOTTISH NATIONAL PARTY, 59 Elmbank Street, Glasgow, C.2
Printed by THE EDINBURGH PRESS, 9–11 Young Street, Edinburgh

SNP election poster, 1936

SNP Electoral Performance 1945–59

General Election	Number of Candidates	% of Votes
1945	8	1.2
1950	4	0.4
1951	2	0.3
1955	2	0.5
1959	5	0.8

Table 8.3

Some historians would argue that the Scots were not ready for radical change. Although many people north of the border felt strongly that Scotland was getting a raw deal, they lacked confidence in Scotland's ability to 'go it alone'. Neither Labour nor the Conservative-dominated National Government had done a lot for Scotland. Could the Nationalists do any better? In addition, the electoral system worked against the newly formed SNP. Who was going to throw away their vote for the relatively unknown and untested Nationalist candidate? It was better to vote for one of the mainstream candidates and have some impact on the outcome of the election. The SNP were simply not credible when they could only put up eight candidates at a general election.

The image of the Nationalists was further dented by the deepening international crisis. Extreme nationalism was associated with fascism and war. By the late '30s, the public gaze was diverted outwards to the danger from Nazi Germany. In contrast, inward-looking nationalism seemed irrelevant to the problems of the day.

THE WAR YEARS– NATIONALISM SPLIT

The SNP did not have a good war. Apart from being divided and lacking in credibility, according to one historian the Party suffered from "uninspiring leadership, poor discipline, low morale, declining branch activity, increasing financial pressures, and last but not least, the stigma of being nothing

more than an inconsequential fringe group in Scottish politics".[27] The SNP's difficulties were further compounded by the fact that in 1939 it was officially opposed to conscription, a highly damaging policy given that the national mood was to give Hitler a bloody nose. The anti-conscription stance had been a victory for the hardline faction of the SNP at the 1937 conference. Now the moderates wanted the policy changed. Because neither side was willing to give in, a so-called compromise position was worked out.

The Party officially pledged its support for the war but fudged the issue of conscription. Scots could be conscripted as long as it was for the defence of Britain. On the other hand, the Party would support members who, for political purposes, refused to be conscripted! This was a classic example of a plaster being applied to a gaping wound. The wound did not heal and the plaster did not hold.

Prominent radical Nationalists like Douglas Young and Arthur Donaldson continued to promote their anti-conscription stance, for which both were jailed. In the moderate camp, John MacCormick was trying desperately to limit the damage to the Party's image. Between 1939 and 1942, he worked away behind the scenes to try to secure a cross-party united front on the Home Rule issue. Yet the more MacCormick attempted to steer the SNP into the moderate centre, the more suspicious and antagonistic the hardliners be-

came. The festering internal divisions opened up afresh at the 1942 annual conference. The anti-war candidate, Douglas Young, was put up by the radical wing for the position of Chairman of the Party in opposition to the moderate candidate, William Power. When Young won the vote, MacCormick took this as a personal rebuff and called on his moderate supporters to resign. About half of the delegates did so. MacCormick then formed the Scottish Convention.

The 1942 split was "arguably the most dramatic turning point in the SNP's history".[28] The SNP, of course, had never been united in its short history. The NPS and the Scottish Party had joined together in 1934 but had not jelled. Radical surgery was perhaps the best course of action for the long-term health of political nationalism in Scotland. The public could now see that there were two competing organisations representing the different wings of the nationalist movement. The SNP contained those who wished to reassert the fundamental policy of complete independence for Scotland, to be achieved by fighting elections against the mainstream parties. John MacCormick's Scottish Convention, on the other hand, aimed for a measure of Home Rule within the UK, to be achieved by pressure on the major UK parties.

In the short term, however, the split clearly damaged the image of Scottish nationalism. Andrew Marr, writing about the importance of the 1942 split, says that "it produced two opposing Nationalist strategies—the small sect (the SNP) and the broad church (the Covention)—and then conclusively demonstrated the weakness of both. In politics it is not always true that somebody wins. The wartime Nationalist split produced only two competing sets of losers."[29]

Marr's view is certainly borne out in the case of the SNP which "was reduced to a very small group of

To the Electors
of
MOTHERWELL
and
WISHAW
from
Dr
ROBERT
McINTYRE

IT is my privilege to have been invited to come before you as the independent Scottish candidate. Scotland means more to me than a shape on the map. A new hope and a high vision must rouse the Scottish people to face our future responsibilities as a nation and the home of a free people.

NOW IS THE TIME FOR SCOTTISH PEOPLE TO TAKE CHARGE OF THE AFFAIRS OF SCOTLAND. THAT IS THE ISSUE AT THIS ELECTION. WE MUST HAVE THE POWER TO PUT OUR HOUSE IN ORDER IN SCOTLAND.

The war is not an Election Issue. The result of your decision on April 12 will have no effect on the war. It will have a very definite effect on the future of our country. If Scotland goes down then we, her citizens, go down with her. We cannot afford to have a repetition of the disasters which followed the last world war and paved the way to the present cataclysm.

The Prestwick Airport and the Forth Road Bridge are important projects in themselves. The opposition shown to those schemes is just the most recent example of British Government antagonism to all Scottish Industrial development. **The London controlled Labour and Unionist Parties are agreed in this barefaced attack on Scottish interests.**

An election leaflet issued by the SNP.

intransigent nationalists" and had become "inward looking and this tended to make it even less successful".[30] On the other hand, the Party organisation had been steadily falling apart for a long time. In 1934, the SNP had ninety operational branches; in 1936, only fifty nine were functioning; in 1940, a mere twenty nine branches carried the nationalist message in Scot-

land. From this low base, the Party lost even more active members during and after the 1942 split. However, in terms of its electoral strategy, the SNP had one brief moment of glory. In April 1945, Dr Robert MacIntyre became the first Scottish Nationalist MP at the Motherwell by-election, only to lose his seat at the General Election in June. The Party fielded

eight candidates at the 1945 General Election, gaining only 1.2% of the votes cast—a low point in its history. (See Table 8.3.)

As for the Convention, John MacCormick worked hard to bring the parties together on the Home Rule issue. Members of the Convention were encouraged to join other parties in order to influence their policies on Home Rule. There were also lots of meetings. In Glasgow for example, monthly meetings were held throughout the war. Pamphlets were also produced, but in the end the Convention was not a political party and it was not fighting elections. It sought to change the minds of the major parties. During the war, Tom Johnstone, the Secretary of State for Scotland, had given some hope that he would support the idea of a Scottish parliament after the war. However, when Labour got into power with a massive majority in 1945, Home Rule was dropped. By the end of the war, MacCormick's strategy of infiltrating and influencing the major parties had failed.

THE TWO FACES OF NATIONALISM 1945–62

The postwar political and economic climate did not help the nationalist cause. Nationalism and devolution seemed irrelevant to the immediate needs of the Scottish people; 'socialism' on the other hand could meet those needs. Labour had been thrust into power in 1945 with a massive vote of confidence by the British people. The wartime spirit appeared to have created a consensus in favour of a 'welfare state' and reconstruction based on central planning. Labour was being entrusted with bringing this about. Because Scotland lagged behind the rest of Britain in terms of health and housing, the prospect of the state delivering improved welfare services throughout the country seemed an attractive prospect for most Scots. In terms of what the government could do for Scotland, a British welfare state

John MacCormick

seemed a better deal than a Scottish parliament. Five years of total war had also conditioned the British people to centralised decision making. Central economic planning, even although based at Westminster, could benefit Scotland since it could be argued that the Scottish economy needed more state help than other regions of the country.

In fact, Scotland did comparatively well in the decade or so after the war. In housing, Scotland was a success story with 230,000 houses (mostly council) built between 1945 and 1951. The coming of the NHS in 1948 undoubtedly improved Scotland's poor health record. Living standards were rising—standards in working-class Scottish households were on average 2.5–3 times as great in 1953 as they had been in 1938. Scotland enjoyed a period of full employment in the late 1940s. Due to the devastation of the German and Japanese shipyards during the war, the Scottish shipbuilding industry once again came into its own with Scottish yards alone launching 15% of the world's ships in 1949–

51. Scotland's other heavy industries (iron, steel, locomotives, coal) were experiencing a revival.

In short, the modest expectations of the Scottish people for a better future were being met. This was bad news for Scottish nationalism. After 1945, the SNP entered its darkest period—in fact, until the mid-1960s it was almost invisible in Scottish politics. Even the Party's Chairman, Arthur Donaldson, could say with a grim sense of humour that "the SNP is not dying, it is merely mummifying".

Officially, the SNP claimed that between 1945 and 1962, there were about twenty branches and 1,500–2,000 members in the Party. (By contrast, there had been 10,000 members in the SNP in 1934.) In fact, the figure was much lower. It is likely that there were no more than seven hundred members in 1959. The Party had never really recovered from the defection of the '55 Group' in 1955—nationalists who advocated racial and hate propaganda and the use of violence. Many of the core branches in Central Scotland were damaged by the '55 Group' breakaway. How could the SNP carry out an effective strategy for fighting elections with so few members and branches? The Party organisation was ramshackle, being highly decentralised thus giving the branches far too much independence. Furthermore, communications were poor and the national leadership was weak and lacking in charisma. Arthur Donaldson colourfully defined the 1950s as years when "all the activists of the SNP could have been the complement of a small passenger aircraft, and had they flown together and crashed without survivors, the cause of independence would have been lost to view for many years".[31]

In 1950, the Party was only able to put forward four candidates at the General Election; in 1951 and 1955 it was down to two. (See Table 8.3.) The electorate understandably re-

jected the SNP as a wasted vote throughout the 1950s. As we have seen, the vast majority of Scots did not want independence—they were more concerned with 'bread and butter' issues such as jobs, housing, welfare and reconstruction.

The torch of Scottish nationalism was carried more effectively by the Scottish Convention in the few years after the war. John MacCormick's all-party organisation held a 'National Assembly' in Glasgow in 1947. The meeting was composed of six hundred delegates from political parties, local authorities, Churches and trade unions. From a publicity point of view, it was a success. *The Scotsman* newspaper called it "perhaps the most representative meeting ever held to discuss Scottish affairs".[32]

The Assembly voted overwhelmingly for the proposition that Scotland should have its own parliament within the UK. A committee was set up to flesh out details for a Scottish Parliament. These proposals were agreed at the second National Assembly in 1948. In order to gain popular support for the Scottish parliament, the Convention drafted a petition which the public could sign. This 'Scottish Covenant' asked supporters to solemnly:

> "... pledge ourselves in all loyalty to the Crown and within the framework of the United Kingdom, to do everything in our power to secure for Scotland a Parliament with adequate legislative authority in Scottish affairs".

The Covenant was a huge success with the Scottish people in 1949. Despite the fact that nearly two million people signed the pledge, the Labour government was unimpressed and unmoved by the groundswell of support for Home Rule. After all, the petition was not supervised by an independent agency, the Scottish Convention had no real democratic credentials (it had no MPs at Westminster) and signatures for the Covenant, however many, did not count.

There was no doubt that the Scottish Convention had mobilised widespread sympathy for Home Rule, but the real test of people's commitment to devolution would come at the ballot box. Here the voters had little choice. The Convention would not fight elections; the SNP could not field even a handful of candidates; the Liberals were seen as a spent force, and Labour and the Conservatives were firmly attached to the Union. It is no surprise, therefore that the Scottish public voted overwhelmingly for the two major parties at the 1950 and 1951 General Elections. Clearly, Scots rated jobs and welfare services above their desire to see a Scottish Parliament. The fact that these elections came so soon after the apparent success of the Covenant only served to underline the shortcomings of the pressure group approach. Keith Webb aptly brands the Covenant a "splendid failure" which was "always doomed to fail".[33]

Now that the Convention approach had failed, John MacCormick resorted to publicity stunts rather than serious politics. He was involved in the prank of stealing the Stone of Destiny from Westminster Abbey on Christmas Day 1950 and smuggling it back to Scotland. In 1953, he took out a lawsuit challenging the right of Queen Elizabeth to be called Elizabeth II in Scotland. When this failed, extremists blew up postboxes with the ERII insignia. Although these episodes were popular with many Scots and served to keep the nationalist issue alive, they did nothing to advance the cause. On the other hand, it could no longer be said that there were two wings to the nationalist movement. The Home Rule approach using pressure group tactics was dead. The only viable alternative was to fight for outright independence for Scotland in electoral contests against the major parties. This was the SNP approach. If the SNP had 'won' the battle for leadership of the nationalist movement in the 1950s though, it won by default—not through its own efforts but simply because the Convention had withered away.

Despite its failure to dislodge the two main parties from their Unionist stance in the 1950s, the Convention nevertheless left behind a considerable legacy. Firstly, the attitude of the public towards Home Rule had changed as revealed in the Covenant. Secondly, the Convention helped to elicit a measure of administrative devolution for Scotland from the Conservative government. In 1951, an additional Minister of State was added to the Scottish Office team. In 1952, the government set up the Balfour Commission to look again at the administration of Scotland. Balfour recommended that highways, the appointments of JPs and the control of animal diseases should be devolved to the Scottish Office. This was duly carried out in the next four years. Although these were modest steps, they indicated that the Conservative government in London was aware of the ebb and flow of nationalist sentiment and the need to respond to it.

By the late 1950s/early 1960s, Scottish nationalism was marginalised in British politics. Not even its most ardent supporters could have predicted that the SNP was on the verge of a breakthrough. In retrospect, a combination of factors can be found to explain the SNP's reversal of fortune. For the first time since 1934, nationalism was united under the SNP flag. The Party could now begin to project its distinctive image unhindered by the antics and distractions of the Convention group. Secondly, the Party started to put its house in order and it attracted new members who were keen to modernise the Party organisation, build up the finances and make it fit to fight elections. Thirdly, by a stroke of good timing, these positive developments coincided with a sharp downturn in the Scottish economy.

Between 1958 and 1959, unemployment doubled from 58,000 to 116,000 and it was the traditional industries, on which Scotland relied too heavily, which were worst hit. To make matters worse, the rest of the UK began to recover from the recession while Scotland continued to suffer. Scotland's standard of living relative to the UK as a whole fell from 92% in 1951 to 88% in 1960. So when Tory Prime Minister Harold Macmillan famously told the British people "You've never had it so good", the slogan had a hollow ring north of the border. For the first time since the 1930s, the SNP had hard economic grievances to add to its nationalist propaganda.

THE RISE OF THE SNP 1962–1974

The first indications that the public were beginning to take an interest in the SNP came at the Glasgow Bridgeton and West Lothian by-elections in 1961–2. Ian MacDonald gained 18.7% of the vote at Bridgeton in 1961—by far the best result since the war. Enthused by the result, MacDonald offered his services to the Party for a token salary of £5 a week. He became the SNP's first full-time National Organiser in 1962.

Immediately, he gathered together a core of young activists who canvassed the West Lothian constituency in a new and vigorous style. Canvassers raised money going round the doors selling cheap, tin SNP badges. Youngsters were given Saltire flags to wave and SNP badges—good free propaganda for the Party. To everyone's amazement, the SNP candidate, William Wolfe, polled 9,450 votes and came second to the formidable Tam Dalyell (Labour). The Conservative and Liberal candidates both lost their deposits. From then on, the major parties could not discount the SNP as an irrelevance and the voting public began to alter their perception of the SNP. A vote for the SNP might not be a wasted vote after all.

After the West Lothian by-election, the SNP turned its attention to increasing Party membership and putting the organisation onto a sound, efficient footing. In 1960, the leadership called for a membership drive. By 1962 and in the wake of the West Lothian 'success', membership had increased to 2,000. Membership then took off, doubling every year until it reached a staggering 120,000 in 1968. (See Tables 8.4 and 8.5.)

On the fund-raising side, the SNP had the services of Angus MacGilliveray, a former baker. He started up the Alba Pools (a lottery system) in 1965. This netted the Party £200,000 in the next five years. Publications run by MacGilliveray turned over more than £50,000. By the end of the 1960s, the SNP could finally boast that it was a 'national' party in the sense that it had branches and members in all parts of the country; it had the finances to get its message across; it had the organisational strength to contest local and national elections like the major parties.

Explaining the Rise of the SNP
We have already identified some of the reasons why the SNP's fortunes changed for the better in the late 1950s and early 1960s:

✳ the rival nationalist organisation, the Scottish Convention, had failed—the SNP was now the only upholder of the nationalist banner;

✳ new personnel came into the Party from a business and professional background who were keen to modernise the Party and create an effective machine for fighting elections;

✳ by-election advances brought the SNP much-needed publicity and membership and finances grew quite considerably;

✳ coincidentally, the Scottish economy was going through a difficult time—the rest of

Britain seemed to be doing better than Scotland.

Historians and political analysts have identified other reasons why the SNP rose so quickly in the 1960s and '70s.

The SNP appealed to
voters of all social classes
For most of the twentieth century, analysts had detected a very strong relationship between social class and voting. For example, an unskilled manual worker tended to vote Labour, whereas a wealthy person running a business was likely to vote Conservative. Labour and Conservative policies were geared to the interests of their supporters. The SNP realised that they could not compete with the two

big parties for the loyalties of the voters in terms of social class. Instead, they decided to adopt a social democratic position between the Labour left and the Conservative right. This 'catch-all' strategy would enable them to attract voters from all social classes. The SNP's image was, therefore, of a 'national' party, not a class party. By the 1970s, the SNP's classless image was paying off. Table 8.7 shows that by 1975, the SNP had been much more successful than Labour and the Tories in attracting support across the whole spectrum of society. Labour still gained much of its support from the working class (C2 and DE) and the Conservatives continued to appeal to the high status professional and business occupations (AB).

Share of the Vote Received by Parties at General Elections in Scotland (%)

Election	Cons.	Lab.	Lib.	SNP	Cons. & Lab.	Lib. & SNP
1964	41	49	8	2	90	10
1966	38	50	7	5	88	12
1970	38	45	6	11	83	17
1974	33	37	8	22	70	30
1974	25	36	8	30	61	39
1979	31	42	9	17	73	27
1983	29	34	25	12	63	37
1987	24	42	19	14	66	34

Table 8.6

The Rise of the SNP

Membership 1962–83

1962	2,000
1963	4,000
1964	8,000
1965 (June)	16,000
1965 (Nov)	20,000
1966	42,000
1967	80,000
1968	120,000
1971	70,000
1974	85,000
1983	c20,000

Table 8.4

GROWTH in Number of SNP Branches

May 1962	18
May 1963	41
1965	140
December 1966	205
December 1967	484
April 1969	500
March 1971	518

Table 8.5

FACTFILE

1964

At the General Election, the SNP put up fifteen candidates and polled 2.4% of the Scottish vote.

1966

At the General Election, the SNP fielded twenty three candidates and gained 5.0% of the vote overall.

1967

At the local elections, the SNP won 16% of the vote and gained twenty three seats. However, the big breakthrough for the Party was Winnie Ewing's victory at the Hamilton by-election. Mrs Ewing was the first SNP MP since the war. This was supposedly a 'safe' Labour seat, but the SNP polled 46% of the vote compared to Labour's 41.5%. Tam Dalyell, the Labour MP for West Lothian said that Hamilton was a turning point in Labour's attitude to the SNP: "The election of Mrs Ewing went off like an electoral atom bomb in the Labour establishment. To say that Party leaders were shell-shocked for weeks is an understatement. After all, Hamilton was not just any old Labour seat ... it embodied the socialist heartland."[34]

1968

At the local elections, the SNP gained one hundred and three seats, mostly at the expense of Labour. SNP councillors now held the balance of power on Glasgow City Council. The SNP had won 30% of the vote overall in Scotland. Again, this created a shockwave because it could no longer be said

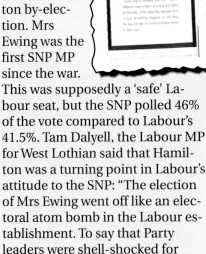

VOTE...
FOR A
CHANGE
VOTE
EWING
SCOTTISH
NATIONAL
PARTY

WILSON'S ADVICE TO HIS PERFORMING POOCHES

EWING...
SWINGS HAMILTON TO THE
SNP

Winnie Ewing's 1967 Hamilton by-election leaflet.

that Hamilton was a 'flash in the pan'. The publicity surrounding the SNP's spectacular gains brought in 40,000 new members to the SNP in 1968.

1969

The SNP fell back. In the local elections, the Party polled only 22% of the vote and made only twenty gains.

1970

At the local elections, the SNP share of the vote was down to 12.6%. At the General Election, the SNP contested sixty five out of the seventy one constituencies and polled 11.4%, the Party's best result ever. Winnie Ewing lost her Hamilton seat, but Donald Stewart gained the Western Isles. Stewart was the first SNP candidate to win a seat at a general election.

1971

The SNP candidate came second to Labour with 34.6% of the vote at the Stirling, Falkirk and Grangemouth by-election—a creditable performance.

1973

Margo MacDonald won a famous victory at the Govan by-election, polling 41.9% of the vote. Like

Hamilton, this had been a safe Labour seat. The SNP now had two MPs at Westminster.

1974

The SNP fielded seventy candidates at the February General Election. Seven of these candidates became MPs. The Party's overall share of the vote was 21.9%. Another general election was held in October and the SNP achieved its best ever result. It gained 30.4% of the vote and returned eleven MPs to Parliament. In forty two out of the seventy one constituencies, the Party was in second place. The SNP was now the second largest party in Scotland after Labour.

It's
Scotland's
Oil

SNP Poster, 1970s

Eleven SNP MPs were elected to Parliament in October 1974.

The SNP appealed to the young

The SNP appeared to be a youthful and dynamic party which compared favourably with the images of the Labour and Conservative parties. Whereas the big two inevitably had to compromise their policies when in power, the SNP at this stage had no prospect of gaining office and seemed to convey an enthusiastic idealism which appealed to a young electorate. During the heady days of the late 1960s, the SNP transformed itself from a fringe party into a mass party. Thousands of young people joined. Many young activists became involved in campaigning at elections. Surveys at this time found that about half of all 18–34-year-olds supported the SNP compared to only 20% for Labour and the Conservatives.

SOCIAL CLASS *and the Vote* June 1975

	AB	C1	C2	DE
Conservative	56	40	23	22
Labour	14	23	39	48
Liberal	10	6	6	6
SNP	20	30	32	23
Other	-	1	-	1

Table 8.7
Source: Based on an ORC survey for the *Scotsman* June 1975

The SNP appealed to those who were socially and geographically mobile

Growing affluence and changes in technology were transforming Scotland's social structure. In the 1920s, Scotland was largely working class with 61% doing manual jobs. By the 1980s, only 39% of workers were in manual jobs. The country had a more middle-class profile. Moving from working-class to non-manual and middle-class occupations tended to weaken the traditional Labour/working class link. Whereas in England this benefited the Conservatives and the Liberals, social mobility tended to favour the SNP in Scotland.

Another factor which helped the SNP was the growth of the new towns after the Second World War. Labour had always done well in the cities, especially Glasgow. Moving to new towns, like Cumbernauld and East Kilbride, had created new opportunities which had served to break the link with Labour.

"The more people left their traditional families and communities, the less they were susceptible to traditional appeals to vote the way 'people like them' had always done".[35]

Voters were disillusioned by the major parties and this benefited the SNP

Evidence for this disenchantment can be seen in Figure 8.1 which shows the two major parties' share of the vote in the UK went down from over 90% in the early 1950s to under 80% after 1974. In Scotland, this trend was more marked. Up until 1964, Scots voted in even greater numbers than the UK as a whole for the two big parties. After 1964, they turned to the Liberals and the SNP. Table 8.6 shows the Scottish statistics for the period after 1964 when the key changes started.

The combined Labour and Conservative vote went down from 90% in 1964 to 73% in 1979. The two 'third parties' picked up the lost votes. The combined SNP/Liberal share went up from 10% in 1964 to 27% in 1979. During most of that time, the SNP gained the bulk of these votes.

The public voted for the SNP, not because they believed in its policies but in protest at the major parties

The explanation often given for the growth of third parties is protest voting. According to this view, those who started voting for the SNP in the late 1960s and early 1970s were not 'genuine' nationalists but people who were temporarily disillusioned with the party in power at the time. Evidence to support the temporary and volatile nature of protest voting can be seen in the fact that the SNP did very well at the Pollock and Hamilton by-elections in 1967, but when it came to the serious business of choosing a government at the General Election in 1970, the voters abandoned the SNP in these constituencies. Furthermore, survey evidence at the time showed that most SNP voters did not support the Party's core policy of independence for Scotland.

The people voted for the SNP to pressurise the British government to do more for Scotland

Whereas the protest vote is seen as a negative tactic, according to this view the public were voting in order to gain a positive outcome. They were sending the government of the day a message—'do more for Scotland'.

"The SNP was an effective party of protest and an even more effective way of making British politicians take note."[36]

By the 1960s, the Scottish electorate had become accustomed to viewing central government as the major supplier of jobs and social services. Voters judged governments on the level of public spending and their effectiveness in dealing with Scotland's intractable problems. If the economy of Scotland was doing badly, it was the government's fault. The Scottish economy had not diversified and still relied on its failing heavy industries. Scotland was also much more dependent on government spending than the rest of the UK. By the late 1960s, the Labour government was spending 20% more per head on Scotland than the British average. Yet this did not dampen nationalist grievances.

Nationalist success at the polls can be explained at the economic level. The SNP did well when the Scottish economy was doing badly and the voters wanted the government to act more vigorously. For example, the Hamilton by-election victory in 1967 took place in the context of rising Scottish unemployment and wages falling behind those of the rest of the UK. One historian, commenting on the SNP victory at Hamilton, says that "given the (economic) record of successive governments, the only surprising feature of this development was that it came so late and was not sustained in the general election of 1970".[37] The Nationalists peaked again in 1974 at a time when the Scottish/ British economy was in crisis.

North Sea oil
The discovery of massive oil fields in the 'Scottish' sector of the North Sea in late 1970 offered the prospect of a huge bonanza of

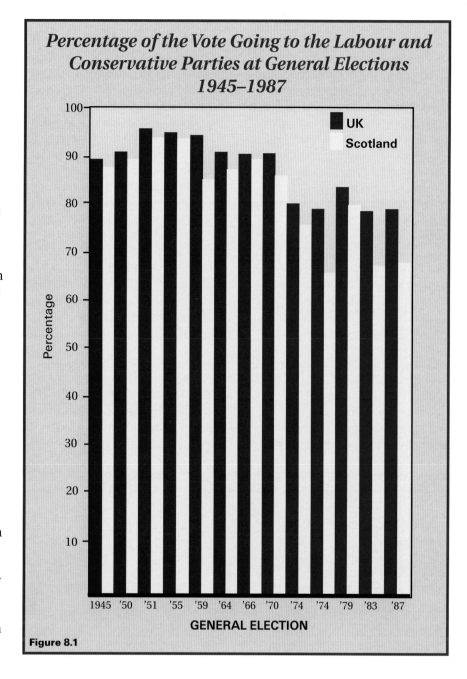

Figure 8.1

Percentage of the Vote Going to the Labour and Conservative Parties at General Elections 1945–1987

wealth—but for whom—Scotland or the whole of Britain? The SNP milked the propaganda value of North Sea oil for all it was worth with slogans such as 'It's Scotland's Oil' and 'Rich Scots or Poor British'. The oil factor undoubtedly helped the SNP although it should not be seen as the cause of the Party's rise. After all, we know that the SNP had made large gains in the late 1960s. The SNP argues that "the oil campaign itself did not persuade Scots to change the way they voted, rather it removed the doubts about the economic viability of an independent Scotland from their minds".[38] Nevertheless,

the SNP went on to its greatest success at the two general elections in 1974 when oil was high on the political agenda. Most of the Nationalist MPs returned that year were on the 'oil' side of Scotland (the east) suggesting that the electorate here may have been influenced by the SNP's oil campaign.

The SNP was lucky
It can be argued that the SNP grew so spectacularly because several helpful factors combined at the right time to benefit the Nationalists. By the 1960s, the nationalist movement was united. It had a clear aim of independence for

113

Scotland. It appealed to all classes at a time when the politics of class was coming under criticism. Voters were becoming disillusioned with both Labour and the Conservatives. The Scottish economy was in poor shape compared to that of the rest of the UK. In spite of all these positive indicators, the SNP advance could have faltered in the late '60s due to inexperienced leadership and lack of resources, but it did not. Even the SNP Leader, William Wolfe, expressed amazement at the near spontaneous growth of the Party in these years. Yes, they had to work hard to expand the organisation, but this alone could not explain the phenomenal increase in numbers of branches, members and votes. The historian David McCrone simply says, "The SNP was in the right place at the right time".[39]

A good example of this lucky timing is the oil issue. 1970 was the year when observers began commenting that the SNP had peaked at a mere 11% of the vote and that there was no prospect of a breakthrough. Then in late 1970 commercial quantities of oil were discovered in the Forties Field off Aberdeen. This gave a huge psychological boost to the nationalist movement when it might otherwise have flagged. Then again, in the run-up to the 1974 Elections, Britain was dogged by an 'energy crisis' brought on by the Arab-Israeli war. Oil was in short supply and the price shot up. North Sea oil became a central election issue which the SNP was in pole position to exploit—and it did so successfully.

In short, the SNP was an opportunist party and by chance, the 1960s and early 1970s provided the Party with unparalleled opportunities to flourish and grow.

DEVOLUTION–THE UNIONIST RESPONSE TO THE NATIONALISTS 1968–1979

From 1889 until 1927, Motions and Bills concerning Home Rule for Scotland had regularly come before Parliament. For the next forty years, Parliament was silent on the issue. Why did Home Rule or devolution come back onto the political and Parliamentary agenda so strongly and so suddenly in 1968? The answer quite simply is the spectacular rise of the SNP which had not gone unnoticed at Westminster. For political parties, nothing concentrates the mind more than losing votes and seats. Both Labour and the Conservatives quickly jumped on the devolution bandwagon in a desperate attempt to stop the Nationalists in their tracks.

Labour was deeply divided on the devolution issue, but in the autumn of 1968, the Labour Home Secretary, James Callaghan, de-

William Wolfe, Wallace Day 1979.

cided to act and set up the Royal Commission on the Constitution. The purpose of the Commission was to come up with proposals for the creation of a Scottish Assembly. The Labour leadership hoped that this would be enough to appease the SNP's supporters and bring them back into the Labour fold. It was also a way of buying time. The Government "... wanted an excuse to do nothing in the face of Nationalist success ... For the period that the Commission sat, the Government had an unimpeachable excuse for taking no action and producing no plans".[40] Prime Minister Harold Wilson put it more cynically—the Commission would spend years taking minutes! Indeed, the Kilbrandon Report finally materialised in 1973—nearly five years after it had been commissioned. It recommended the setting up of a directly elected one hundred seat Scottish Assembly with very limited revenue-raising powers.

The Scottish Conservative and Unionist Party, like Labour, felt obliged to react to the rise of the SNP. After all, it had been steadily losing ground at the polls. At their peak in 1955, the Conservatives had gained 50% of the Scottish vote, but by 1966 their share had dropped to 38%. They had lost sixteen seats since 1955. One response to this decline was to ditch the 'and Unionist' part of their title in 1965 even although most of the Party members were still staunchly anti-devolution. It also came as a shock to the faithful when their Leader Edward Heath announced his support for a Scottish Assembly at the Scottish Party conference at Perth in 1968. An internal Party committee was set up to look at proposals, chaired by former Prime Minister Sir Alec Douglas Home. Two years later, the Home Committee came out with the idea of a 'Scottish Convention'. One writer at the time called it "no more than a powerless, debating chamber". However, since most Scottish Conservatives were unionist to the core, the Convention

was as far as the Party was likely to go along the devolution road.

The Home proposals became Party policy and the Conservatives fought and won the 1970 General Election pledged to bring about the Scottish Convention. In the event, devolution was quietly shelved by Prime Minister Heath. Why did this not happen? The SNP challenge which had been threatening in 1967/8 seemed to evaporate at the General Election when they only returned one MP. In 1973, the Conservative Party conference drew back from its stance on devolution and threw out the Home Report proposals. When the Kilbrandon Commission finally reported its findings in October 1973, the Conservative government was in the middle of reorganising Scottish local government (the two-tier regions and districts) and Britain had just joined the European Community. In this context, they were unwilling to contemplate the creation of yet another layer of government (a Scottish Assembly) on top of this.

It was Labour's turn in power between 1974 and 1979. After the October 1974 General Election, the SNP had eleven MPs in Parliament and their presence ensured that devolution dominated the Parliamentary agenda for the next five years. The government's proposals for Scotland appeared in November 1975. The Scottish Assembly would have few significant responsibilities and only very limited tax-raising powers. Eventually, the Scotland and Wales Bill got under way in Parliament in December 1976. However, the government was bedevilled with problems. Its majority in Parliament was tiny and increasingly it had to rely on the Liberals and the SNP for its survival. Labour itself was badly split over the devolution scheme. In 1976, the Labour MPs Jim Sillars and John Robertson broke away to form the more socialist/nationalist Scottish Labour Party. Labour's majority was wiped out when two other Labour MPs left the Party.

The passage of the Bill through Parliament was now under threat. Several Labour MPs abstained on the Second Reading and as a concession, the Government agreed to hold a referendum in Scotland if the Bill was passed. Another problem was that the Bill was, according to one historian "literally incomprehensible" and "sank into a quagmire of 350 amendments".[41] In February 1977, debate on the Bill was so delayed that a vote was taken to cut short (or 'guillotine') the Bill. The Government lost by 312 to 283 votes, effectively killing off the Bill. Almost immediately, Labour felt the cold blast of disapproval from the Scottish electorate. The SNP rose to 36% in opinion polls and the local elections in May saw the Nationalists taking one hundred and thirty one seats from Labour.

As a last ditch measure to keep the devolution issue alive, the Government divided the Scotland and Wales Bill into two separate Bills and gave the proposed Scottish Assembly more powers. In November 1977, the Scotland Bill passed its Second Reading but the Government was forced to accept a new amendment to the Bill. This was the now infamous '40% rule' whereby 40% of the total elector-

REFERENDUM 1979

... different reactions from the cartoonists

"I'm feart" — cartoon by Turnbull for *Glasgow Herald*, 2 March 1979

Cartoon from *The Scots Independent*, April 1979

ate had to vote 'yes' at the referendum for the Scottish Assembly to come about. The Scotland Bill finally passed all its stages through Parliament in July 1978. The final hurdle was the referendum, scheduled for 1 March 1979. This turned out to be a huge disappointment for the devolution campaigners. Although 51.6% voted 'Yes' for the Assembly, that figure was only 32.9% of the total electorate and so failed to meet the 40% rule. The Scottish Assembly was dead. In the aftermath of the referendum, pro-Assembly sympathisers vented their anger and frustration at the unfairness of the 40% rule which effectively counted those who did not vote as 'No' voters and which had not been applied to the only other referendum to take place in Britain to agree to continued membership of the European Community. Nevertheless, the vote had shown that the Scots were deeply divided about the Assembly.

Historians put the 'defeat' down to a number of issues. The 'Yes' campaign was split. Labour and the SNP would not be seen campaigning on the same platform. Labour itself was divided, with several prominent Labour MPs joining the 'Labour Vote No' campaign. The SNP campaigned on the 'Yes' side but provided only lukewarm support as the Party had yet again developed a split between the fundamentalist believers in outright independence and those who supported devolution as a step on the road to independence. The 'Yes' camp also lacked the money and organisation which were behind the 'No' campaign. Another factor which may have affected the outcome was the weather. It snowed on the day of the vote which may have deterred many from venturing out to the polling booths. Remember that a large turnout was essential for the success of the 'Yes' campaign. The referendum result may also have been the Scottish electorate's verdict on the Labour government's performance during the 'winter of discontent' when public sector strikes led to school closures, rubbish piled high on the streets and the dead left unburied. A more exotic but less plausible explanation for the downfall of the Assembly blames Scotland's humiliating exit from the 1978 World Cup in Argentina which led to a collective loss of national self-confidence! (See Turnbull cartoon on page 116.)

Whatever the reasons, the SNP went into the 1979 General Election campaign with the referendum defeat ringing in its ears. The Election was disastrous for the Nationalists. Only two of the eleven SNP MPs were re-elected and the SNP's share of the vote fell from 30% (1974) to 17%. Although Britain as a whole voted in a new Conservative government, the Scots shifted from the SNP to Labour whose vote went up from 36% (1974) to 42%.

Why did the Scottish electorate not punish Labour for its handling of the British economy and why did it desert the SNP? The leading historian on Scottish nationalism, Richard Finlay, explains that most SNP voters were never in full agreement with its main policy of outright independence. However, from the late 1960s onwards, they were willing to vote SNP in order to put pressure on London to deliver more public spending and more government intervention in the Scottish economy. Nationalism appeared to grow up until 1974 because successive governments failed to solve Scotland's particular economic problems. Voting SNP sent a powerful message of disapproval. In 1979, Margaret Thatcher headed the Conservative Party and she was campaigning strongly for cutbacks in public expenditure—a heresy for most Scots. SNP voters therefore turned or returned to Labour as the only viable UK party which could meet their economic aspirations. The SNP was no longer useful as a vehicle for tactical or protest voting. Finally, voters rejected the SNP for the simple reason that devolution was off the political agenda for the foreseeable future.

... AND FINALLY A SCOTTISH PARLIAMENT

THE 1979, 1983, 1987 and 1992 General Elections saw the Conservative Party win power in Britain as a whole only to be rejected on each occasion north of the border. The 1997 Election brought Labour back with a landslide majority. Labour had gone into the Election pledged to legislate on a Scottish Parliament in the first year of office, which it duly did. This was followed by a referendum asking Scots whether they wanted a Scottish Parliament and whether they wanted it to have tax-varying powers. The answer to both questions was 'yes'.

Scotland is therefore about to enter a new and exciting era in its history. For the first time since 1707, it has its own Parliament. What direction this will take is difficult to detect at present. It will be for the next generation of Scottish historians to judge whether a devolved Scottish legislature is sufficient to satisfy the political and economic needs of the Scottish people or whether this merely whets the appetite of the nation for full independence.

Changing Britain 1850–1979

Changing Scottish Society 1880s–1939

This chapter is made up of the following sections:

- **Urbanisation (Case Study: Urban Housing)**

- **Education in Scotland**

- **Leisure & Popular Culture in Scotland**

- **Religious Identity in Scotland**

WHAT YOU WILL LEARN

- ■ *The meaning, causes, consequences and process of urbanisation in late nineteenth and early twentieth century Scotland.*

- ■ *The consequences of urbanisation in late nineteenth and early twentieth century Scottish society in the areas of leisure, popular culture, education and religion.*

Urbanisation 1880s-1939

T HE POPULAR IMAGE of Scotland across the world is of a small country made up of moors, lochs and glens. While this picture continues to serve the interests of the contemporary tourist industry, the fact is that 80% of the population are urban dwellers whose links with the countryside have long since disappeared.

The Image of Scotland
Until the 1980s, Scottish historians and academics tended to perpetuate the 'rural myth' by spending more time researching rural rather than urban Scotland. The studies of the last two decades have somewhat redressed the balance, unveiling an urbanisation process which, in its complexity and uniqueness, is now seen to be a major force in the formation of contemporary Scottish society.

For the purposes of this study, 'urban' refers to "a distinctive physical environment noted for its relative size, density and complexity. It also refers to a specific form of local authority, located in space and associated with distinctive powers; in Scotland that meant the burgh in all its different forms".[1]

In common with North America and Western Europe, Scotland experienced a period of enormous social and economic change during the nineteenth and early twentieth centuries. Industrialisation, population growth, internal migration, immigration, and emigration changed the way in which Scottish society was organised as it moved away from its rural/agricultural/mercantile past into an urban/technological/industrial age with all its attendant problems.

The National Picture
The period 1880 to 1939 sees the urbanisation process in Scotland reach its peak of intensity, slowing down thereafter. In 1911, Scotland (49.5% urbanised) was second

only to England and Wales (60.6% urbanised) in a European rank ordering of population living in towns and cities of more than 20,000. The Scottish situation at this time was dominated by four centres, Edinburgh, Glasgow, Dundee and Aberdeen. This was markedly different from England where London (5.9 times larger than any other English city) led the way. It would, however, be misleading to view Scottish urbanisation as exclusively limited to four cities. Smaller urban centres, each distinct for its own local reasons, were also growing at this time. Ayr and Perth were industrial and textile centres. Coatbridge and Hamilton developed into centres for heavy industry. Peterhead and Fraserburgh were fishing ports. Haddington and Dumfries became farming, market and service centres.

Nevertheless, the 'big four' dominated the Scottish urban landscape. The Census of 1901 records that Scotland's population was 4.6 million, of whom 784,496 lived in Glasgow. The city's population had increased in size over the previous century by almost 1,000%. While Edinburgh, Aberdeen and Dundee had also grown significantly, Glasgow was the largest and most dynamic city at the turn of the century. The historian RJ Morris argues that these cities were expanding because "part of the power of a developed urban economy was its ability to generate economic development from a

URBANISATION 1891-1911

Percentage of the Scottish Population in Settlements of more than 5,000, 1891–1911

Year	Total (%)
1891	3.5
1901	57.6
1911	58.6

Table 9.1

Tenement housing at Dowanhill, Glasgow.

variety of economic resources and relationships".[2]

What were these "economic resources and relationships" which fuelled the urban development of Scotland? There are similarities and differences between the 'big four' in Scotland.

Glasgow's main economic activities were based on engineering, shipbuilding, coal, steel, textiles and trade. Its mercantile links were literally global between 1880 and 1939. It could boast of a workforce of whom fewer than 30% were unskilled, approximately 60% were skilled, and about 10% were professional. In addition, 37% of the city's women were in employment of which 20% was domestic service. Glasgow's population of 784,000 in 1901 grew to 1,128,000 by 1939. The city expanded during this period to such an extent that it annexed nearby burghs like Govan and Partick in 1912.

Edinburgh's profile was different. By the early twentieth century the city, while second in size to Glasgow, had become the financial, political and authority centre of Scotland. Its main industries were engineering, brewing, printing and publishing, rubber vulcanisation, banking and administration. The workforce was less than 30% unskilled, 55% skilled and 15% professional. Like Glasgow, 37% of females were in employment, but 40% of that total were in domestic service. In 1911 Edinburgh's population stood at 320,000, but by 1939 this had increased to 472,000.

Dundee's economy was particularly biased towards textile manufacturing based on jute, coarse linen and engineering. The workforce was dominated by females. In 1911, for every one hundred females there were seventy four males in Dundee. Accordingly, 52% of females were in employment, a far higher proportion than in any other Scottish city. The city's population had increased rapidly between 1861 and 1911 from 91,000 to 165,000, the rate of increase then slowing between 1911 and 1939. Aberdeen was the hub of the north-east corner of Scotland. Its main industries were shipbuilding, fishing, trade, regional services for its agricultural hinterland, and the production and export of granite. Again, 37%

Highland **Population** *in towns, 1891*

Town/City	Total Population	Number of Highlanders	% Highlanders
Greenock	63,423	3,810	6.0
Stirling	16,776	376	2.24
Perth	19,919	1,117	3.73
Dundee	155,985	1,277	0.81
Aberdeen	112,923	1,257	1.1

Table 9.2
Sources: *Scottish Population History:17th Century to the 1930s* Ed. Michael Flynn; *Highland Migration* in *Journal of Historical Geography* by CWJ Withers.

Edinburgh, from the Calton Hill, looking to Granton.

of the city's females were in employment and of that total 23% were in domestic service. Like Dundee, Aberdeen's population increased dramatically between 1861 and 1911 from 74,000 to 164,000, slowing thereafter to reach 180,000 by 1939.

By 1914, these four cities along with the seventy five or so burghs of 5,000 or more inhabitants formed the intricate network of urban Scotland. By the outbreak of war, however, the pace of urbanisation had begun to slow. Richard Rodger in *Urbanisation in Twentieth Century Scotland* argues that in the years immediately prior to 1914, "the unmistakable message was of a slackening in the rate of urban expansion in the industrial heartlands of Scotland. The decade of World War I did prove something of a watershed for the pattern of Scottish urban expansion though this probably had more to do with the structure of Scottish industry, foreign competition and economic depression than the war itself."[3] Nevertheless, there are signs that the pace of urban growth was again beginning to pick up in the years immediately preceding the outbreak of World War II as the economy began to recover.

POPULATION, MIGRATION AND IMMIGRATION 1880–1939

A major factor in Scotland's urbanisation was a rapid increase in population. In 1801, the population stood at approximately 1.58 million. The 1911 census counted a population of 4.76 million. Between the years 1871 and 1911, the population increased by 1.4 million, but thereafter slowed and actually decreased by 1% in the 1920s. The largest increase in population during this period took place in the central belt, Scotland's industrial urban heartland. By contrast the numbers living in the Highlands, Borders, Western and Northern Isles fell markedly after 1911.

Added to the general population increase, migration within Scotland swelled the population of the already growing towns and cities. During the nineteenth century, 'push' factors such as famine, overcrowding, lack of land ownership, clearances, dwindling economic opportunities and increased education combined with the 'pull' of the towns and cities led to a considerable exodus from the Highlands. In the west of Scotland, Glasgow and smaller towns such as Greenock and Paisley were popular destinations for the High-

landers. In the east, Dundee, Perth, Stirling and Aberdeen had a significant Highland presence by 1891. (See Table 9.2.)

Overall, more Highland migrants settled in Glasgow and the towns of the west than in the east. Research shows that there is a pattern to the settlement of Highlanders in the Lowlands. Aberdeen, for example, was a magnet for migrants from the eastern parts of the Northern Highlands and between 1850 and 1900 drew, "hardly at all from the south and central Highlands, and only later drew in any number from the north and west mainland and islands".[4] By contrast, Glasgow and towns in the west such as Paisley and Greenock attracted migrants from Argyll and the West Highlands.

Who were the migrants? Initially it was men who left the Highlands, but increasingly in the later part of the nineteenth and early twentieth centuries, more women than men were leaving for the Lowland towns and cities. Overall, Highland migrants were to be found in unskilled and skilled work, professional and management positions.

Migration also affected the rural Lowlands at this time. In the sec-

IRISH-BORN IN SCOTLAND, ENGLAND AND WALES 1841–1931

| Date | ENGLAND & WALES | | SCOTLAND | |
	Number Irish-born	% Total Population	Number Irish-born	% Total Population
1841	289,404	1.8	126,321	4.8
1851	519,959	2.9	207,367	7.2
1861	601,634	3.0	204,083	6.7
1871	566,540	2.5	207,770	6.2
1881	562,374	2.2	218,745	5.9
1891	458,315	1.6	194,807	4.8
1901	426,565	1.3	205,064	4.6
1911	375,325	1.0	174,715	3.7
1921	64,747	1.0	159,020	3.3
1931	81,089	0.9	124,296	2.6

Table 9.3
Source: John Arthur Jackson, *The Irish in Britain* 1963.

ond half of the nineteenth century, the proportion of the population engaged in agriculture declined from 25% in 1850 to approximately 11% in 1911 and this trend accelerated more dramatically between 1918 and 1945.

What caused this decline in the importance of the rural way of life? Firstly, the replacement of traditional country crafts and occupations by modern industry forced people who had been a rich resource of seasonal farm labour away from the countryside. Secondly, the application of science and mechanisation again reduced the need for labour on Scotland's farms. Finally, improvements to transport, particularly refrigeration and improved, faster, rail links, brought the spectre of harsh competition to Scottish farmers. Foodstuffs were imported in greater variety and quantity and at a competitive price from other parts of the UK and beyond.

Was the process of migration to urban Scotland inevitable, and if so, what was the most important cause? TC Smout argues that "as the city rose the countryside, ultimately, declined".[5] Until 1890, depopulation of the rural Lowlands, it is argued, was no more pronounced than in the Highlands. However, in the Highlands, depopulation was associated with the clearances—the forced removal of people from the land—whereas in the Lowlands, "it just occurred and was accepted". Surprisingly, the depopulation of the Highlands continued after the 1886 *Crofters' Holdings Act* which gave the Highland crofters fixed rents, fair rents and security of tenure. The population of the Highlands and Islands counties declined by 26% between 1891 and 1931.

Other historians argue that the causes of rural depopulation are linked to agrarian change and the social consequences of that change. This process which increased the size of farms and gradually introduced mechanisation in the late nineteenth and early twentieth centuries, disrupted and eventually led to the break-up of stable rural communities.

In the last thirty years of the nineteenth century, approximately one-third of farm workers left the land. Some historians, such as TM Devine, say that the mechanisation argument is far too simplistic. They cite higher wages in the mines as factors in attracting Lanarkshire's farm workers, and more attractive employment in the railways and police as incentives for the farm hands of the north-east to move to towns such as Aberdeen, Elgin, Inverurie and Keith.

"Conditions of employment in agriculture were seen by an increasing number of farm workers as less attractive than life in industry and the towns. Significantly the rural trade unions of the late nineteenth century were not concerned with raising wages ... Life on the land had improved but advances were still patchy and failed to keep pace with the rising expectations of many workers of the later nineteenth century. There was a new awareness of what constituted comfort.

Officially farm workers worked a ten-hour day but this did not take into account the early morning feeding and preparation of the horses and evening grooming. As late as the 1930s some farmers in the northeast insisted on horses being 'suppered' as late as 8.00 pm. Increasingly too the lack of community and social life in agriculture attracted criticism."[6]

At the same time female farm servants were leaving the land to go to urban areas. As with men, pay and conditions were a source of discontent, but as women increasingly articulated their grievances, they talked of agriculture as an unfeminine occupation which was dirty and rough unlike the more attractive urban occupations such as domestic service.

"No educated country girl with a spark of ambition and pride about her need toil among the 'tatties' for lack of opportunities to better herself in a different branch of employment. The structural change in the Scottish economy ensured that farmers in the later nineteenth century faced greater competition than ever before from urban and industrial employers for women workers. The days of cheap and abundant supplies of women, eager to labour in the countryside for paltry earnings were gone forever." [7]

What fuelled the "rising expectations" and the "new awareness of what constituted comfort" for both male and female farm workers in the late nineteenth and early twentieth centuries?

TC Smout highlights popular culture and education as factors which led to an exodus of the young from the countryside.

"Rural depopulation therefore occurred when the young, in particular, felt their need to associate could only be met by going to town. For them, the rural 'community' had ceased to be a community they cared about ... seventy years of uniform education ... tended to produce a uniform culture in which the ways of the town were given a higher value than those of the countryside. At the same time the cultural influence of the churches as centres of local life gradually diminished, while after the First World War the influence of the radio and cinema rose in prestige to portray a metropolitan and essentially big-city culture." [8]

By 1881, Scotland's growing towns and cities were populated by increasing numbers of Irish as well as smaller numbers of immigrants from mainland Europe. Irish immigration to the UK mainland increased dramatically during the 1840s as a result of famine. Between 1881 and 1931 immigration decreased, but as the figures in Table 9.3 reveal, Irish immigration to Scotland had a far greater impact than in England and Wales since the proportion of Irish in Scotland's population was higher.

The strength of the Irish community in Scotland, and therefore its influence, is probably much greater than these figures reveal, as they do not take into account those who had Irish parentage but who were born in Scotland.

Why did the Irish come to Scotland and where did they settle?

Table 9.3 shows that Irish immigration to Scotland was at its highest point in the decades following the famine of the 1840s. While significant immigration continued well into the twentieth century, by 1939 the figures stood at just over 100,000. As Figure 9.1 illustrates, the Scottish picture is very different from that of England and Wales, where the decline in Irish immigration bottomed out in the 1920s then increased sharply.

KEY POINTS
Urbanisation 1880s–1939

 Urbanisation accompanied economic, industrial and population growth in the nineteenth and early twentieth centuries.

 Scotland's urbanisation centred around the growth of four industrial cities—Edinburgh, Glasgow, Dundee and Aberdeen—along with a series of seventy five smaller towns and regional centres.

 Improvements to transport eg. railways, refrigerated transport, roads and general infrastructure facilitated the urbanisation process.

 Internal migration from the Highlands and rural Lowlands contributed to urban growth at this time.

 'Push' factors which caused migration from the countryside at this time were: lack of economic and employment opportunities; the increasing mechanisation of some agricultural processes; the amalgamation of small farms into larger units; lack of land tenure, low wages and long hours; a less attractive lifestyle; increased education and access to the media which tended to promote a uniform 'big-city' culture, downgrading the value of rural life.

 'Pull' factors from the cities and towns at this time were: increased economic opportunities; better pay, conditions, holidays and shorter working hours; improved, cheaper transport; improved social contact with access to leisure and cultural pursuits.

 Immigrants from Ireland came to Scotland in the late nineteenth and early twentieth centuries in declining numbers.

 Irish immigrants came to Scotland for improved economic opportunities, and settled mainly in the central belt urban industrial areas.

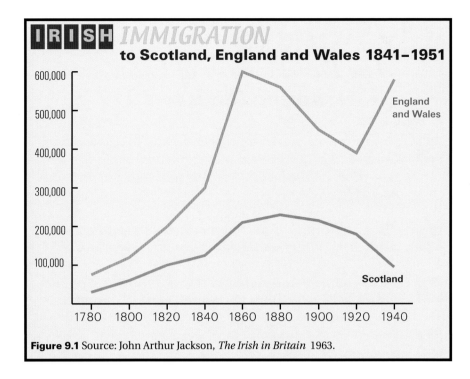

Figure 9.1 Source: John Arthur Jackson, *The Irish in Britain* 1963.

"The 1880s and the first three decades of the twentieth century all showed reductions in the Irish-born population of such magnitudes as to indicate substantial emigration. The annual series of emigrants from Irish ports for Scottish destinations confirms the relatively low level of movement after 1876. By the late nineteenth century, the influx of Irish had effectively ceased and the earlier generation of immigrants had become assimilated into the Scottish population." [9]

Like the Highlanders, the Irish who came to Scotland settled in urban areas for a variety of similar reasons. Poverty and lack of economic opportunities, combined with cheap transport, brought Irish immigrants to Scotland either on a seasonal/temporary basis into occupations such as railway building or seasonal farm work, or on a permanent basis into Scottish industry.

The Irish who settled permanently in Scotland did not distribute themselves evenly across the country. As employment opportunities were paramount, immigrants settled in urban areas, concentrating in the west of Scotland in towns and cities such as Glasgow, Paisley and the mining towns of Lanarkshire. Smaller numbers of Irish immigrants settled in Edinburgh and in Dundee where there were employment opportunities particularly for women in the textile industry.

One peculiarity of Irish immigration to Scotland is that while overall numbers were declining in the latter decades of the nineteenth century, the greatest proportion of immigrants were Protestants from Ulster. In 1876, there were 8,807 immigrants from Ireland of whom 8,191 were natives of Ulster. In 1900 there were 1,968 Irish immigrants of whom 1,646 were from Ulster. Like their predominantly Catholic counterparts from the south of Ireland, these immigrants brought with them their culture, religious traditions and their disagreements, the effects of which on Scottish society will be examined in a later section.

MEETING THE CHALLENGES OF URBANISATION—THE DEVELOPMENT OF LOCAL GOVERNMENT 1880s–1939

"The brutalism associated with urban development has been a recurrent and international experience. As with the nineteenth century, when uncontrolled urban development brought environmental damage and public health risks on an unprecedented scale, so in the twentieth century, urban change has in some cases been drastic." [10]

As Scotland's towns and cities expanded during the nineteenth and early twentieth centuries, the need for a municipal authority structure which would provide public utilities such as water, sewage and waste disposal, regulate building and oversee public health requirements also grew. The scale of the public health problems created by urban growth and industrialisation alone demanded that a laissez-faire approach at a local level could not be sustained and indeed was being eroded from the 1850s onwards.

The historian RJ Morris argues that at the close of the nineteenth century the "Scottish perception of urbanisation increasingly identified the urban place with higher levels of authority and order than was expected by the English. The Scots accepted and expected strong, positive forms of locally specific authority in their towns. The town was a place of order. The countryside and the unbounded mining settlements like Blantyre were the sources of violence and chaos. In Scotland, urban traditions of authority were strong whilst central direction was weak. Scotland's image of its towns was as places of order and discipline." [11]

What were these "positive forms of locally specific authority in their towns"? Essentially the Royal Burgh was the main form of urban authority in the nineteenth century. All building within a burgh was technically regulated by Dean of Guild Courts, institutions which dated back to the seventeenth century, but which by 1850, in many cases, had ceased to exist. After 1833, the Royal Burghs were elected by the ratepayers, but the Dean of Guild courts were not elected and were almost closed, self-appointed bodies. In addition, local police forces in Scotland had a wide remit which included law and order, lighting and paving as well as issues of public health. Glasgow Corporation used the police to enforce its 'ticketing' legislation after 1866. Houses not exceeding 2,000 cubic feet had a metal ticket placed on the door stating the maximum number of occupants. The system was intended to combat overcrowding, and extended to all burghs after 1903, enabling police and sanitary inspectors to raid a house at any time, day or night.

The development of a specific Scottish local government response to urban health and social problems between the 1880s and 1939 thus began in a rather piecemeal and patchy fashion, with very little central direction prior to World War I. However, by 1939 there was a clearly delineated and recognisable system funded from local rates and supported by central government.

KEY POINTS
The Development of Local Government 1880s to 1939

✔ *Urbanisation caused local government to develop and expand in order to deal with problems such as overcrowding, public health, housing and law and order at a local level.*

✔ *The main catalysts for improvements in local government were public health, housing and civic pride.*

✔ *Local councils had some success in improving public health before 1914, but many problems still remained.*

✔ *The emerging system of local government was patchy and uneven across Scotland prior to 1914.*

✔ *Through the Local Government (Scotland) Act, 1929, central government put in place a recognisable system of Scottish local authorities. This system was supported by central funding.*

Urban Housing 1880s–1939

'Too little too late!'

AS SCOTLAND'S cities grew in the nineteenth century they came to be dominated by tenement-style blocks of working-class housing, which was erected by speculative private builders and landlords. In the second half of the century, urban expansion led to an enormous demand for working-class housing. By 1914, it is clear that the poorest classes lived in the worst housing.

Scotland's developing municipal authorities had attempted to deal with housing problems before this time with legislative support from central government. The main motivation for municipal intervention and housing reform before 1914 was sanitation and public health, but success was limited due to the costs involved. In most cases intervention meant demolition or improvement of defective houses, not the construction of new houses.

The *Nuisances Removal & Contagious Diseases Act* (1846) was used by local authorities to demolish dangerous or insanitary property up to the beginning of the twentieth century.

The *Burgh Police Acts* (1866 & 1892) were used by local authorities to combat overcrowding by attempting to regulate the numbers of people living in slum dwellings. In Glasgow a system of 'ticketing' houses was adopted, and the police carried out raids to enforce the regulations. This practice enraged many poor people who supplemented their incomes by taking in lodgers.

The *Housing of the Working Classes Act* (1890) and The *Housing & Town Planning Act* (1909) gave burghs the power to improve, close or demolish houses for the working classes.

Despite growing municipal intervention to attempt to deal with the worst of Scotland's urban housing problems, little impact was made prior to World War I. The key issues of shortage of housing supply, affordable accommodation for the unskilled labouring classes, defective housing, overcrowding and insanitary living conditions remained.

According to a Glasgow Medical Officer of Health in 1888, overcrowding was the key problem:

> "Of all the children who die in Glasgow before they reach their fifth year, 32% die in houses of one apartment ...There they die and their bodies are laid on a table or on a dresser so as to be somewhat out of the way of their brothers and sisters, who play and sleep and eat in their ghastly company."[1]

Between 1875 and 1915, the average annual supply of new dwellings in Scotland was 10,727 but there was a marked decline in house building after 1904. In the years 1911–1912 and 1912–1913, the figures fell to 2,757 and 2,990 respectively.

The Decline in House Building

The political environment of the day seemed to favour a growing state interest in matters related to poverty, particularly housing. The rise of Labour inevitably led the Liberals towards a positive, more interventionist stance on social issues in order to compete for the working-class vote. However, government action pre-1914 and economic conditions during the war badly affected the main providers of housing—the speculative builder and the private landlord.

Between 1880 and 1904, private house builders had enjoyed almost boom conditions. However, a tax on vacant land and the effects of the 'People's Budget', which made it unprofitable to hold on to or speculate in land, dealt a severe blow to speculative building in Scotland.

The years immediately preceding 1914 were depressing times for private landlords. Rents were low, properties were vacant and, consequently, profits were low. War reversed the situation.

Demand for property increased, particularly on Clydeside with an increase in the numbers of munitions workers. House building did not, however, increase, and there was soon a shortage of housing combined with rapidly increasing rents. By 1915 the worst affected groups were skilled and semi-skilled workers. In protest, they organised rent strikes in Glasgow and other parts of Scotland. Supported by the 'Red Clydesiders', over 20,000 tenants refused to pay rent in Glasgow alone. One banner carried by a female protester during a march at this time summed up the anger of the rent strikers: "Our husbands are fighting Prussianism in France, and we are fighting the Prussians of Partick." Eventually, working-class militancy forced the government to intervene with the *Rent and Mortgage Restriction Act* of 1915 which kept rents at reasonable levels. As a result, the future for private landlords seemed to be increasingly uneconomic.

Towards the end of the war, the true picture of Scotland's housing was revealed when the report of the Royal Commission on Housing in Scotland (set up in 1912) was finally published in 1918. It catalogued a devastating list of deficiencies, confirming the enormity of the problems which Scotland's often ill-equipped municipal authorities had been trying to solve.

Indicators of OVERCROWDING pre–1914

1911
Size of dwellings occupied by two or more people

1 room dwellings	56%
2 room dwellings	47%
3 room dwellings	24%

Table 9.6

20% of all 'single ends' were occupied by five or more people including one lodger.

1901
Percentage of Scotland's Population Living in Single Room Accommodation

Paisley	**13.5**
Greenock	**11.3**
Kilmarnock	**18.9**
Scotland	**11.2**

Table 9.4

1901
Housing Distribution Among Families

	Aberdeen	Dundee	Edinburgh	Glasgow
1 room	13.1	19.7	17.0	26.1
2 rooms	37.3	52.1	31.4	43.6
3 rooms	26.2	16.5	19.2	16.5

Table 9.5

1912
Death Rate (per 1,000) by Age Group and House Size for Glasgow

Rooms	Under 1 Year	1–5 Years	10–15 Years
1	187.0	39.0	4.5
2	143.5	28.5	3.0
3	114.5	16.5	2.0
4+	88.0	10.0	1.5
City	151.0	28.5	3.0

Table 9.7

Figures in Tables 9.4, 9.5 and 9.6 are from the Census of 1901 and 1911.
Figures in Table 9.7 are from *Glasgow The Making of a City* by Andrew Gibb, page 132.

ROYAL COMMISSION ON HOUSING IN SCOTLAND REPORT: 1918

Unsatisfactory sites and insufficient water supplies.

Unsatisfactory provision of drainage.

Grossly inadequate provision for the removal of rubbish.

Widespread absence of decent sanitary conveniences.

The persistence of unspeakably filthy privy–midden areas.

Whole townships unfit for human occupation in the crofting counties and islands.

Gross overcrowding and huddling of the sexes together in congested industrial villages and towns.

Occupation of one-room houses by large families.

Groups of lightless and unventilated houses in older burghs.

'Clotted masses' of slums in the great cities.

Adapted from J Butt Working-Class Housing In Scottish Cities, in Scottish Urban History Eds.G Gordon & B Dicks, page 236.

POSTWAR HOUSING LEGISLATION

Successive governments legislated between the wars to improve Scotland's housing.

1919 Housing Act (Liberal)

This landmark Act took central government into the housing arena for the first time. Local authorities were required to submit plans for house building, and government subsidies were provided to assist their realisation. For the first time local authorities became the providers of affordable rented housing. Even before the legislation was in place, 297 out of Scotland's 313 local authorities had prepared schemes for house building. Unfortunately, government subsidies to the programme were reduced through the 'Geddes Axe —public spending cuts of 1921–22.

1923 Housing Act (Conservative)

This Act attempted to stimulate private house building in the hope that government spending on housing could be reduced. Local authorities could apply for a subsidy of £6 per annum per house built if they could prove that private builders either could not or would not build in their area. The scheme was a failure in Scotland with only seventy three houses being built for rent in the month of November 1924.

1924 Housing Act (Labour)

In order to stimulate local authority house building for rent, Labour increased the subsidy to £9 per annum per house built for forty years (£12.50 in rural areas). In addition, for the first time central government provided subsidies to help maintain rents at acceptable levels. Local authorities in Scotland built 75,000 houses under the terms of this Act.

1930 Housing Act (Labour)

In an attempt to deal with urban slums, the government began to provide subsidies for their clearance. Under the Act, cities were given powers to clear slum areas for redevelopment. They were also given a subsidy of £2.50 for forty years for each person they rehoused.

1933 Housing Act (National Government)

Once again government finance intervened to slow down housing activity. The National Government's policy was to leave slum clearance to local authorities and house building to the private sector. Consequently, subsidies were once again reduced.

1935 Housing Act (National Government)

As the national economic situation brightened, the National Government relaunched subsidies with a scheme for all housing. A subsidy of £6.75 per annum for forty years was offered for every unit built to rehouse slum dwellers and those living in overcrowded, but good, accommodation.

1938 Housing Act (National Government)

As war approached and rearmament began in earnest, some subsidies were scaled down, and others were only paid in relation to the size of the houses built.

INSURANCE AGAINST REVOLUTION?

There is some debate amongst historians about the political motivation for the government's interventionist stance on housing in the interwar years, particularly the 1919 *Housing Act*.

Was the 1919 *Housing Act* put in place as an "insurance against revolution"? The historian R J Morris supports the proposition when he says that:

● The phrase 'homes for heroes' used by the government with reference to the 1919 Act was well chosen.

● "These homes were ideological artefacts, visible proof that working people were being offered better conditions."[2]

J Butt put forward the following argument. Politicians in 1918 recognised that one of the main causes of unrest during the war was the issue of housing. Butt cites evidence from the 1918 Parliamentary Commission into Industrial Unrest and the Royal Commission on Housing in Scotland.

"Industrial unrest, whatever its ultimate causes, undoubtedly is stimulated directly and indirectly by defective housing."[3]

"We have had startling revelations of the acute need of houses in industrial centres. The want of housing accommodation is undoubtedly a serious cause of unrest."[4]

Sean Damer offers a left-wing analysis when he argues that:

● Housing was a key issue of class conflict during and after World War I.

● The working class gained major concessions from the state in the years 1915–20 in the area of housing.

● Any gains were whittled away in the next twenty years by the effect of market forces on national and local government.

● Housing policy did not 'evolve' in the interwar years, rather it "lurched through a series of contradictions and crises as different forces were brought to bear on it".[5]

SCOTLAND'S FOUR CITIES IN THE INTERWAR YEARS

The cities of Glasgow, Edinburgh, Dundee and Aberdeen all had similar housing problems in 1918, although the difficulties faced by Glasgow were far greater than those of the others. When Scottish local authorities submitted house building plans to the government in January 1918, the total need was for 99,000 new dwellings, most of which were required in the main urban centres. How successful were these four cities in solving their housing problems in the interwar period?

Glasgow

In 1918 Glasgow submitted its plan to build 57,000 new houses immediately, plus 5,000 per annum thereafter. Most of the new houses were to have a minimum of three apartments as the biggest problem was overcrowding. In the years 1920–29, Glasgow Corporation built 21,939 new houses and between 1930 and 1939, 28,338 new dwellings were built. A survey in 1935, based on the very lax standards of the 1935 *Housing Act*, showed that 82,109 families (31% of all Glasgow families) were living in overcrowded conditions. When Glasgow Corporation closed its waiting list for housing in 1933, it contained 80,000 applications. While the intentions of Glasgow Corporation were good, it was simply overwhelmed by the scale of the problem.

Edinburgh

Edinburgh did not have a vast problem of industrial slum housing on the scale of Glasgow or Dundee. Pressure from the ratepayers and a 'weak civic will' meant that Edinburgh Corporation had to rely on private house builders to increase its housing stock. Under the terms of the 1923 *Housing Act*, 2,000 houses were built, each subsidised to the tune of £70. The Corporation's major house building effort came in the 1930s. In total 14,816 new houses were built in the years 1919–1939 for working-class tenants, one-third by the Corporation and two-thirds by private builders. However, Edinburgh consistently failed to meet its housing targets in the 1930s, and overcrowding remained a serious problem.

Dundee

As early as 1918 Dundee set out to build well-planned housing estates. The Corporation succeeded in erecting 10,000 houses during the interwar years, many of which were of very high quality. Despite this effort, a survey in 1931 showed that 56% of the population still lived in two apartment houses. For many Dundonians overcrowding, lack of basic amenities and defective houses was a way of life in the interwar years.

Aberdeen

Aberdeen initially underestimated the scale of its housing problem at the end of World War I and in the early 1920s increased its estimate from 1,500 new houses to 4,000. The rate of house building increased after 1924, and a total of 11,000 new houses were built in the interwar years, 60% by the Corporation. Middle-class owner-occupiers benefited during this time with the construction of bungalows in the west end of the city. Many problems remained, however. A 1938 survey revealed that over 20% of all houses were overcrowded, 26,000 lacked proper sanitary facilities and 4,905 had no indoor water supply or sink.

SCOTLAND'S CHANGED URBAN LANDSCAPE

The interwar years brought great changes to the style, amenities and form of Scottish housing. The historian Richard Rodger has provided an excellent overview of this change. He argues that:

- The designs of the new working-class housing estates owed more to the English tradition than the Scottish.

- As a result, traditional working-class urban life was disrupted when people were uprooted from their familiar environment of "tenement close social relationships" to vast housing estates on the edges of the cities which lacked the traditional working-class support mechanisms.

- "The dominant housing ideology was based upon garden city principles and influenced by English middle-class suburban values."[6]

- Centralised decision making by London through the Scottish Office was crucial in determining the form of Scottish public housing between the wars. The English tradition of the two-storey 'semi' replaced the Scottish four and five storey tenement. 'Four in a block' cottage and villa style flats, largely absent before 1914 therefore became common features in Scotland's towns and cities.

- In the private sector the fashion for bungalow building was popular in the 1920s and '30s. Scotland's new middle-class suburbs were dominated by this type of housing.

- Bungalow-dominated suburbs segregated the middle classes from the workers, and early council estates were let to skilled workers in stable employment, separating them from the poor and less skilled.

"Housing developments allied with changing bus transport and car ownership in the interwar years formalised social fissures within Scottish society."[7]

Education in Scotland 1880s–1939

THE ORIGINS OF THE Scottish educational system go back to the Reformation in the sixteenth century when Protestantism overtook the Roman Catholic Church in Scotland. The New Faith emphasised personal reading of the Bible as opposed to the Catholic reliance on the priest for spiritual guidance. John Knox, the leading figure of the Scottish Reformation, set out his ideas for education in 1560. In order to achieve a level of literacy whereby every Christian could read the Scriptures, every parish in the country would have to set up a school.

By the end of the seventeenth century, Knox's vision was reality thanks to a partnership between Church and State. By law, the landowners in each parish had to appoint a schoolmaster, and provide him with a house and a small salary. Education was available to both boys and girls for a small fee. Pupils received an elementary education based around the three Rs—reading, writing and arithmetic. They also had to learn by heart the Church's basic set of beliefs called the Shorter Catechism. Throughout the eighteenth and early nineteenth centuries, the parish school system worked well. Organised by the Established Church of Scotland and supported by the State, it supplied a basic schooling for a largely rural, agrarian population.

Many of the schoolmasters could also teach Latin and Greek and so were able to prepare their most talented pupils for university. This strong link with university was a distinctive feature of the Scottish educational system. It provided access to higher education which was denied in other countries to all but the upper and middle classes. In Scotland, it was possible for able pupils of humble origins to gain admission to a university and from there into respectable employment in the professions. Scots took great pride in the opportunities available to the 'lad o'pairts' to climb the social ladder. In the period after the Act of Union (1707), when Scotland had lost its political independence, Scots could still celebrate their separate educational system which seemed to be more egalitarian and progressive than its English counterpart.

EDUCATION IN THE NINETEENTH CENTURY

The nineteenth century brought rapid industrialisation and urbanisation to Scotland. It was inevitable that the parish system of education, based as it was on a stable rural population, would not be able to cope with the influx of people into the industrial towns and cities. Because there was no national authority with the responsibility or financial resources to oversee the changing needs of the new urban masses, educational provision in the towns was a growing cause for concern. A bewildering variety of different types of school emerged to meet the demand and to cater for the social and economic problems of early urban life. Factory and mill schools for child labourers, burgh schools for the middle class, ragged schools for destitute street children, adventure schools for children in the poorest districts of the cities, sessional, mission and Sunday (or Sabbath) schools run by the Churches—all of these institutions competed for the services of the rich and poor, but together they amounted more to a patchwork than to a well thought out system geared to the needs of all.

The picture was further complicated by the Disruption of 1843 when the Church of Scotland's dominance over education was abruptly ended. Now the Free Church and the United Presbyterian Church competed in the educational marketplace for the hearts and minds of the population. Both started to build and run schools. Added to this, the potato famine of 1844 brought thousands of Irish immigrants into Scotland, which in turn created a demand for separate Catholic schools. The Episcopalians also ran their own schools. By the 1860s, there were far too many denominational schools overlapping each other and providing a similar service in the same area.

However, over-provision did not mean that schooling was universal. There were significant gaps, especially in the cities. Fewer than half of the children of Glasgow between the ages of five and ten were reckoned to be going to school in 1857. Provision of education for the bottom end of the urban market was either non-existent or extremely patchy. Already in 1843, the Rev. George Lewis felt it necessary to entitle his book *Scotland a Half-Educated Nation*, and commented on the "entire impotency of the voluntary system to educate either an entire nation, or an entire city".[1] In the cities, private adventure schools with unqualified and unscrupulous teachers presented "extraordinary scenes of wretchedness, stench and disorder".[2] Attendance at school was lower in mining and factory towns than in the countryside—government inspectors found that "the period of attendance is very often cut short at eight or nine".[3] TC Smout concludes that "Scottish education at mid-century was extremely inegalitarian, mainly because the economic pressures on the great mass of the population put anything apart from the acquisition of the most basic literary skills far beyond their reach".[4]

Although Scotland compared favourably with England on basic education with half its rate of illiteracy, there were still huge regional variations eg. 79% of women could write their own name in the Borders (rural) compared to only 69% in Lanarkshire (industrial) and a mere 49% in the Highlands. Again, Scotland provided more places at university (1 place for every 1,000 of the population) than England (1: 5,800) and the ratio of places in secondary schools was better in Scotland

THE EDUCATION ACT (1872)

☑ *Education was made compulsory between the ages of five and thirteen.*

☑ *Schools were to be managed at the local level by elected school boards whose job was to ensure efficient education, enforce attendance, provide additional accommodation and fix school fees.*

☑ *The Scotch Education Department (SED) was set up to oversee the Scottish educational system.*

☑ *Public schools were open to all denominations, but denominational schools did not have to join the public system. Roman Catholic and Episcopalian schools remained independent until 1918.*

☑ *Public schools would be subject to inspection.*

than in England (1:140 compared to 1:1,300). On the other hand, only about 10% of working-class Scots had access to these secondary schools.

The reality was that education in nineteenth century Scotland was a long way from offering equal opportunities for all. Evidence of the 'lad o' pairts' emerging out of rural poverty thanks to an open door from parish school to university is harder to come by than the mythology might suggest. And what about the 'lass o' pairts'? She did not exist because university education for women was banned until 1893.

FACTORS LEADING TO THE EDUCATION (SCOTLAND) ACT 1872

➤ There was a need to rationalise educational provision under one national authority instead of the mess arising from competing voluntary, charitable and private efforts.

➤ School attendance had to be improved which could only be achieved by the State making schooling compulsory.

➤ All parts of Scotland—urban,

rural, Lowlands and Highlands needed to have equal access to education.

➤ The Church of Scotland, which had pioneered the Scottish educational system, could no longer claim to be the 'national' Church. By 1851, fewer than one-third of churchgoers and one fifth of the population as a whole attended the Church of Scotland; in Glasgow and Edinburgh and in the Highlands, fewer than 10% of the population worshipped in it. The authority of the 'State' Church to guide the nation's education had been steadily eroded since the 1830s by secularisation and the Disruption.

➤ More generally, there was growing concern about the key role played by the Churches as a whole in education. Calls were being made for 'national' (meaning 'non-denominational') education.

➤ The Churches were no longer capable of financing the education of the nation. Only the State could do this. The State had been taking a growing

TYPICAL
Elementary Public School *in the 1880s*

EXTERIOR

Stone-built and surrounded by railings. The date of the building was cut in stone above the entrance. There were two entrances —one for boys and one for girls.

CLASSROOMS

High ceilinged rooms painted in brown or green. Rows of desks clamped to the floor. Each desk seated two pupils. There was an open fire for heating; those at the back of the room were cold. Unplaned floorboards; windows were set high so that pupils could barely see out so that they were not distracted.

HALL

This was located in the centre of the school and was surrounded by classrooms. The hall was used as a gym, a dining hall and for assemblies.

PLAYGROUND

Boys and girls were segregated by high walls; play area was concrete in towns, grass in the country.

TEACHING

All grades were taught by the same teacher using the 'chalk and talk' method. It was possible to have up to sixty pupils in the one classroom using a pupil-teacher as an assistant. Most of the lessons were the three Rs—taught by drilling, repetition and copying. Geography would be learning the names of continents and countries from the wall map of the British Empire. History was learning the dates of battles, names and dates of kings and queens. Religious teaching involved memorising Psalm 23 and later studying "the history of Judah from Hezekiah to the Captivity". Other subjects taught were physical exercises, drawing, poetry, singing, and needlework for girls. Pupils were expected to be quiet and obey instructions; the tawse (belt) was frequently used to keep order and discipline. Writing was done on slates in the early stages and later in copybooks using pen and ink from the inkwell sunk into the desk.

HOURS AND HOLIDAYS

9.00am till 4.00pm. Ten days holiday at Christmas, a week at Easter and two months at summer (late June till early September—up to a month later in the north of Scotland to coincide with the later harvest.)

Senior Certificate in Musical Attainment issued by Rosemount Public School, Aberdeen, June 1888.

A classroom in an Aberdeen school

interest in education. In 1839 building grants were given to the Churches to build schools. Grants were given to encourage 'approved' methods and properly qualified teachers in schools. Her Majesty's Inspectorate was set up and made annual inspections of grant schools.

➤ The *Scottish Education Act* of 1872 should not be seen in isolation but within the wider historical context of social, economic and political developments occurring in Britain and abroad. RD Anderson summarises these trends in the following passage:

"… the construction of State systems of elementary education was a general phenomenon of the age. It can be related to the rise of political democracy, marked by the Second Reform Act of 1867; to the evolution of the modern nation-state, in the age of industrial and military rivalry between the great powers, requiring both more highly educated workers and the inculcation of loyalty and citizenship into the masses; and to the general advance of secularisation, transferring social functions from Church to State under the guidance of the liberal bourgeoisie."[5]

ELEMENTARY EDUCATION 1872-1918

The aim of the 1872 Act was to establish a national system of education. This meant ensuring that all pupils throughout Scotland attended school and that once inside school, they received an efficient education in the basics. In this section, we will find out how effective the public school system was in fulfilling this aim between 1872 and 1918.

Attendance

It would be wrong to portray the 1872 Act as bringing mass education to an unschooled nation. After all, census figures show that only about 10% of Scottish 8–10-year-old children were escaping education before the 1872 Act.

Skene Square School, Aberdeen.

Nevertheless, it took another thirty years to bring about full and regular attendance. Barriers to attendance were gradually removed—for instance from 1890, elementary schooling was free. It was more difficult to convince parents of the benefits of free education when contrasted with the drop in family income which occurred when they withdrew their children from factory or farm labour.

Employers, facing the loss of cheap labour, also needed to be convinced of the merits of schooling. The textile industry, in particular, continued to take on children as young as ten on a half-time basis. In 1883, about 27,000 children were working under 'half-time certificates' ie. they had reached Standard III at school. The Dundee jute industry had 4,500 children (mostly female) on half-time work at this time. This was more than half the children employed in Scottish factories and for this reason, contributed to Dundee's reputation as an "educational black spot"[6] in the pre-1914 period.

Casual and seasonal work continued to undermine regular attendance. Weeding, harvesting and herding took pupils away from the country schools. So many children were needed for the potato lifting

that the school authorities in the east of Scotland arranged for the summer holiday to be split in two, with a later 'tattie holiday' in October. In the cities, pupils earned money from running errands and delivering milk and newspapers. However, opportunities for children to escape school in favour of paid work before the age of twelve were increasingly blocked off by legislation. The battle for attendance had been won. By the beginning of the twentieth century, nearly all 6–12-year-olds went to school. Apart from France, "Scotland had more children in the age group 5–14 attending school than all other advanced European countries in 1910–11".[7]

School Building

Making school compulsory brought its own problems. Large numbers of new pupils now had to be catered for. In 1874–5 alone, there was a 23.3% increase in the number of children attending school. Between 1872 and 1914, the Scottish public elementary school population rose from 515,000 to 840,000. School Boards struggled to extend existing schools and build new ones. The problem was especially acute in the cities—Glasgow needed to build thirty new schools to meet the shortfall; Edinburgh and Dundee each required seven. However, by the 1880s the building programme had succeeded in housing the urban scholars, albeit often in large, three or four storey buildings containing over a thousand pupils.

Class Sizes

Overcrowding was an ever-present issue in both town and country. Early school classrooms built by School Boards were intended for eighty pupils, but this number could often rise to over a hundred with the teacher and pupil-teacher struggling to keep control of the pupils. These conditions were tolerated under the 1870 Code which allowed a ratio of sixty pupils per adult teacher along with forty pupils per pupil-teacher. The SED took steps to improve the class size issue in 1906 by setting the maximum at sixty pupils per teacher. They also abolished the pupil-teacher. From now on, all teachers would be adult and qualified. However, the cost implications of building new classrooms/schools as well as training more teachers meant that the ideal of average class sizes of fifty taught by qualified teachers had not been achieved by 1914.

The Supply of Trained Teachers

The 1872 Act aimed to provide professional training for all new teachers and to gradually phase out the use of pupil-teachers. However, the Act left the training to the existing Presbyterian and Catholic colleges. Because of the expansion of the educational system and the demand for trained teachers, the colleges struggled to cope, and in 1907 the State took over the running of the Presbyterian colleges. The number of certificated teachers rose from 2,500 in 1870 to 20,000 in 1914. By that time, there were only twenty four untrained pupil-teachers left in Scotland. By contrast, over 3,000 teachers were graduates. The Scottish educational system had made great strides in forty years and school teaching was now a profession.

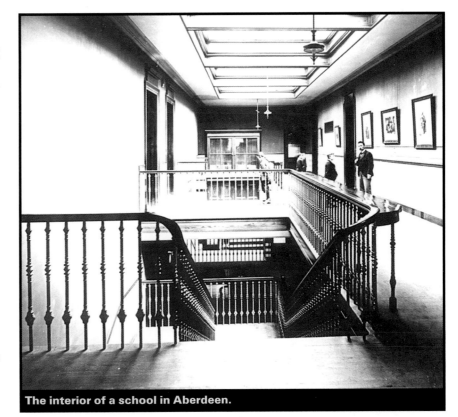

The interior of a school in Aberdeen.

Women and Teaching

In 1872, teaching was mainly a man's job—only 33% of certificated teachers were women; by 1918 most teachers were women (74%). The reason given by Smout for this transformation was that women "were cheap to employ, willing and plentiful, and the school boards needed an immediately augmented supply of inexpensive labour".[8] On average, women were paid half the salary of men for doing the same job. This glaring inequality had not improved by 1914. In that year, a male principal certificated teacher could expect to get £192 a year, whereas a woman in a similar position might only receive £98. Incredibly, the female leadership of the teachers' union, the Educational Institute of Scotland (EIS) publicly opposed equal pay right up to 1914. The inferior status of Scottish women teachers was further highlighted by the fact that, despite having higher qualifications, they were paid less than their female colleagues south of the border. Male teachers in Scotland also found it much easier to get promoted. Despite the fact that 74% of certificated teachers were

female, only 42% of principal teachers' posts went to women. Men had a monopoly on headships.

Clearly then, the traditions of democracy and equality of opportunity which were said to characterise the Scottish educational system did not extend to women teachers. Women were further discriminated against after 1915 when new regulations came in barring married women from teaching.

Payment by Results

The 1872 Act set up a system of 'payment by results' for allocating funds to schools. Under this system, an Inspector would visit the school annually and test each pupil on the three Rs. Parliamentary grants would then be given on the basis of these results. Schools were not slow to realise that they needed to drill pupils using rote memorisation in preparation for the HMI inspection. Gearing up for the inspection became the main focus for school work. Consequently, subjects other than the three Rs were neglected. These distortions were ironed out in 1898

Literacy of Brides and Bridegrooms 1870–1900

(% able to sign their name*)

	SCOTLAND		ENGLAND & WALES	
	Men	Women	Men	Women
1870	90	80	80	73
1875	91	83	83	77
1880	92	85	86	81
1885	94	89	89	87
1890	96	93	93	92
1895	97	95	96	95
1900	98	97	97	97

Table 9.8 Source: Anderson *Education and the Scottish People* page 305

*NB Ability to sign one's name is a very crude measure of literacy, but the only reliable statistical evidence available to historians.

when a new system of block grants based on attendance were brought in for elementary schools. Schools could now concentrate on "permanence, intelligence and development of the whole child's nature".

THE AIMS OF EDUCATION

Before 1872, parish schools aimed to give pupils a basic education in the three Rs as well as solid religious instruction. With the coming of State control, the picture became more complex. Schools were not just there to improve pupils' minds and morals, they were there to produce useful, productive and obedient citizens. Running parallel with politicians' fears for Britain's industrial position compared to Germany came calls for more technical education in schools. Woodwork and elementary science were gradually introduced into the curriculum for boys in the hope of matching Germany's skilled workforce. Prominent Scottish feminists also campaigned successfully for more technical education for girls. They argued that cookery, laundering and other domestic subjects were useful for girls, especially since domestic service was the main source of employment for girls leaving school. Cookery schools to train teachers were established in Edinburgh, Glasgow, Dundee, Aberdeen and Elgin.

Victorian concerns about national efficiency and the physical deterioration of the working class prompted the introduction of physical education into the curriculum. One school inspector as early as 1875 wrote about the need for military drill because the "physique of the working class in this part (Renfrewshire) is degenerating and ... it is desirable to educate a nation vigorous in body as well as mind".[9] 'Drill' became a compulsory subject in 1895. Fears about the degeneration of the urban working class were borne out by the poor physical condition of recruits for the Boer War in 1900. The SED reacted to this by advising schools to pay more attention to the physical training of boys because the defence of the Empire depended on them. Concerns about national efficiency were also behind the *Education Act* of 1908 which brought in school meals and medical inspection of pupils in Scotland.

Education in the State sector was clearly no longer just about the intellectual development of the young. Schools were expected to fulfil the wider aims of government policy such as turning out young adults for the industrial labour market. These young people were being prepared at school to do their duty for King and Country.

Of course, government policy was felt in schools throughout Britain, not just in Scotland, and the effect was to erode the separate and distinctive character of Scottish schools.

Literacy

It is clear from the figures in Table 9.8 that Scotland already enjoyed a high degree of literacy prior to 1872. Nine out of ten boys could write in the 1860s—testimony to the effectiveness of the three Rs taught under the parish school system. Although the 1872 Act had little effect on male literacy, merely continuing an existing trend, it was successful in closing the gender gap by the end of the nineteenth century. The table also shows higher literacy rates for Scotland compared to England and Wales before legislation came in. Again, we see the effect of compulsory education, which had eradicated national differences by 1900.

Catholic Schools

Pupil to teacher ratios could be as high as 150:1. Catholic teachers were paid less than their equivalents in the State sector. The number of Catholic schools rose from sixty five in 1872 to two hundred and twenty six in 1918. By 1918, one pupil in eight was educated in a Catholic school. The 1918 *Education Act* brought Catholic schools under the control of the new Education Authorities without interfering with the religious character of the schools.

SECONDARY EDUCATION 1872–1918

The 1872 *Education Act* is generally viewed as being a success because it achieved its aim of bringing in universal elementary (or primary) education for the masses. Secondary education, on the other hand, was considered to be more of a luxury and certainly not to be subsidised by the State. After all, the dominant belief in late nineteenth century Britain was in laissez-faire and self-help. Middle-class people were expected to pay for their higher education. Consequently, the 1872 Act had little to say on secondary schooling. Burgh schools which had an 'advanced' curriculum could transfer over to the new School Boards, but they would receive no government grants or any funding from the rates. Only a few transferred, and they suffered in competition with private schools. The latter had flourished in the nineteenth century, responding to the needs of the expanding urban middle class who no longer wished to send their children to private schools in England.

Modern historians are, on the whole, critical of the development of government policy on secondary education in the late nineteenth century. It can be argued that the main effect of the 1872 Act

was to block off traditional opportunities for educational advancement for the less well off. As we have seen, under the old parish school system, the schoolmaster often taught the classics to his ablest pupils, however poor, thus enabling the 'lad o' pairts' to gain access to university. After 1872, these schools were given no financial help to progress beyond the three Rs and so a traditional route out of poverty into the professions was closed up.

The strong link between parish school and university was further weakened in the late nineteenth century by the introduction of entrance examinations and the raising of the age of entry to university to seventeen or eighteen. As most pupils left elementary school at fourteen with no qualifications

(there was no leaving certificate), university was beyond their reach. As one historian points out, "For the great mass of school-leavers, it was the field, the pit, or the factory which beckoned, and universities and secondary schools were part of an alien world".[10]

Unlike today where all pupils progress from primary to secondary school at eleven or twelve, in the late nineteenth century, the State school system was structured vertically whereby most pupils either went to an elementary school or to a secondary school—transfer from the former to the latter was rare. However, access to secondary education gradually improved in the years up to the war. In 1897, only 5% of Scottish pupils went to secondary school; by 1914, the figure had gone up to 15%.

LANDMARKS *in Scottish Education*

Public school, Alyth.

1888 A Scottish Leaving Certificate was introduced for all secondary pupils, public and private. Now the great variety of secondary schools would have one standard to aim for. The new Leaving Certificate was the ancestor of today's Highers.

1892 The SED was granted £60,000 for the extension of secondary education. Annual grants were to follow. Thirty five Secondary Education Committees were set up with the aim of establishing secondary schools capable of preparing pupils for university in every county and burgh.

1898 Advanced Departments were set up in elementary schools to provide practical courses for the mainly working-class pupils.

1901 All pupils had to stay on at school until the age of fourteen.

1903 New 'supplementary courses' were introduced into elementary schools to cater for the needs of pupils who had to stay on. These non-academic courses assumed that "the boys will become ploughmen, crofters, farmers, artisans; the girls will go into shops or factories or into domestic service." (HM Paterson *Incubus and Ideology in Scottish Culture and Scottish Education 1800–1980* page 207.)

This compared favourably with England where fewer than 5% had access to a secondary education.

Although the number of public secondary schools had grown from fifty nine in the 1860s to two hundred and forty nine in 1912, what had also developed was a two-tier class-based system—secondary schools for the middle class preparing them for university, and second-rate elementary schools with supplementary courses preparing the working class for manual employment. The issue of equality of educational opportunity was still to be resolved. On the other hand, Scotland was no different from most countries in the nineteenth century where "education systems developed on marked lines of social class, with little connection between 'popular' and 'élite' education".[11]

THE UNIVERSITIES
Apart from medicine, where Scottish universities are estimated to have turned out 95% of British doctors in the mid-nineteenth century, the quality of university education in Scotland was generally poor. Students could start as early as fourteen years old; no entrance qualifications were needed; the arts degree, based on philosophy, was not specialised enough and graduates often had to go south to obtain further training. By the end of the century though, the Scottish universities had been thoroughly reformed (or anglicised, depending on your point of view). A new Honours Degree was in place, offering a mixture of general and specialised study; efforts were made to improve teaching and research; examinations made entrance to university more exacting; women were at last allowed entry in 1893.

Scottish universities were certainly accessible to a wider cross-section of society than Oxford and Cambridge, but they were still largely middle-class institutions—"The reality was that the son of a minister had a hundred times better

chance of going to university than the son of a coalminer."[12] By no stretch of the imagination could a Scottish university education be called 'democratic' when fewer than 2% of the population were able to access it by 1914.

EDUCATION 1918–39
The 1918 *Education Act* set out a number of important reforms of the Scottish educational system.

➤ Secondary education from now on was to be made available without charge.

➤ The Act proposed to raise the leaving age to fifteen, but this was delayed until after the Second World War.

➤ Catholic schools, which had struggled to resource the education of the mainly Irish immigrant population of south-west Scotland, were now brought into the State system.

➤ Schools Boards were abolished, to be replaced by directly elected county and city education authorities.

The 1918 Act did not, however, address concerns about the structure of secondary education. Given that the universities had been reformed and mass elementary education was well established by 1918, post-primary education became the pressing issue of the interwar years. The debate centred on whether secondary education should be available for all pupils or just for the élite preparing for higher education.

After the war, there was a growing demand among parents for increased access to secondary schooling as of right, but obstacles lay in the way. In the interwar economic climate, governments were unwilling to finance such a costly venture. Under government regulations, secondary schools got more money for teachers, classes and facilities than primary schools. Allowing more secondary schools would inevitably be expensive. Furthermore, the policy makers in the SED favoured the élitist approach of limiting access to secondary schooling only to the

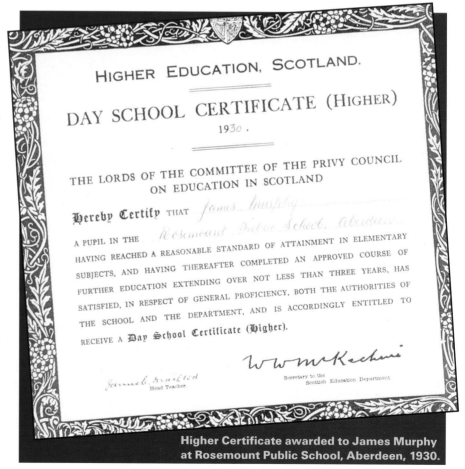

HIGHER EDUCATION, SCOTLAND.

DAY SCHOOL CERTIFICATE (HIGHER)

1930.

THE LORDS OF THE COMMITTEE OF THE PRIVY COUNCIL ON EDUCATION IN SCOTLAND

Hereby Certify THAT *James Murphy*

A PUPIL IN THE *Rosemount Public School, Aberdeen*

HAVING REACHED A REASONABLE STANDARD OF ATTAINMENT IN ELEMENTARY SUBJECTS, AND HAVING THEREAFTER COMPLETED AN APPROVED COURSE OF FURTHER EDUCATION EXTENDING OVER NOT LESS THAN THREE YEARS, HAS SATISFIED, IN RESPECT OF GENERAL PROFICIENCY, BOTH THE AUTHORITIES OF THE SCHOOL AND THE DEPARTMENT, AND IS ACCORDINGLY ENTITLED TO RECEIVE A **Day School Certificate (Higher)**.

W W McKechnie
Secretary to the
Scottish Education Department

James Crawford
Head Teacher.

Higher Certificate awarded to James Murphy at Rosemount Public School, Aberdeen, 1930.

academically gifted. The SED view was that "... the school population falls into two parts—the majority of distinctly limited intelligence, and an extremely important minority drawn from all ranks and classes who are capable of responding to a much more severe call".[13] The SED was plainly more concerned to provide for the "extremely important minority" than for the majority.

The SED set out its blueprint for secondary education in Circular 44, issued in 1921. This controversial document organised secondary education into a rigid, two-tier system. The minority would have access to a full five-year course leading to the Leaving Certificate; the majority would be taught two-year supplementary courses renamed 'Advanced Divisions' in their elementary school. Here, "the standard of work was poor ... since the staff were not sufficiently qualified to go beyond the requirements of primary education".[14] Clearly then, the position of the majority was essentially the same as it had been at the turn of the century—second-class pupils in receipt of second-rate education. They were 'non-secondary', 'non-academic', 'non-certificate'. According to the historian Andrew McPherson, the division of post-primary schooling implemented by the SED in the 1920s, "set the pattern of ... schooling for the next half century." This pattern condemned the majority of school pupils to the 'failure' of leaving school 'early' with no qualifications. On the other hand, the SED greatly increased the number of schools it recognised as secondary (from fifty five to two hundred and fifty). Scottish pupils also had better access to a secondary education than their counterparts in England and Wales.

The SED was forced to admit to its bias in 1936 when it had to reply to the accusation made in Parliament that secondary schools were better funded than 'Advanced Division' schools. Its own evidence showed that building costs per pupil for secondary schools were double those for Advanced Division schools. The pupil to teacher ratio was also better in the secondaries—twenty four pupils per teacher compared to thirty per teacher in the Advanced Departments.

The 1936 *Education Act* did little to narrow the gap. All post-primary schools were renamed secondary schools. Nevertheless, this did not mean secondary education for all. The same old divisions remained. There would be three-year 'junior' secondary schools for the majority (no leavers qualification) and five-year 'senior' secondary schools for the minority with 'natural ability' (leaving certificate leading to university entrance). A 'clean cut' would be made between primary and secondary school at age twelve. The problem of allocating pupils to the two sectors was 'solved' by the introduction of the Intelligence Test which was supposed to be able to determine which pupils had 'natural ability'. In fact, this spurious, 'scientific' test helped to shore up the social divisions in Scottish education right up until the coming of comprehensivisation in the mid-1960s.

EDUCATION AND SCOTTISH IDENTITY

"One thing the Scots can never be said to have lacked is identity."[15]

So wrote Tom Nairn in an influential book entitled *The Break-up of Britain*. Historically, education has played a vital role in keeping this sense of identity alive since the Act of Union. As part of that Union 'deal' in 1707, Scotland retained for all time its own legal system, its Established Church and its separate educational system. These institutions became the "transmitters of Scottish national identity from one generation to the next".[16] How important was the educational system in shaping Scotland's self-image between 1880 and 1939? Generally speaking, writers during that time saw it as central to the nation's distinctive identity. Modern historians are much more sceptical.

In the period 1880–1939, Scots in general showed pride in their educational heritage. Frequent reference would be made to the more 'democratic' qualities of Scottish education such as the "relative absence of class barriers and the encouragement of social mobility".[17] These 'democratic' characteristics were also supposed to be a hallmark of the Scottish people in general. The following passage, written in 1912, is typical of Scottish attitudes at the time:

"Other countries may have shown a finer flower of scholarship, but in none has the attitude towards education been so democratic, so thoroughly imbued with the belief that learning is for the whole people, so socialised as to afford the spectacle of the sons of the laird, the minister, and the ploughman, seated on the same bench, taught the same lessons, and disciplined with the same strip of leather."[18]

Never far away from discussion of Scottish educational achievements was the 'lad o' pairts'. Anderson says, "Such myths are often central to the identity and self-image of nations".[19] As we have seen though, the Scottish educational system was neither 'democratic' nor egalitarian. According to the historian Helen Corr, gender inequalities were rife in Scottish schools and universities and women teachers were even more oppressed than their colleagues in England. The 'lass o' pairts' does not feature in the literature of the period which revolves around the achievements of men. Corr argues that educationalists in the twentieth century helped to sustain the myth that "the Scottish educational tradition reflects the finest qualities of Scottish national identity".[20]

Between 1880 and 1939, Scottish education was regularly compared in a favourable light to its English counterpart by Scottish writers.

George Lewis, writing about the parish schools says "… in these alone we survive as a nation—stand apart from and superior to England".[21] Behind this boasting lay the ever present threat of assimilation from the larger neighbour south of the border. 'Anglicisation', whether real or imagined, was strongly resisted. In an influential book on the history of Scottish education, George Davie says that "Throughout the nineteenth century … in spite of increasing assimilation … the Scots stuck to this policy of apartness in social ethics … (which rested on) … the distinctive life of the country … in the mutual interaction of religion, law and education".[22] Having and retaining a separate educational system was for many Victorian Scots "a vital element in the preservation of Scottish identity".[23]

In recent years, historians have been reassessing the role of education in shaping Scotland's national identity. Michael Lynch, for example, downgrades the importance of the established institutions and says new organisations were rising up to replace them. The "renewed sense of Scottish identity (which appeared in the period 1850–1920) depended not so much on official institutions as on various agencies in civil society, ranging from friendly or temperance societies to the Boys' Brigade. These new developments were all the more important because by 1850 the three main institutions which had protected Scotland's identity since 1707—the Church, education and the law—were already on the retreat"[24] and were "buckling under the strain of urbanisation and industrialisation".[25]

There can be no doubt that the teaching of Scottish history in schools was and is a powerful means of transmitting Scotland's distinctive national identity from generation to generation. However, Scottish history was certainly on the retreat for a time after 1886 when mainly British history was taught. According to one inspector, learning about Scottish history only encouraged Scots to resent the English. Instead, Scots should be taught that they were citizens of a greater Britain and should learn about the achievements of the Empire. Only after a campaign by organisations like the Scottish Patriotic Association and the St Andrews Society was the teaching of Scottish history restored to the curriculum in 1907.

The position of Scottish history was again eroded between the wars. According to the historian Richard Finlay, "the teaching of Scottish history was not encouraged, except within the opportunity offered by the Scottish Education Department for 'local history'—a notion that offended many".[26] Finlay argues that the dislocations caused by the First World War and the economic decline suffered by Scotland during the interwar years brought about a loss of national self-confidence—an identity crisis—and this was reflected in the downgrading of 'national' history teaching in schools. War and Depression, not the educational system, were the determinants of Scotland's changing identity in the interwar years.

With education increasingly anglicised and the other traditional, middle-class Scottish institutions under pressure, the working class became "the true heirs to authentic Scottish traditions, particularly in the field of popular culture and sport".[27]

Leisure and Popular Culture in Scotland 1880s–1939

WHAT YOU WILL LEARN

- ■ The main factors influencing changes in leisure patterns in Scotland between 1880 and 1939.

- ■ The main reasons why many sports became professional and commercial.

- ■ An understanding of why drink played a major part in popular culture and the response of authority to the drink culture.

- ■ An explanation of why gambling, dancing and the cinema grew in popularity during this period.

- ■ A knowledge of how and why tourism spread to the working class.

- ■ The arguments for and against the proposition that Scotland developed a distinctive culture during this period.

WE LIVE IN AN AGE where mass entertainment and the leisure 'industry' are big business. We take all of this for granted, but it was not always so. The last century has seen massive changes in our pattern of culture in Scotland. Historians have only recently latched on to 'popular culture' as a major theme for research. There is considerable academic interest in the period 1880–1939 because many of the modern forms of sport and entertainment were forged during that time.

The general trend in late nineteenth century Scotland and Britain away from laissez-faire towards more intervention was mirrored in the fields of leisure and popular culture. Repeated attempts were made by the State, local authorities, Churches and the middle class to control the 'rough' aspects of popular culture such as drinking and gambling and to divert the working class towards more 'rational' forms of recreation which, it was hoped, would educate, civilise and improve the masses. The years between 1880 and 1914 saw the growth of public parks, swimming baths, libraries, art galleries and museums where

A variety of social, economic, cultural and technological factors which affected the way Scots spent their 'leisure' time in the late nineteenth and early twentieth centuries can be identified.

- ● Working hours were shortened from sixty a week in the middle of the nineteenth century to fifty four in the 1880s, with workers being given a half-day off on a Saturday. These two factors, combined with the trend towards holidays with pay and the gradual improvements in overall standards of living and affluence, created more disposable income for the workforce to enjoy their time away from the factory or office.

- ● A more energetic working class emerged thanks to better diet, social welfare and health.

- ● Women gained greater freedom which allowed them to increase their participation in leisure pursuits.

- ● The decline in the rural way of life and the growth of urban society created a mass audience for new forms of entertainment.

- ● The coming of steam ships, trains and motor vehicles provided new opportunities for away-days, sightseeing trips, excursions and holidays.

- ● There is evidence of a growing secularisation of society. The Churches, therefore, had to respond to this competition for the hearts and minds of their clientele.

- ● The Great War and the Depression also had an impact.

- ● Mass education and the response of newspapers and publishers to new readership markets affected the people of Scotland.

- ● Sectarianism existed in the south-west of Scotland and had an impact on sport.

- ● Local authorities had to respond to the dangers perceived in 'the rougher aspects of working-class culture'.

- ● Concerns were voiced at the turn of the century about the physical deterioration of the nation and the need to involve the working class in healthy and uplifting activities.

- ● The coming of cinema and radio had an impact on people's lives—in particular the pervasive influence of Anglo-American culture.

the lower orders were expected to pass their time. Public parks were "laid out to ensure orderly walking past labelled flowers and shrubs. In rational leisure, disorder was to be avoided and no opportunity for improvement was to be missed".[1]

By and large, such attempts to 'elevate' the masses failed. By the 1930s, the whole nature of recreation had changed—instead of something you did yourself, "it became something that others were paid to organise on your behalf".[2] Leisure and sport had become 'industrialised' and commercialised. The key was profit. The growth areas in entertainment—the cinema, dance hall, music hall and football—were ones which catered for 'popular' or working-class tastes. By 1939, there was an unspoken acceptance of working-class 'rough' culture by the social élite. After all, many of the middle class by then went to the cinema and dance hall, placed legal bets and drank in licensed restaurants. To condemn and try to control such activities smacked of hypocrisy.

SPORT

"Sport, in its modern, organised, commercialised and extensive form, was truly an 'invention' of the Victorian and Edwardian age."[3]

In the fifty years prior to the First World War, sport underwent a 'revolution'. Out went the amateur, localised pastimes and in came national leagues, rules and regulations governing field sports, permanent stadiums, commercialisation, professionalism, vast spectator interest, and rising levels of popular participation in new as well as in older sporting activities.

Football

Football is the clearest example of a sport transformed out of all recognition during the period under study. Initially an upper-class game whose rules were codified in the rarefied atmosphere of England's top public schools, soccer was rapidly adopted by the labouring masses as the game to play and

ATTENDANCE AT SCOTLAND V ENGLAND INTERNATIONALS 1872–1939			
1872	4,000	1904	40,000
1874	7,000	1906	102,000
1876	16,000	1910	110,000
1878	15,000	1912	127,307
1880	10,000	1914	120,000
1882	10,000	1921	100,000
1884	10,000	1923	71,000
1886	11,000	1925	92,000
1888	10,000	1927	111,000
1890	30,000	1929	111,214
1892	21,000	1931	129,810
1894	46,000	1933	134,710
1896	57,000	1935	129,693
1898	40,000	1937	149,547
1900	64,000	1939	149,269
1902	15,000		

Table 9.9 Source: Figures from Andrew Ward *Scotland: the Team*

watch. Unlike cricket and rugby which required specially prepared grounds, football could be played in the back court or in the street and for this reason gained the loyalty of the workers. Games were easily organised, the rules were not difficult to understand and no expensive equipment was needed. By the 1880s, it is reckoned that one in four males in Central Scotland was a member of a football club.

THE IBROX TIE.

'Parting at the Bank.' *Scottish Referee,* 10 February 1908.

From its amateur and middle-class origins at Queen's Park, football in Scotland developed a professional and working-class profile, responding to the new realities of competition, commercialism and increased spectator support. The football winter season was gradually extended and ambitious clubs bought their own grounds, enclosed them and built stadiums. Staff were appointed to maintain the pitch and other facilities and spectators were charged for entry to games. Appearance money and illicit fees were paid to attract better players. By the 1870s, many of Scotland's quality players were moving to English clubs where professionalism was accepted and large fees were available. Finally in 1893, the Scottish Football Association followed England and legalised the professional game. The number of professional players in Scotland rose from 560 in 1893 to 1,754 in 1914. The successful teams were also city clubs which benefited from large gate receipts and fan expectations. By the early twentieth century, the main Glasgow sides, Hearts, Hibs and Dundee were all trophy winners. By the First World War, football had estab-

Milestones in SCOTTISH FOOTBALL

1867   Foundation of the first Scottish club—Queen's Park. First matches were between the club's own members—smokers versus non–smokers!

1870   Queen's Park competed in the first FA Cup competition in England.

1872   Glasgow Rangers founded at Kinning Park. First International: England 0 Scotland 0 (attendance 4,000)—Queen's Park provided all the Scottish players.

1873   Scottish Football Association and the Scottish Cup competition were formed but Scottish clubs still played in the English FA Cup.

1874   Hearts founded (Edinburgh).

1875   Hibernian founded (Edinburgh)—for Catholic players only.

1878   First Scotland v England International at Hampden (attendance 15,000, score 7–2).

1888   Celtic founded as a charitable organisation to help the Catholic Irish in Glasgow.
        Rangers moved to Ibrox Stadium.
        SFA ordered Scottish clubs to withdraw from the FA Cup competition—Scottish clubs could no longer be members of the FA.

1890   Scottish League set up with regular fixtures.

1893   Hibs reconstituted as a non-sectarian club. Professionalism legalised in Scotland. Dundee FC founded.

1902   Twenty five people died in the Ibrox Stadium disaster.

1903   Aberdeen FC founded.
        New Hampden stadium opened.

1906   102,000 attended International against England.
        116 clubs affiliated to the SFA.

1937   A record 149,547 attended the Scotland versus England match at Hampden. (Score 3–1)

International—Scotland and England, 1898.

"THE CROWD."

lished itself as the premier spectator sport, with average attendances at Scottish Cup Finals rising spectacularly from 8,500 in the 1880s to 51,000 by 1914. The 'people's game' was now firmly rooted in Scotland's urban, male working-class culture.

Early on in football's history, sectarian rivalry emerged between Dundee and Dundee Hibs and in Edinburgh between Hearts and Hibernian (who only allowed Catholic players until 1893). However, the 'Old Firm' held centre stage in the sectarian battle. The origins of the Rangers–Celtic 'bad blood', first reported in 1896, can be summarised as follows: "Celtic became the champions of the Irish Catholic immigrants, and Rangers the flagship of the native Scottish Protestants who feared this influx."[4]

Celtic got off to a flying start. The club, founded by Brother Walfrid as a charity, was quickly taken over by members of the local Irish-Catholic business community and run for profit. By 1893, Celtic had won all the major trophies—the Scottish Cup, the Glasgow Cup, the Scottish League Championship and the Charity Cup. Success on the pitch enabled the club to build a 70,000 capacity stadium—the largest in Britain at the time. In 1898, the club recorded a healthy profit of £16,000.

Rangers did not start off as an overtly Protestant club. However, in the 1890s it became the main focus for a strong, working-class Protestant identity (which was anti-Catholic and anti-Irish). Quite simply, Rangers were the only team who could halt Celtic's success, seen in nationalist terms as Irish dominance of Scottish football. When Rangers began to challenge 'the Irishmen' in 1894, winning the Scottish and Glasgow Cups, many supporters were attracted to Rangers as the defenders of 'native prestige'. Reflecting as it did the wider tensions between Protestants and Catholics in

Rutherglen Hockey Club, First Eleven, seasons 1913–1914.

south-west Scotland, the 'Old Firm' divide developed into "the most intense and enduring sporting symbol of sectarian rivalry in not only Scottish but western European society as a whole".[5]

Football was also tarnished with its fair share of hooliganism and violence. There was no 'age of innocence' when fans behaved impeccably. Disorder and wilful disruption of games were commonplace in the late nineteenth century. Scottish football crowds were generally less well behaved than their English counterparts, unlike today. Attacks on referees occurred; bottles were thrown onto the pitch. Crowd violence was at its worst in the decade prior to the First World War. Sectarianism added to the problem. During the 1909 Cup Final between Celtic and Rangers, "spectators invaded the pitch, uprooted the goal posts and tore off the nets, set pay-boxes on fire, broke gaslights all round the ground, and united to throw stones at police and firemen (who threw them back), inflicting injuries to 130 people, 30 of whom went to hospital".[6] However, incidents like this were rare. Neil Tranter's research in the Stirling

area suggests that crowd troubles were only a problem at one in every two hundred matches involving football clubs of senior status. Nevertheless, by the 1890s the middle class had already given up on football as a game prone to violence and one which had failed to elevate and civilise the working class as either players or spectators.

Other Sports
Although football eclipsed or marginalised other sports during this period, there was still a general increase both in the watching and playing of sport. Cricket, for example, was widely played in the eastern part of Scotland where the chances of rain stopping play were less than in the west. Quantitative evidence of uptake for sport is thin on the ground but, if Tranter's research on the Stirling area is in any way representative, it shows that, over a wide range of sports, late nineteenth century Scotland saw an unprecedented growth in popular enthusiasm for sporting activity.

"... the number of curling clubs rose from twenty five in the 1830s ... to roughly one hundred in the 1870s, angling clubs from one in the 1840s

DRINK
in Scotland 1880–1939

Date	1	2	3	4
1880-9	1.69	31.2	72	105
1890-9	1.63	18.2	88	103
1900-9	1.60	16.1	103	107
1910-9	1.00	14.2	75	76
1920-9	0.55	12.4	45	47
1930-9	0.35	12.0	27	37

1 Consumption of spirits (gallons) per head of population per year
2 Publicans' spirit licences per 10,000 of population
3 Convictions for drunkenness per 10,000 of population per year
4 Alcoholic mortality per 1 million per year

Table 9.10
Source: Adapted from GB Wilson, *Alcohol and the Nation (1940)*.

to twenty eight in the 1880s, bowling clubs from five in the 1840s to forty three in the 1890s, cricket clubs from five in the 1840s to one hundred and seventy three in the 1870s, quoiting clubs from ... thirteen in the 1840s to forty five in the 1890s and golf clubs from one in the 1850s to thirty one in the 1890s ... Between the 1870s and the 1890s the number of cycling clubs rose from four to thirty, lawn tennis clubs from three to thirteen, amateur athletics meetings from six to thirty three."[7]

A few sports did suffer as the market-place expanded. Shinty retreated into the Highlands and professional rowing also decreased in popularity. Professional athletics attracted large crowds up until the turn of the century. Twenty five thousand punters attended the opening of the new Powderhall Stadium in 1870. In 1884, Harry Hutchens of Putney set a world best of 30.00 seconds in the 300 yards race—a record which still stands today. However, the nobbling of races to line the pockets of betting syndicates became too prevalent and pedestrianism (professional athletics) was discredited and went into decline. Cricket, which had become a popular

working-class game by the 1880s had lost its appeal by 1939.

One historian, WH Fraser, argues that sports like cricket, rugby, athletics and rowing failed to acquire a mass following because the middle-class cliques which dominated them refused to give up the amateur ideal in favour of professionalism. Behind their high-minded beliefs lay a social snobbery and a reluctance to spread their sport to the lower orders. Unlike football, which embraced professionalism, rugby remained amateur until 1995 and its middle-class, public school image undoubtedly hindered its development. Only in the Borders did rugby secure popular support where it was "seen as part of a tradition of rough athleticism harking back to the 'mass football' ... of the early nineteenth century".[8] Other sports like professional boxing, which lost its upper-class image, attracted strong working-class loyalties in Scotland. A record forty thousand watched the Benny Lynch fight in 1937.

Sport in Scotland, as in the rest of Britain, remained male-dominated throughout the period. Cricket, rugby and football were largely closed to women players. More genteel games like golf, swimming and tennis did allow

inroads. Female swimmers were competing in Scotland as early as 1892. A small minority of curling and golf clubs had women members. Gradually women gained entry to games requiring more physical exertion (and hence less decorum). The first lacrosse International against England was held in 1913. Badminton became a popular female sport.

DRINK
Nineteenth century popular culture in Scotland was steeped in alcohol—mainly whisky. At its peak in the 1830s, Scots were consuming on average 2.5 gallons of whisky per head of population per year. Drink was cheap and easily obtained in licensed premises. In the cities, the 'local' was always within staggering distance of home. Dundee had one public house for every twenty four families!

The 'demon drink' was condemned by the Churches and a temperance movement grew from the 1830s, associating alcohol abuse with poverty, violence and moral decay. The attack on the 'rough culture' associated with drink took two forms. The first was to provide uplifting, rational recreation in the form of alternative, drink-free venues—concerts, lectures, dances, tearooms and temperance hotels—for those who had turned their backs

A 'ROUGH' GUIDE TO THE DRINKING HABITS OF THE SCOTS

Lowland Scot	*Drinks spasmodically but intensely for complete release and to obliterate the miseries of industrial life—whisky makes drunks more excitable*
Highland Scot	*Can drink vast quantities of whisky without apparent ill-effect*
Middle-class Scot	*Drinks privately—if drunk in public, tries to conceal the fact*
Working-class Scot	*Drinks publicly—openly and publicly flaunts his drunkenness*

Adapted from TC Smout and S Wood, *Scottish Voices 1750–1860* pages 151–3

Advertisement for Sandeman's whisky, 1903.

on the bottle. A youth section of the temperance movement, called the Band of Hope, organised 'magic lantern' shows. From 1883, the Boys' Brigade provided another diversion from the temptation to drink. When the BBs introduced Saturday football leagues in 1893, membership shot up and by 1934 had reached 36,000 throughout Scotland. A second, more direct attack on the drinking class came with legislation which, in 1920, allowed 40 out of 586 local wards to ban the sale of drink in their area.

The dramatic decline in the consumption of alcohol which took place between 1880 and 1939 owed more to state action than to the efforts of the temperance movement. In particular, drink simply became too expensive thanks to steep rises in excise duty.

The direct link between price and consumption was first observed in 1909 when duty on whisky went up by 34%, resulting in an 18% drop in sales. In 1860, tax on a gallon of whisky was 10 shillings; in 1920, it was 72 shillings. Consumption was also hit by high levels of unemployment in the interwar years as well as by alternative leisure pursuits. Quite simply, going to the cinema was better value for money. For the price of a pint, you could get two or three hours of entertainment in more wholesome

surroundings than the pub. Instead of it being an end in itself, drink in Scotland became part of the more diverse, recreational culture of the 1930s.

GAMBLING

Although gambling was never restricted to one social class, Victorian and Edwardian society was particularly concerned about the effects of betting on the morals of the working class and the young. In this respect, Scotland was later than England in intervening in the 'rough' culture of gambling. The *Betting Act* of 1874 made most forms of betting illegal. Between 1880 and 1939, the only way the ordinary punter could place a legal bet was to go to a horse-racing course (there were few in Scotland and these were difficult to get to for the urban workers) or arrange credit with a bookie and make the bet by phone, letter or telegram. Even coin-operated fruit machines were banned in Scotland in 1917. These restrictions were clearly designed to discourage working-class gambling. However, like other aspects of popular culture under legal assault, then as now, working-class betting was not eradicated but simply driven into the illegal sector.

Between the wars, recreational gambling grew with the introduction of nationally-run football pools and the building of greyhound-racing tracks. The pools were legal because the coupons were a postal bet. It is estimated that, by 1939, ten million households in Britain were doing the pools. Even the unemployed, who could not afford to go to the match, were able to put a small stake on the outcome of the Saturday fixtures. Dog racing was first introduced in 1926 with the electric hare. By 1932, there were twenty two dog tracks in Scotland, usually in the working-class inner city areas. By the 1930s, gambling had become a huge industry and the authorities privately recognised that it could not be suppressed. The courts continued to

convict for gambling offences but fines were mostly for a token amount.

THEATRE/ MUSIC HALL

The music hall grew in popularity in the cities from the 1880s and reached its peak in the years prior to World War I. The 'penny gaffs' as they were called, attracted a mainly working-class audience. The atmosphere was noisy, smoke-filled, drunken, vulgar and sometimes disorderly. On stage dancing, singing, comedy, magic, hypnotism, conjuring, ventriloquism and 'electrical wizardry' were performed to notoriously fickle audiences who "struck terror into English entertainers as artistic judgment was displayed by way of pennies and rivets on the stage".[9]

Variety theatre appeared at the turn of the century to challenge the music hall and provide a more wholesome and reputable entertainment for the middle class. Impresario HE Moss established a chain of variety theatres throughout Britain—the Moss Empires. Efforts were made to control or filter out the rough element by providing ornate interior design with fixed rows of seats, banning standing audiences, making the new

Charlie Chaplin and Harry Lauder

HM Theatre in Aberdeen early 1900s.

first decade of the century) in working-class districts of the city.

As the 'pictures' grew in popularity, purpose-built cinemas catering for a more middle-class clientele were sited in the city centres with ornate decor, wall-to-wall carpeting and plush seats. The first of these was the Electric Theatre in Glasgow in 1910. By the 1920s and '30s—the heyday of the cinema, picture houses were in every town and even larger villages had one. Big city cinemas could seat thousands and were luxuriously appointed. In 1939, Glasgow could boast one hundred and fourteen

His Majesty's Theatre
ABERDEEN
OF FREDK. MELVILLE'S NEW SENSATION.

Monday, April 5th, 1909
And during Week.

THE UGLIEST WOMAN ON EARTH
FRED MELVILLE

THE WOMAN WHOSE FACE HAS NEVER BEEN SEEN

The Veiled Woman, will make her Appearance at His Majesty's Theatre, Aberdeen in the new and Original Play of Extraordinary Interest,

THE UGLIEST WOMAN ON EARTH

The New and Original PLAY OF EXTRAORDINARY INTEREST,
BEST DRAMATIC COMPANY OUT OF LONDON

theatres alcohol free, by ending encores and censoring stage material. Family entertainment became the order of the day. Popular acts knew how to manipulate the emotions of the audience by portraying a distorted, sentimental image of a 'tartanised' Scotland which bore little relation to the contemporary, urban reality—and was the more effective because of that. The foremost exponent of this tradition was the comedian and singer Harry Lauder.

"The ower thrifty wee mannie with his crooked stick, his cackling voice and his pawky humour, was a superficial caricature, and his jokes, like the words of his sentimental songs, lie leaden on the printed page."[10]

Nevertheless, Sir Harry, the former miner, was idolised wherever he played, whether it was Glasgow, London or America and his songs *I Love a Lassie* and *Roamin' in the Gloamin'* were the big hits of the time.

The turn of the century also saw the development of the pantomime tradition, which drew a wider audience than the 'serious' theatre. Pantomimes were popular in Scotland because the storyline was often given a local, topical dimension. Good stunts and special effects were also laid on. Pantomimes in the Royal Princess Theatre in Glasgow often ran from December until the summer.

CINEMA/ DANCING

The popularity of variety and music hall went into decline in the 1920s and 1930s with the rise of the cinema. The 'movies', however, go back as far as 1895 when travelling showmen introduced moving pictures as side shows in fairground booths. By the following year, most towns and many villages had been introduced to the motion picture. Soon they were put on as part of variety or music hall performances in the cities. By the early twentieth century, cinema companies were looking for permanent premises. The first 'cinemas' were converted factories, shops or derelict roller skating rinks (a short-lived craze in the

cinemas—more per head of population than any other city in the world. Unlike other forms of entertainment, going to the cinema was not confined to one social class—it was a mass activity. Cheap, diverting and warm, the picture house became a weekly habit for 80% of the young unemployed during the Depression.

The early films were, of course, silent. Charlie Chaplin and Laurel and Hardie were the big film stars of that era. Silent films were often enlivened by a piano accompaniment and the largest city cinemas even had an orchestra. Sound did not come of age until the late 'twenties, but an enterprising Aberdonian elocution teacher by the name of Dove Paterson gave an early glimpse of the talkies by standing behind the screen during the showing of *Oh, What a Night After a Fish Supper* and talking the audience through the story! His 'real' talking pictures were an instant hit and Paterson was able to open his own cinema, the Gaiety, in 1908. The first full-length talkie, combining dialogue and music, to reach Scotland was *The Singing Fool* in January 1929. It ran five times a day to accommodate the queues.

Film output was quickly dominated by Hollywood, especially during the First World War when all the European film studios closed. There was, nevertheless, a small, indigenous Scottish film industry. Early films concentrated on Scottish topics. Short features appeared on the bagpipes, Highland Dancing and Gretna Green. Several versions of *Macbeth* were made and Walter Scott's *Rob Roy* and *The Heart of Midlothian* were also turned into films. According to one writer, "The cumulative effect of these films was to build up an image of Scotland as a wild, romantic country, rich in pictur-

esque drama and blessed with magnificent scenery".[11] In a sense, the early cinema mimicked the music hall's sentimentalised portrayal of Scotland.

A more realistic view of contemporary Scotland was given by John Grierson, the founder of the documentary film movement. His film *Drifters* (1929) on the Scottish herring fishing fleet was followed in the 1930s by a group of films recording the country's industry, history, farming, health, education and sport. These films were intended to "tell the world the other side of Scotland, tear away the tartan curtain of romance and show a nation fighting for its existence".[12] Another popular phenomenon of the 1920s and '30s was the craze for dancing. City culture replaced Highland and Scottish country dancing with the more raucous, jazz-influenced sounds and steps imported from America. Establishment disapproval ('It stinks! Phew open the windows' on the arrival of the Charleston) only served to increase the popularity of the dance hall among the young. Like the cinema, dancing was a cheap

night out and throughout Britain became a national pastime. Glasgow was 'dancing mad' with one hundred and fifty nine registered dance halls in 1934.

HOLIDAYS AND THE GROWTH OF POPULAR TOURISM

Technology and commercialism came together to organise the workers' weekend leisure hours and their annual paid holidays. Improvements in transport opened up the countryside for the urban masses and spawned a new holiday industry in the late nineteenth century. Trips 'doon the watter' started in the 1820s, transporting Glasgow's middle class on day excursions down the Clyde to Largs, Millport, Ardrossan, Dunoon and Rothesay. By the 1870s, the service had been expanded to cater for the 'respectable' working class.

"The cult of Victorian respectability pervaded these day excursions; they were to be a form of rational recreation, educational, healthy and vigorous for the mind and body."[13]

This may have been the intention but commercial reality intruded—many of the steam ships became floating public bars which gave a new meaning to the word steamin'.

Railways opened up the Highlands and north-east of Scotland to the holiday maker. Seaside resorts at Nairn, Lossiemouth and Cruden Bay, and Highland health spa towns such as Strathpeffer provided uplifting and healthy destinations for the middle class. However, Scotland had no equivalent to Blackpool, where millions of workers enjoyed open-air swimming pools, 'pleasure beaches', fairgrounds and cinemas. The first Butlin's all-in workers' holiday camp was built at Skegness in 1937. It was a further ten years before Butlin's started in Ayr.

Appreciation of the 'great outdoors' had, until the 1880s, been the preserve of the better-off.

Car used by the Highland Railway Company to advertise fishing holidays by rail, 1908 or after.

However, increased leisure time and new forms of transport opened up the countryside to a wider range of people. While mountaineering remained an upper-and middle-class activity in Britain, by the 1930s the unemployed in the West of Scotland were gaining access to the hills through the Craig Dhu and Lomond Clubs.

"They met at night at the Craigallion fires near the loch in Milngavie, they read the poetry of Robert W Service and disliking youth hostel rules they slept in the hills on their climbs, in caves, barns and howffs."[14]

The battle for greater access to roam Scotland's private estates without fear of prosecution was taken up by the Scottish Rights of Way and Recreation Society.

The availability of cheap bicycles (£5) added to the mass weekend exodus from the towns in the 1930s. Although the motor car was still outwith the reach of the working class (£100 for a Ford 8 in the late 1930s), private ownership mushroomed (100,000 cars in Britain in 1919; 2 million in 1939). However, the long-distance coach gave the humbler tourist a cheaper alternative to the train for day trips and excursions and enabled more football supporters to attend 'away' matches.

THE IMPACT OF LEISURE AND POPULAR CULTURE ON SCOTLAND'S IDENTITY

The search for Scotland's national identity became something of an obsession for academics in the run-up to the establishment of a Scottish Parliament in 1999. Many felt the need to demonstrate that Scotland was a distinct national entity even after nearly three hundred years without statehood. The historian Tom Nairn accurately sums up the motivation behind this search: "Identity," he says, "is what frustrated nationalities want and nation–states possess".[15]

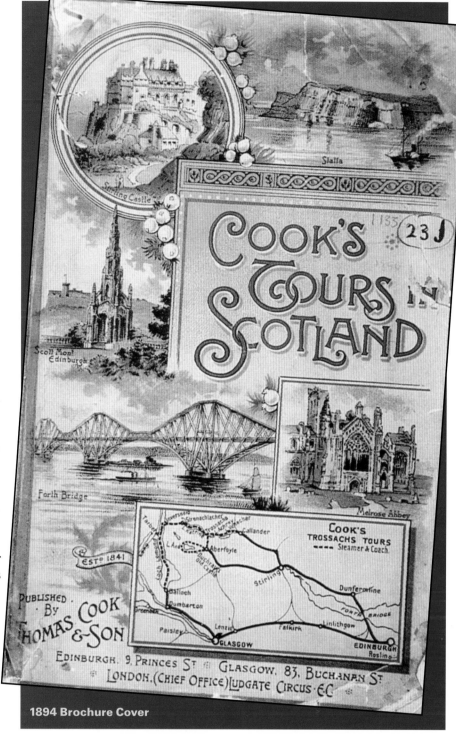

1894 Brochure Cover

The period 1880–1939 is interesting because new organisations associated with the leisure industry began to challenge the Church, the law and education as the standard-bearers of Scotland's identity. Popular culture came to displace élite, middle-class culture. By the 1930s, the working class were, arguably, "the true heirs to authentic Scottish traditions, particularly in the field of popular culture and sport".[16] However, just how distinctive and unified Scotland's national identity became during this time is a matter of debate.

... A DISTINCTIVE CULTURE?

Arguments which support the view that Scotland did develop a distinctive culture

- The traditional middle-class institutions failed to provide leadership in the nineteenth century but Scotland remained distinctive because the 'cultural vacuum' was filled in the 1880s by the "treacly effluent of the Kailyard".[19]

- A renewed sense of Scottish identity did develop from the 1890s, culminating in the 'Scottish Literary Renaissance' of the 1920s. The reaction against 'tartanry' and the Kailyard started with a renewed interest in the works of Robert Burns. After the war, great Scottish writers like Lewis Grassic Gibbon and Hugh MacDiarmid emerged to confront the Scottish people for the first time with their own social condition. Stark realism replaced the romantic escapism of the Kailyard school of writers.

- New national institutions such as the Scottish National Portrait Gallery (1882) and the Scottish History Society (1887) sprang up "giving a renewed focus for Scottish identity and culture".[20] In the postwar period, the tourist industry brought about new national organisations to protect and enhance Scotland's rural heritage eg. the National Trust for Scotland (1931).

- Local identity had not been snuffed out by the forces of modernisation. Instead, locality had transferred from the countryside to the town. "Scottish cities were socially and culturally distinct from English cities."[21] Aberdeen and Edinburgh remained regional centres with "traditional Scottish values". Glasgow's cultural profile was "closer to Europe or America than to England".[22]

- National consciousness depended on this renewed local identity. Evidence of this could be found in the growth of popular local newspapers like the *Aberdeen Free Press* and the Dundee based *People's Journal* which "printed not news as such but a pot pourri of Scottish national, local and literary history, folk tale and popular fiction, mostly in vernacular Scots".[23]

- Contrary to the evidence given opposite about the origins of the SFA, one writer asserts that the schism was about "the nationalism of Scottish football enthusiasts, who preferred to have nothing to do with English football".[24] Football "became a focus for a Scottish national identity ... observable especially at the annual match with England, which in the late thirties attracted 60,000 Scots on trips to Wembley".[25]

Arguments which support the view that Scotland did not develop a distinctive culture

- Scotland's rich local traditions, language and customs had been eroded by 1939 due to urbanisation and mass communications. The new 'national' culture of Scotland was both bland and British.

- The popular Scottish culture which remained (music hall, sentimental 'Kailyard' novels about rural Scotland) was vulgar and a distortion of a former way of life. "New cultural institutions such as the BBC (radio) made few concessions to Scottish national identity."[17]

- Developments in leisure and popular culture were no different from those in the rest of Britain. Football had become Scotland's 'national game', but it was also Britain's national game. Similarly, enthusiasm for the cinema was not just confined to the north of Britain.

- Scotland did not come together as a nation in its leisure time. To a large extent, recreation was divided along class lines: the working class gambled, went to the dog races and watched football; the middle class frequented concerts, art galleries and, apart from in the Borders, provided most of the spectators at rugby matches. In this sense too, Scotland was no different from England.

- The establishment of a separate Scottish Football Association in 1873 is not evidence of a new national consciousness. Rather it was simply the acceptance of reality—cost and distance made it prohibitive for clubs like Queen's Park to compete in the FA Cup and they withdrew. Between 1878 and 1939, there was no clamour for a separate national anthem for Scotland before the annual football International. Scottish fans were as respectful as the English in their rendition of *God Save the King*.

- Football did not contribute to the rise of Scottish nationalism. Despite the massive rivalry surrounding the Scotland-England match, especially in the interwar years, political nationalism failed to take off until the 1960s. It is probably more accurate to see Scottish football fans during that time as 'ninety-minute patriots'.

- The new loyalties were neither to Scotland nor Britain, but to the city where 40% of the population lived by 1900. "Urban life, rather than Scottish identity, was the central fact of late nineteenth century Scotland."[18]

Religious Identity in Scotland 1880s–1939

WHAT YOU WILL LEARN

- **The main features of the Scottish religious landscape.**

- **The attempts of religion to cope with social change.**

- **The growth of secularism.**

- **Sectarianism— Protestant and Catholic identities.**

FROM THE SIXTEENTH century Protestant Reformation to the early twentieth century, religion was a key factor in the shaping of Scottish society.

THE NINETEENTH CENTURY SCOTTISH RELIGIOUS LANDSCAPE

The dominant Christian denomination, the Church of Scotland, was, by the early nineteenth century, the largest of a number of Presbyterian denominations. Its organisational and power structure centred around the members of local churches grouped together in presbyteries. The presbytery had the power to appoint ministers and elders and to deal generally with all Church business at a local level. Each year, every presbytery sent representatives to the General Assembly of the Church of Scotland in Edinburgh. This body discussed and made decisions on all matters, religious and secular, which concerned the Church.

In the Presbyterian system, power rose from the bottom up. In essence it was 'democratic', in contrast with Church organisation in the rest of the UK. The protestant Church of England's leaders (Bishops) were appointed by the state, and the Roman Catholic hierarchy drew its authority from the Vatican. Presbyterianism was therefore an indication of Scotland's religious distinctiveness.

Nineteenth century Presbyterianism was characterised in belief, practice and culture by:

- A fundamentalist approach to the Bible leading to a culture and lifestyle which was strict and prohibitive and particularly 'anti-drink'.

- A Calvinistic theology. This meant that Presbyterians believed that God predetermined or 'predestined' people to go to either heaven or hell.

- Sabbatarianism—strict observance of Sunday as a day of rest and worship.

- 'Hair-splitting' on theological matters. Presbyterians at this time were notoriously unwilling to compromise which eventually led to numerous splits within the Presbyterian denominations.

At the beginning of the nineteenth century the Church of Scotland seemed to be in a position of unassailable strength, providing the Scottish people with a sense of values and permanence in the face of the upheavals of industrialisation and urbanisation. Figures from 1830, however, show that this was not the case. One-third of the population at this time owed alle-

THE 1843 DISRUPTION

Cause
The issue of patronage. This meant that the Crown, the town council and local landowners could select and impose a Minister of their choice on a congregation against its wishes.

Course
A growing group of evangelicals within the Church of Scotland opposed patronage and used the courts between 1833 and 1843 to have it abolished. At the 1843 General Assembly 37% of the Ministers and almost 50% of the members left the Church of Scotland to form a new denomination, the Free Church of Scotland.

Effect
The Church of Scotland was weakened in terms of members, finance and influence. In the Highlands defections to the new Church were high, and in the Lowlands higher in urban than in rural areas. In Aberdeen, the defectors were from the new rising middle class of merchants and entrepreneurs, and were essentially suburban in character.

ries of decline, almost tripled its membership between 1877 and 1914. The Episcopal revival was fuelled by the unhappiness of landowners with developments in the Presbyterian Churches, combined with aggressive evangelism in urban working-class areas. Additionally, the smaller dissenting denominations such as the Baptists, Congregationalists and Methodists were also increasing. Thus, by the turn of the century, the Church of Scotland's dominance was no longer assured.

RELIGION AND SOCIAL CHANGE
How did Scotland's religious community deal with the rapid changes which took place between 1880 and 1939?

As towns and cities grew in size and population, social class divisions between their inhabitants grew. The ministers, elders and deacons in the Presbyterian Churches were essentially middle class. They saw the growing urban working class, who lived in crowded and insanitary conditions, as immoral 'heathens' who were given to drunkenness and violence and who were a threat to ordered capitalist society. In this situation there were three distinct responses from the Churches.

✝ Some saw it as an opportunity for a social and evangelistic 'mission' to the poor, heathen unchurched. By the 1880s many of the Presbyterian Churches, influenced by the revivalist campaigns of the Americans Moody and Sankey in the 1870s, had spawned a multitude of para-Church agencies, for example City Missions, Bands of Hope, Sunday Schools, the Boys' Brigade and many others. These organisations bombarded the poor with religious tracts (leaflets), tea and testimony evenings, and exhortations to temperance.

> "There were missions to seamen and railwaymen, shipyard workers and businessmen as well as evangelistic tents in the major cities for the very poor. Before the advent of secular

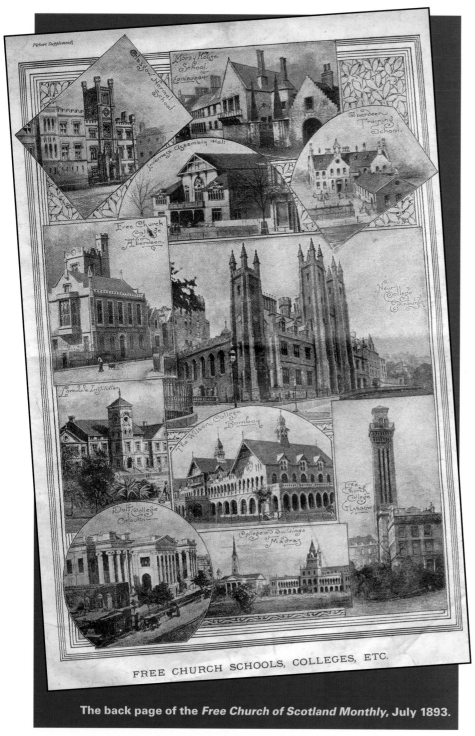

FREE CHURCH SCHOOLS, COLLEGES, ETC.

The back page of the *Free Church of Scotland Monthly*, July 1893.

giance to the dissenting Churches, notably the Episcopalian, Roman Catholic, Secession and Relief Churches. (The Secession and Relief Churches united in 1847 to become the United Presbyterian Church.)

The dominant position of the Church of Scotland came under more pressure with what came to be known as the Disruption of 1843, described by the historian Calum Brown as "the most spec-

tacular Church split in British church history". "Schism," Brown argues, "was endemic in Scottish Presbyterianism".[1]

The other main development during the nineteenth century was the growth of the Roman Catholic and Episcopalian Churches. Catholic growth was caused by the large influx of Irish immigrants in the 1840s and '50s, precipitated by the famine of 1845–46. The Scottish Episcopal Church, after two centu-

sports and the commercial leisure revolution in the late 1880s, organised 'respectable' recreation was dominated by religious occasions like Sunday School excursions, and temperance walks; leisure venues were mostly churches or church halls, or else municipal halls where 'sacred concerts' were a staple until the First World War."[2]

Were these activities effective? The evidence shows that a number of mission stations did eventually become self-financing congregations in their own right, and the statistics of increased Church adherence until the turn of the century indicates that the evangelisation of the working class had some success. Where initiatives by the Churches amongst the poor failed, it was due to the patronising middle-class carriers of the message rather than the message itself.

✝ A number of individual Presbyterian congregations, however, acted in a way which reinforced social class divisions. The system of 'pew rents', whereby an individual rented his or her pew or seat in the church building (this system lasted until the 1960s in some congregations), served to discourage rather than attract working-class adherents. Some congregations even raised pew rents to prevent the working classes from using their church! Other, more middle-class congregations, fearing that they would be engulfed in the process of 'urban sprawl', simply moved to the suburbs where they built new churches out of reach of the poor.

"Where church attendance required either payment for seats or the stigma of occupying the niggardly ration of free sittings, and in any case respectable Sunday clothes, anyone familiar with the incomes of unskilled workers will readily see how unlikely it was that the masses should attend church regularly."[3]

Nevertheless, the Presbyterian middle classes did have a great deal of influence on the shaping of late Victorian Scotland. While some did not wish the working

'Administration of Sacrament in Gravel Pit near Achnacroish, Mull.' Part of the front page of the *Free Church of Scotland Monthly*, July 1893.

classes to share in their worship, they certainly wished the poor to adopt their values. Hence, ministers and elders were well represented on Town Councils, Licensing Courts, School Boards and other municipal bodies.

✝ The experience of the Roman Catholic Church in the nineteenth and early twentieth centuries was different from that of the Presbyterian Churches. While numbers of adherents increased markedly in mid-century through the large influx of Irish immigrants, and continuously but slowly thereafter by 'natural increase', the Church adopted a defensive and 'inward-looking' strategy.

Presbyterian Scotland at this time was an inhospitable environment for Irish Catholic immigrants who, together with internal migrants from the Highlands, settled in its urban areas. In this situation, they gravitated to the Church, whose clergy encouraged a Church-centred lifestyle based on Catholic Young Men's societies and branches of the League of the Cross. Apart from the culture of the Church, life was difficult. In employment there was sectarianism and job-segregation with Protestants dominating

the skilled jobs in engineering and shipbuilding while Catholics dominated the workforce in labouring and carting.

The clergy, however, encouraged assimilation, and in many ways the values of 'respectability', sobriety and self-help which they promoted were similar to those of the Presbyterian community. However, for some ambitious Catholics, gradual assimilation was not enough and by the turn of the century, they had concluded that the only way to 'get on' in society was to 'get out'. Thus they chose to emigrate to the USA, Canada and Australia.

While the Churches did try to meet the challenge of social change, it was clear by the end of the 1880 to 1914 period that the battle was being lost in some areas, and the process of secularisation—the displacement of religious values by those which were more humanistic and materialistic—was beginning to gather pace.

Attendance of Protestant churches and affiliated organisations had ceased to grow and in some areas was in decline. Sunday Schools were losing members. Movement in population was beginning to loosen religious affiliation, and class was beginning to replace the traditional ideas of community. Non-religious marriage ceremonies were becoming more popular. The long-accepted literal interpretation of the Bible was being cast in doubt by individuals within the Church.

State interventionism began to challenge the value of self-help as a route to the improvement of society. Socialism, with its emphasis on equality and community appeared to offer more to the poor than the religious values of self-help and self-denial. During the industrial unrest pre-1914 and the rent strikes and union militancy on Red Clydeside during World War I, the Protestant Churches increasingly appeared to be the enemies, rather than the friends, of organised Labour.

Splits among the Presbyterian denominations made them less effective at dealing with the challenges of industrialisation and urbanisation.

However, by 1914 working-class adherence was still strong amongst the Protestant Churches, and the Catholic Church was continuing to grow in numbers and

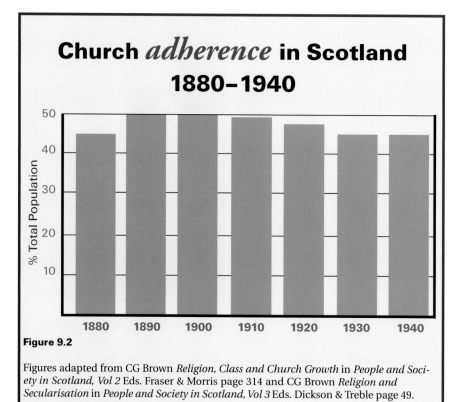

Church *adherence* in Scotland 1880–1940

% Total Population (y-axis: 10, 20, 30, 40, 50)

(x-axis: 1880, 1890, 1900, 1910, 1920, 1930, 1940)

Figure 9.2

Figures adapted from CG Brown *Religion, Class and Church Growth* in *People and Society in Scotland, Vol 2* Eds. Fraser & Morris page 314 and CG Brown *Religion and Secularisation* in *People and Society in Scotland, Vol 3* Eds. Dickson & Treble page 49.

Today, Scotland is a society in which a minority of its citizens have any direct religious affiliation. In attempting to explain this situation, historians have concentrated on two questions: when did the process of religion's decline begin, and what were the causes?

There are two schools of thought in this debate. The traditionalists or 'pessimists' locate the roots of decline at the beginning of the nineteenth century (around 1830) as a direct result of industrialisation and urbanisation. The 'optimists', on the other hand, argue that the decline in religion is a twentieth century phenomenon (the catastrophic fall in Church of Scotland membership did not begin until the 1960s), and cite reasons such as disunity and the failure of the Presbyterian Churches to meet the challenges posed by industrialisation and urbanisation.

Figure 9.2 shows that religious adherence in Scotland was rising during the nineteenth century, reaching its peak around 1905 (the 'pessimist' thesis would expect a fall). Thereafter decline was slow and long, interspersed with spurts of growth.

"After the Second World War, resurgent growth up to 1956 produced a level of adherence only marginally lower than it had been in 1905." [4]

Recent research shows the 'pessimist' argument on the timing of the decline to be misplaced. As to the causes of decline, there are merits to both the 'optimist' and the 'pessimist' arguments. Industrialisation and urbanisation caused tremendous upheaval and fundamental change to a relatively stable society in which religion was at the core. Equally, the failure of the Churches to address those changes and consequent challenges to their legitimacy in a manner which was relevant to the lives of ordinary people must also be seen as contributing to their long-term decline. What is clear is that twentieth century Scotland has been transformed from a largely Presbyterian-dominated society into one in which secular values dominated.

confidence with an improved organisational structure.

THE RISE OF SECULARISM

The rise of secularism in twentieth century Scotland was much slower than in other European countries. The Reverend John White argued that while the 'rot' of secularism had set in before 1914, it was the experiences of many men and women during the conflict which shook their faith in religion, and thus accelerated Scotland's drift away from the Churches and their values.

> "... the shock many people experienced on the discovery of the incompetence of the generals and politicians: religious leaders who blessed the guns and criticised pacifism in the name of Christ rightly shared the general odium."[5]

Thus, given the effects of the war, the growth of alternative ideologies such as Socialism and increased state interventionism, coupled with the general social and economic uncertainties of the period, a widespread collapse in religious adherence might reasonably have been expected. Remarkably, this was not the case in Scotland. The statistics of Church membership and attendance at Communion services show that even though there was a slow decline in the Presbyterian Churches, it was uneven and discontinuous. While membership of the United Free Church declined, and overall Sunday School attendance fell, there was an increase in adherence to the Church of Scotland between 1918 and the early 1930s.

Indeed, recent research has shown that periods of economic hardship in the 1920s produced some outbursts of quite intense religious revivalism in the fishing ports of the north-east and in Lanarkshire mining villages. These upsurges of popular religion occurred outwith the control or leadership of the established mainstream Protestant denominations.

RC Church, Fochabers

By contrast, the hardships of the coal miners in the 1920s, culminating in the General Strike of 1926, also produced a backlash against the Presbyterian Churches, with a decline in numbers attending Communion as a protest against ministers who opposed industrial action.

The Catholic Church fared much better in the interwar years, with a modest but sustained rise in adherence in Scotland's urban areas. In the Western Isles, Catholicism remained very strong on the island communities of Barra and South Uist, where the influence of the Church permeated most aspects of life.

Of the smaller Protestant denominations, the Baptists fared best in the interwar years. While the larger Presbyterian and Catholic denominations were very slow and cumbersome in their approach to church building to accommodate a migrating population, the smaller denominations, being less centralised, adopted a much more flexible strategy. The Baptist Union of Scotland responded by building four new churches in the 1920s (three in Glasgow's new housing schemes and one in Rosyth) which combined with some aggressive evangelistic campaigning, pushed Baptist membership to an all-time high in 1935.

Twentieth century social change, however, worked against religion. Increased leisure time was no longer being devoted to Church activities by the outbreak of World War II. Perhaps this was an inevitable result of better education which led a younger and more self-confident generation to make choices which they found to be more attractive. For the Churches, the reality was that working-class people simply chose to do other things with their time such as cycling, going to the cinema and the dance hall and playing and watching football. In the face of this challenge, the Presbyterian Churches responded negatively, condemning those who organised and took part in such activities.

> "Ministers were especially jealous of football, for it above all aroused exactly the heart-warming zeal and total devotion which they themselves had tried so hard, so painfully and so totally unsuccessfully to arouse for God. Undoubtedly football was the new opiate of the people. But such observations, however true, all begged the question of why these new activities were more addictive than church. In all the investigations there was one hard and unattractive fact which ministers kept striking: the working class could no longer see the point of the kind of church they were faced with in the towns and villages of Scotland."[6]

Even in the Presbyterian heartlands of the Western Isles, the power of religious influence on the young was beginning to erode as the secular culture of the city reached out to Scotland's peripheral areas.

> " ... a visitor to Lewis in the Second World War found an army hut used by the island youth for monthly dances: 'When I asked a young crofter invalided from the navy whether the Elders of the Kirk made no protest, he replied that they had, but had to give it up: They see that we won't stand for it.' This would have been unthinkable during the First World War or after."[7]

The Churches did try to face up to social change. Between 1880 and the 1920s, some clergy and lay members of the Church of Scotland, assisted by some in the Congregational, Free, and United Presbyterian Churches, tried to address the problem of working-class alienation from religion. They argued that the root causes of working-class apathy were the effects of free market capitalism on people's lives and living conditions. This led to the development of Christian Socialism, in which the Churches attempted to take up the cause of the poor, and to distance themselves from the interests of business and property owners. Popular with some ministers and church members for a time, the political and economic upheavals of the interwar period effectively killed off Christian Socialism, although its idealism remained through the work of the Revd. George MacLeod with the unemployed in Govan in the late 1930s with the Iona Community.

In the areas of more popular pursuits, some Churches tried to offer more non-religious activities, attempting to compete with secular society for the hearts and minds of the people. Such strategies did not always produce the desired effect of increased religious commitment.

> "Churches became entertainment centres, and sites of church halls appeared in the 1920s and 1930s: many churches had as many as five halls for their various organisations. The Churches were starting to suffer serious 'goal displacement' where the religious objective of their activities was being overtaken by 'secular' enticements."[8]

As overall religious adherence in Scotland began its slow decline from the early years of the twentieth century, there were also changes in the role played by the Churches in the national life of the country. From 1870 onwards, the Presbyterian Churches had played a significant role in local government, and on a variety of other bodies which gave them a voice in matters such as poor relief, sanitation, health, and education. In education they were represented on the popularly elected School Boards until their replacement by elected county education authorities after the First World War. Church influence continued in this area until the government, fearing that sectarianism was creeping into the triennial education authority elections, legislated to bring education under County Council control in 1929.

After the First World War, the issue of alcohol became a campaigning issue for Presbyterians. The *Temperance (Scotland) Act* of 1913 provided for local veto referendums from 1920. By this legislation, voters in a Ward (a sub-division of a Burgh, Town or County Council area) had the right to vote their district 'dry', that is, free of public houses or off-licences. Extensive Church campaigning at the beginning of the 1920s led to thirty out of Scotland's five hundred Wards being declared 'dry' in local referendums. This early triumph of Presbyterianism in the political arena was short-lived. By the end of the decade, the brewing and distilling lobbies had regrouped and, gaining support from Labour voters in particular, almost completely reversed the result of the early 1920s.

In summary, the interwar period was a time of mixed fortunes for religion in Scotland.

† The experience of people in World War I eroded their faith in religion.

† The institutional role of the Churches in society diminished as national and local govern-

WHAT WERE THE CAUSES OF INTERWAR SECTARIANISM?

Recent research points to the following main factors

1 The economic downturn of the interwar period, with severe and prolonged periods of unemployment in urban Scotland fuelled latent sectarian feeling. Job segregation between the skilled Protestant and unskilled Catholic workforce broke down leading to unrest in the workplace and other meeting places such as dance halls, the streets and at football matches.

2 Large-scale emigration (392,000 between 1921 and 1931) dented Protestant self-confidence and fuelled the sectarian myths of growing Catholic dominance, none of which were based on reality.

3 Protestant influence was strong in Scotland's political parties, particularly the Conservatives, who by the twentieth century had joined forces with the Liberal Unionists (the Liberals who split from their Party over the issue of Irish Home Rule). The Unionists in the interwar period became a vehicle through which the prejudices of some Protestant working-class voters in the West of Scotland found expression. Labour, however, also inherited the votes of many Protestant and Catholic workers at this time, which countered some of the sectarianism of the political right.

4 The existence of extremist political parties, like the Scottish Protestant League and Protestant Action, provided a political home for some voters in the 1930s. These parties had some local success in Edinburgh and Glasgow in the '30s.

5 Politically influential elements of the Scottish business élite in organisations like the West of Scotland Association of Foremen Engineers identified strongly with Protestant loyalism.

6 Local government reorganisation in 1929 finally removed much of the Prebyterian Churches' influence in the areas of education and welfare.

7 Parliamentary legislation in 1921, known as the Declaratory Articles, confirmed the Church of Scotland as the National Scottish Church, reinforcing its freedom from state interference.

8 The reunification of the larger Presbyterian denominations with the Church of Scotland in 1929 boosted the ideology of 'Protestantism'.

"it was an assertion of Protestantism as the guardian of the nation's welfare and identity in the face of a range of threats which included secularisation trends, a growth in communist and socialist politics, and most far-reachingly, the presence of a sizable Catholic community of Irish origin which was considered 'alien'." [11]

ment increased their influence in society.

† There was a slow but uneven decline in adherence and attendance amongst the Presbyterian Churches.

† Churches attempted to compete with secular society through initiatives such as Christian Socialism and increased secular activities in church buildings.

† There were isolated outbreaks of popular religious revivalism and some small denominations enjoyed considerable success.

† Increased education and leisure time gave more opportunity for young people to indulge in various secular pursuits.

SECTARIANISM

Religion in the form of presbyterianism served as a unifying influence in Scottish society in the nineteenth and early twentieth centuries. However, it was also a source of division. Sectarianism in Scotland has a long history and is principally centred around antagonism which existed between the majority Protestants and the minority Catholics. From the early nineteenth century, anti-Catholicism came to be equated with anti-Irish feeling. This was particularly true after the 1840s, although at least one-third of Irish immigrants from this time onwards were Protestant. Additionally, it should be noted that by 1900, Scotland's Catholic population was not exclusively Scottish or Irish, but also comprised Italians, (3,000 in Glasgow and 1,000 in Edinburgh) and Polish and Lithuanian refugees who had found work in the Lanarkshire coalfields.

Until the outbreak of World War I, sectarian antagonism was evident in Scotland's growing urban industrial heartlands. Historians are nevertheless divided on this issue. Some argue that in Scotland pre-1914, sectarianism was subdued compared to events in Liverpool and Lancashire, where chapels were burned and there was large-scale mobbing and rioting from time to time.

> "it is far more appropriate to describe Victorian Liverpool rather than Glasgow as a sectarian city."[9]

Glasgow, it is argued, was a city without ghettos whose workers were more attracted to socialism than to sectarianism pre-1914. Others argue that sectarianism was a widespread and deep-rooted malaise in urban Scotland before 1914. They cite evidence such as job segregation in Greenock, where Protestants monopolised the skilled jobs and Catholics the unskilled dock-labouring occupations; in Airdrie and Coatbridge where employers, with the acquiescence of the unions, ensured that workers were separated on religious grounds through the allocation of jobs and housing. Cases of sectarian violence in urban Lowland Scotland are also well documented in both the local and national newspapers of the day.

> "No proper geography of religious sectarian violence has been drawn up, but the frequency of recorded confrontations ... suggests that the unrecorded cases represented an artery of hatred operating throughout Scottish urban industrial society."[10]

While Scotland's Protestant and Catholic workers fought and died side by side during World War I, the issue of sectarianism returned with a renewed intensity in the interwar years.

IN WHAT WAYS WAS SECTARIANISM MANIFESTED DURING THE INTERWAR PERIOD?

Protestant reaction to the 1918 *Education Act* was the catalyst which reignited sectarian friction in postwar Scotland. This landmark piece of legislation brought Catholic schools fully into the state system, guaranteeing them funding from the state while at the same time allowing the Catholic Church to retain control of staffing and the curriculum. 'Rome on the rates,' became the rallying cry of some Protestants who opposed the beginnings of equal educational opportunities for all. The historian Graham Walker argues that Protestant reaction to the 1918 *Education Act* was symptomatic of a general Protestant loss of self-confidence in the interwar period.

> "Education, it must be remembered, had a totemic significance; the Presbyterian Churches felt that Catholic control of education ... rubbed salt in the wound of their loss of educational influence."[12]

Irene Maver has found that the Irish origins of a majority of Scotland's Catholic community provoked a form of "ethnic stereotyping ... which could appear to those outside the faith as both subversive and conservative, exotic and forbidding ... Ironically, in view of the often observed Catholic defensiveness over their minority status, it was the defensiveness of the majority which helped to shape the image."[13]

While some historians emphasise the 'tribal' violence which accompanied ritual events such as 'Old Firm' football matches, and the gang violence in Glasgow during the 1920s and 1930s as popular manifestations of sectarianism, two other events exemplify the fundamental and explosive nature of interwar sectarianism. In 1923 the General Assembly of the Church of Scotland published a blatantly racist report which "identified the Catholic presence as subverting and corroding the Scottish national identity".[14] Rhetoric such as this merely served to legitimise and underpin the violent activities of extremist groups such as John Cormack's Protestant Action. This organisation orchestrated the now infamous Caanan Lane riot in 1935 in Edinburgh, when a Protestant mob of many thousands attacked worshippers at the Catholic Eucharist Congress.

For the Catholic community, the interwar period was a time of transition from a position of defensiveness to one of increased consolidation in Scottish society. The 1918 *Education Act* undoubtedly increased educational opportunities for Catholics leading to middle-class status for growing numbers of people. Teachers were leading figures in the interwar Catholic middle class. The 1926 *Roman Catholic Relief Act* removed some of the last outdated discriminatory aspects of the 1829 *Catholic Emancipation Act* allowing Catholic clergy equal rights with the clergy of other denominations to parade in public wearing formal vestments.

World War II led to a lowering of sectarian intensity in Scotland, although there were anti-Italian riots during that time which had sectarian undercurrents. Postwar slum clearance and redevelopment led to a dispersal of Catholic communities from areas like Gorbals in Glasgow to the large peripheral housing estates. At the same time, increased welfare provision helped bring new opportunities, upward social mobility and assimilation for Scotland's Catholic community.

REFERENCES

CHAPTER 1
DEMOCRACY AND THE BRITISH PEOPLE 1867–1928

1. DG Wright *Democracy and Reform 1815–1885* page 64. Published by Longman.
2. ibid Wright pages 71–72.
3. Sir David Lindsay Keir *The Constitutional History of Modern Britain* page 467. Published by Adam and Charles Black.
4. TC Smout *A Century of the Scottish People 1830–1950* pages 245–246. Published by Collins.
5. DG Wright *Democracy and Reform 1815–1885* page 105.
6. Quoted in KO Morgan *The Age of Lloyd George* page 39. Published by Allen & Unwin, 1971.
7. ibid *The Age of Lloyd George* page 40.
8. Robert Pearce *Britain: Domestic Politics 1918–39* page 8.

CHAPTER 2
THE GROWTH OF THE LABOUR MOVEMENT 1890–1922

1. James Hinton *Labour and Socialism* page 13. Published by Wheatsheaf Books.
2. ibid Hinton page 13.
3. Peter Lane *The Labour Party* pages 16–17. Published by Batsford.
4. op. cit. Hinton page 15.
5. Tom Mann & Ben Tillet *The New Trade Unionism 1890* page 15. Quoted in Keith Laybourne *British Trade Unionism 1770–1990* page 86. Published by Alan Sutton.
6. Cole and Postgate *The Common People* pages 414–415. Published by University Paperbacks.
7. Henry Pelling *The Origins of the Labour Party* page 34. Published by Oxford.
8. ibid Pelling page 77.
9. JP Nettl *Socialism to 1914–The Leadership Analysed* in *History of the 20th Century* Eds. Taylor & Roberts page 271.
10. Henry Pelling *The Origins of the Labour Party* page 64. Published by Oxford.
11. op. cit. Cole and Postgate page 423.
12. op. cit. Hinton page 72.
13. John Maclean *In the Rapids of Revolution* page 13 of biographical introduction by Nan Milton. Published by Allison & Busby.
14. Hyman Shapiro *Keir Hardie and the Labour Party* page 86. Published by Longman.
15. Harry McShane *No Mean Fighter* page 97. Published by Pluto Press.
16. Martin Shaw *War and Peace and British Marxism*, in Richard Taylor and Nigel Young *Campaigns for Peace* page 172.
17. AJP Taylor *English History 1914–45* page 70.
18. Robert Pearce *Britain: Domestic Politics 1918–39* page 45.

CHAPTER 3
THE MOVEMENTS FOR WOMEN'S SUFFRAGE 1850–1928

1. Angela Holdsworth *Out of the Doll's House* page 28. Published by BBC 1989.
2. Quoted in E Royston Pike *Human Documents of the Age of the Forsytes* page 142. Published by Allen & Unwin 1969.
3. Sarah Harris *Women at Work*. Published by Batsford 1981.
4. Healy Heriman *A 'Guid' Cause— the Women's Suffrage Movement in Scotland*.
5. GM Cuddeford *Women in Society*. Published by Hamish Hamilton 1976.
6. Jennifer Harris and Alistair Wisker *Marriage*. Published by Batsford 1976.
7. op. cit. Holdsworth.
8. op. cit Holdsworth page 180.
9. Adapted from Elizabeth Wilson *Women and the Welfare State* pages 40–41. Published by Tavistock Publications Limited, 1977.
10. Christabel Pankhurst in Martin Durham *Suffrage and After: Feminism in the Early Twentieth Century* page 183.
11. Martin Durham *Suffrage and After: Feminism in the Early Twentieth Century* in *Crisis in the British State 1880–1930* Eds. Langan & Schwarz (1985).
12. Paula Bartley in *Votes for Women 1860–1928* page 100 (1998).
13. op. cit. Holdsworth.
14. Arthur Marwick *The Deluge* pages 97–98. Published by Penguin.
15. ibid Marwick.
16. Gerard De Groot *Blighty: British Society in the Era of the Great War* page 135 (1996).
17. Martin Pugh *Women and the Women's Movement in Britain 1914–59* page 35.
18. ibid Pugh page 38.
19. ibid Pugh page 36.

CHAPTER 4
BRITAIN IN 1900—LAISSEZ-FAIRE IN DECLINE

1. *The Charity Organisation Register*, 27 September 1884, quoted in K Woodroffe *From Charity to Social Work in England and the United States* page 23.
2. *Charles Booth's London* selected and edited by A Fried and M Elman 1971 pages 54–55.
3. N Lowe *Mastering Modern British History* page 297.
4. D Fraser *The Evolution of the British Welfare State* page 139.
5. Henry Pelling *Popular Politics and Society in Late Victorian Britain* page16.

CHAPTER 5
THE LIBERAL WELFARE REFORMS 1906–1914

1   Sidney Webb, September, 1901 quoted in K Morgan *The Age of Lloyd George* pages 126–127.
2   Albert Mansbridge *Margaret Macmillan, Prophet and Pioneer* pages 41–2 (1932).
3   T Ferguson *Scottish Social Welfare, 1864–1914* page 565.
4   P Thane *The Foundations of the Welfare State* page 75.
5   HV Emy *Liberals, Radicals and Social Politics 1892–1914* page 150.
6   J R Hay *The Development of the British Welfare State, 1880–1975* page 59.
7   T Ferguson *Scottish Social Welfare 1864–1914* page 571.
8   Quoted in JR Hay *The Development of the British Welfare State 1880–1975* page 73. Published by Edward Arnold.
9   Lloyd George's speech at Cardiff 1906, quoted in *The Evolution of the Welfare State* page 144. Published by McMillan.
10 RS Churchill *Winston Churchill Vol.II* quoted in *Evolution of the British Welfare State* page 152. Published by McMillan.
11 RS Churchill *Winston Churchill Vol. II* quoted in K Benning *Edwardian Britain* page 20. Published by Blackie.
12 Chamberlain's evidence to the Royal Commission quoted in Sir A Wilson and G S Mackay *Old Age Pensions—An Historical and Critical Study, 1941*, page 27.
13 ibid Wilson and Mackay pages 27–8.
14 ibid Wilson and Mackay pages 27–8.
15 ibid Wilson and Mackay pages 38–9.
16 *Foresters' Miscellany*, Leader (June 1894) quoted in J R Hay *The Development of the British Welfare State, 1880–1975* page 17.
17 EP Hennock *The Origins of British National Insurance and the German Precedent 1880–1914* in WJ Mommsen *The Emergence of the Welfare State in Britain and Germany* page 87.
18 op. cit. Wilson and Mackay page 43.
19 M Bruce *The Coming of the Welfare State* page 180.
20 ibid Bruce page 100.
21 *Hansard*, 25 May, 1908.
22 *Hansard*, 29 April, 1909.
23 Quoted in D Fraser *The Evolution of the British Welfare State* pages 156–157. Published by McMillan.
24 Quoted in E Royston Pike *Human Documents of the Lloyd George Era* page 110. Published by Allen & Unwin.
25 Quoted in HV Emy *Liberals, Radicals and Social Politics 1892–1914* page 154.

CHAPTER 6
THE NATIONAL GOVERNMENTS OF THE 1930s

1   LCB Seaman *Post-Victorian Britain* page 206.
2   P Adelman *The Rise of the Labour Party 1880–1945* page 73.
3   AJP Taylor *English History 1914–1945* page 365.
4   R Skidelsky *Politicians and the Slump* page 12.
5   op. cit. Seaman page 222.
6   op. cit. Taylor page 373.
7   A Marwick *The Explosion of British Society 1914–70* page 74.
8   op. cit. Taylor page 403.
9   Stephen Lee *Aspects of British Political History 1914–1995* page 120.
10 op. cit. Seaman page 232.
11 op. cit. Taylor pages 417–418.

12 op. cit. Marwick page 73.
13 R Blake *The Decline of Power 1915–1964* page 169.
14 AJP Taylor *English History* page 426.
15 A Wood *Great Britain 1900–1945* page 282.
16 op. cit. Taylor page 411.
17 Harry McShane *No Mean Fighter* page 184.
18 Aneurin Bevan, Labour MP, writing in the *Daily Express* 23 April, 1937 quoted in J Patrick and M Packham *Years of Change* page 253.
19 George Orwell *The Road to Wigan Pier* pages 70–1.
20 Gordon Brown *New Leader* 23 December 1932 quoted in *Maxton* page 251.
21 George Orwell *The Road to Wigan Pier* pages 76–77.
22 JB Priestley *English Journey* page 238.
23 RJ Cootes *The Making of the Welfare State* page 68.
24 *The Listener*, 26 October 1961, quoted in John Stevenson and Chris Cook *The Slump—Society and Politics during the Depression* page 6.
25 George Orwell *The Road to Wigan Pier* page 48.
26 ibid J Stevenson page 223.
27 Lowe *Mastering Modern History* page 487.
28 Ibid Lowe page 360.
29 ibid Stephen Lee pages 120–121.
30 RAC Parker *Chamberlain and Appeasement* page 276.

CHAPTER 7
THE ARRIVAL OF THE WELFARE STATE 1940–1951

1   D Fraser *Evolution of the British Welfare State* 4th ed. page 210.
2   AJP Taylor *English History 1914–45* page 556.
3   Quoted in Paul Addison *The Road to 1945* page 72.
4   JB Priestley quoted in Addison *The Road to 1945* page 162.
5   CJ Bartlett *A History of Postwar Britain 1945–74* page 6.
6   M Bruce *The Coming of the Welfare State* page 293.
7   ibid Bruce page 295.
8   Titmuss *Evolution of the Welfare State* quoted in D Marsh *The Welfare State 2nd ed.* page 22.
9   ibid D Fraser page 211.
10 P Addison *The Road to 1945* page 227.
11 Pauline Gregg *The Welfare State* page 25.
12 Pat Thane *The Foundations of the Welfare State* page 241.
13 ibid Thane.
14 Churchill radio broadcast 4 June 1945 quoted in L Coate and A Pike *Life in Britain 1945–60* page 5.
15 Quoted in R Eatwell *The 1945–51 Labour Governments* page 54.
16 J Heb *The Social Policy of the Attlee Government* in WJ Mommsen's *The Emergence of the Welfare State in Britain and Germany* page 306.
17 Bevan in the House of Commons debate 30.4.46, quoted in M Bruce (ed), *The Rise of the Welfare State* pages 260–261.
18 Paul Addison *Now the War is Over* pages 104–105.
19 RC Birch *The Shaping of the Welfare State* page 63.
20 E Royle *Modern Britain* page 367.
21 LCB Seaman *Post-Victorian Britain* page 454.
22 Eatwell *The 1945–51 Labour Governments* page 67.
23 Robert Pearce *Attlee's Labour Governments 1945–51* page 45.
24 Quoted in article by Paul Addison *A New Jerusalem* page 96, in *Britain 1918–51* Peter Catterall (ed).
25 M Bruce *The Coming of the Welfare State* page 326.
26 D Fraser *The Evolution of the British Welfare State* page 207.

Changing Britain 1850–1979

27   Nick Tiratsoo *The Attlee Years Revisited* page 114, in *Britain 1918–51* Peter Catterall (ed).

28   Robert Pearce *Attlee's Labour Governments 1945–51* page 48.

29   Kevin Jeffreys *The Attlee Governments 1945-51* page 62.

30   John Macnicol quoted in article by Paul Addison *A New Jerusalem* page 45 in *Britain 1918–51* Peter Catterall (ed).

31   ibid Catterall page 95.

CHAPTER 8
THE GROWTH OF POLITICAL NATIONALISM IN SCOTLAND 1880–1979

1   HJ Hanham *Scottish Nationalism* page 10.

2   H J Hanham *The Creation of the Scottish Office* in *Judicial Review* page 205 (1965).

3   Keith Robbins *Nineteenth Century Britain* page 28.

4   M Lynch (ed) *Scotland, 1850–1979: Society, Politics and the Union* page 6.

5   ibid Lynch page 5.

6   RJ Morris and Graeme Morton in Lynch ibid page 14.

7   Christopher Harvie *Scotland and Nationalism* page 40.

8   Sir Reginald Coupland *Welsh and Scottish Nationalism* page 295.

9   ibid Coupland page 295.

10   HJ Hanham *The Creation of the Scottish Office* in *Judicial Review* page 229 (1965).

11   James Kellas *Modern Scotland* page 96.

12   Michael Lynch *Scotland–A New History* page 416.

13   HJ Hanham *Scottish Nationalism*.

14   Michael Fry *Patronage and Principle* page 209.

15   ibid Fry page104.

16   Keith Webb *The Growth of Scottish Nationalism in Scotland* page 39.

17   Michael Fry *Patronage and Principle* page 128.

18   *Daily Record*, 31 December 1929. Quoted in R Finlay, *National Identity in Crisis: Politicians, Intellectuals and the 'End of Scotland', 1920–1939* Historical Association 1994.

19   Andrew Marr *The Battle for Scotland* page 54.

20   R Finlay *A Partnership for Good?* page 83.

21   ibid Finlay page 89.

22   ibid Finlay page 111.

23   J Kellas *Modern Scotland* page 98.

24   SNP Research Department *A Short History of the SNP*.

25   K Webb *The Growth of Nationalism in Scotland* page 52.

26   RJ Finlay *Scottish Nationalism and Scottish Politics 1900–1979* page 22 in *Scotland 1850–1979* Michael Lynch (ed).

27   R Finlay *Independent and Free* page 206.

28   op. cit. Finlay page 126.

29   Andrew Marr *The Battle for Scotland* page 93.

30   Jack Brand *The National Movement in Scotland* page 242.

31   W Wolfe *Scotland Lives* page 17.

32   ibid Marr page 96.

33   K Webb *The Growth of Nationalism in Scotland* page 61.

34   T Dalyell *Devolution–The End of Britain?* page 76.

35   David McCrone *The Unstable Union: Scotland since the 1920s* page 47 in *Scotland, 1850–1979: Society, Politics and the Union* edited by Michael Lynch.

36   op. cit. Finlay page 148.

37   Bruce Lenman *An Economic History of Modern Scotland* page 262.

38   *A Short History of the Scottish National Party* page 3.

39   ibid McCrone page 47.

40   H Drucker and G Brown *The Politics of Government and Nationalism* page 54.

41   C Harvie *No Gods and Precious Few Heroes* page 162.

CHAPTER 9
CHANGING SCOTTISH SOCIETY 1880s–1939

Urbanisation

1   RJ Morris *Urbanisation In Scotland*.

2   ibid Morris.

3   Richard Rodger in *Urbanisation in Twentieth Century Scotland*.

4   CWJ Withers *Highland Migration to Aberdeen*.

5   TC Smout *A Century of the Scottish People 1830–1950*.

6   TM Devine (Ed) *Farm Servants and Labour in Lowland Scotland 1770–1914*.

7   TM Devine (Ed) *Farm Servants and Labour in Lowland Scotland 1770–1914*.

8   ibid TC Smout

9   Michael Flinn (Ed) *Scottish Population History from the 17th Century to the 1930s*.

10   Richard Rodger *Urbanisation in the Twentieth Century* in *Scotland In The Twentieth Century* TM Devine & RJ Finlay (Eds).

11   RJ Morris *Urbanisation and Scotland* in *People and Society in Scotland* Vol 2. Eds. WH Fraser and RJ Morris.

Case Study: Urban Housing

1   Richard Rodger *The Pursuit of Urban History* quoted in review article *Materialism & Tenements* by RJ Morris in the *Scottish Economic & Social History Journal Vol 1, No 1 1981*, page 74.

2   RJ Morris *Journal of Scottish Economic and Social History, Volume 2, 1982* page 91.

3   J Butt *Working Class Housing in Scottish Cities* in *Scottish Urban History*, Eds. George Gordon & Brian Dicks.

4   From the 1918 report of the *Royal Commission on Housing in Scotland*; quoted in Butt, page 242.

5   S Damer in *Housing, Social Policy and the State* Ed. Joseph Melling.

6   Richard Rodger *Urbanisation in Twentieth Century Scotland* in *Scotland in the Twentieth Century* Eds. TM Devine & R J Finlay page 136.

7   ibid Rodger page 143.

Education in Scotland

1   Quoted in RD Anderson *Education and the Scottish People 1750–1918* page 44.

2   ibid Anderson page 97.

3   TC Smout *A Century of the Scottish People* page 214.

4   ibid Smout page 216.

5   RD Anderson *Scottish Education since the Reformation* page 26.

6   op. cit.RD Anderson page 231.

7   WW Knox *The Scottish Educational System 1840–1940* in *The Scottish People 1840–1940* CD ROM by the Scottish CCC.

8   op. cit. TC Smout page 220.

9   op. cit. RD Anderson page 200.

10   op. cit. RD Anderson page 263.

11   RD Anderson *Education in Modern Scottish History Vol. 2* page 241.

12   WW Knox *The Scottish People 1840–1940* CD ROM.

13 HM Paterson, *Incubus and Ideology* page 208 in *Scottish Culture and Scottish Education 1800–1980* by W Humes and HM Paterson (eds).
14 ibid Knox.
15 Tom Nairn *The Break-up of Britain* page 131.
16 J Kellas *The Scottish Political System* page 2.
17 RD Anderson *Education in Modern Scottish History* Vol. 2 page 235. A Cooke et al (eds).
18 WJ Gibson, quoted in RD Anderson *In Search of the 'Lad o' Pairts'; the Mythical History of Scottish Education* page 271, in *Modern Scottish History Vol. 4*. A Cooke et al (eds).
19 op. cit. RD Anderson page 254.
20 Helen Corr *Where is the Lass o'Pairts? : Gender, Identity and Education in Nineteenth Century Scotland* page 220, in *Image and Identity*, R Finlay et al (eds).
21 Quoted in Keith Robbins *Nineteenth Century Britain* page 134.
22 George Elder Davie *The Democratic Intellect* page xv.
23 op. cit. K Robbins page 132.
24 M Lynch *Scotland 1850–1979* page 6.
25 R Finlay *National Identity: From British Empire to European Union* page 28 in *Modern Scottish History*
26 op. cit. Finlay page 20 in *Modern Scottish History Vol 4*.
27 ibid Finlay page 38.

Leisure and Popular Culture in Scotland

1 WH Fraser, *Developments in Leisure* page 248.
2 Robert Lambert *Leisure and Recreation* page 258 in *Modern Scottish History Vol 2*.
3 Neil Tranter *Sport, Economy and Society in Britain 1750–1914* page 16.
4 ibid Lambert page 260.
5 Callum Brown *Religion in Modern Scottish History Vol 2* page 158.
6 T C Smout *A Century of the Scottish People* page 154.
7 N Tranter *Sport, Economy and Society in Britain 1750–1914* page 24.
8 op. cit. Lambert page 262.
9 WH Fraser *Developments in Leisure* page 261.
10 CW Hill *Edwardian Scotland* page 60.
11 Forsyth Hardie *The Cinema* page 268 in *Scotland—A Concise Cultural History*, PH Scott (ed).
12 ibid Hardie page 269.
13 op. cit. Lambert page 258.
14 op. cit. Lambert page 27.
15 Tom Nairn *The Break-Up of Britain* page 172.

16 ibid Finlay page 38.
17 RJ Finlay *Modern Scottish History Vol 4* page 38.
18 C Harvie *Scotland and Nationalism* page 109.
19 ibid Harvie page 141.
20 M Lynch *Scotland, 1850–1979*.
21 op. cit. Harvie page 109.
22 op. cit. Harvie.
23 op. cit. Lynch page 6.
24 J Kellas *Scottish Political System* page 168.
25 Callum Brown *Popular Culture and the Continuing Struggle for Rational Recreation* page 215, in *Scotland in the Twentieth Century* TM Devine and RJ Finlay eds.

Religious Identity in Scotland

1 CG Brown *Religion, Class and Church Growth* page 317, in *People and Society in Scotland Vol 3* Fraser and Morris Eds.
2 CG Brown *Religion, Class and Church Growth* page 329, in *People and Society in Scotland Vol 3* Fraser and Morris Eds.
3 Rosalind Mitchison's review of *The Social History of Religion in Scotland since 1730* by CG Brown in *The Journal of the Economic and Social History Society of Scotland, Volume 9*, 1989 page 109.
4 CG Brown *The People in the Pews* page 44.
5 TC Smout *A Century of the Scottish People 1830–1950* pages 206–207.
6 ibid TC Smout page 202.
7 ibid TC Smout page 184.
8 CG Brown *Religion and Secularisation* in *People and Society in Scotland* A Dickson and JH Treble Eds page 69.
9 T Gallacher *A tale of two cities: communal strife in Glasgow and Liverpool before 1914* in *The Irish in the Victorian City* Eds. Swift & Gilley page 123.
10 C G Brown *The People in the Pews* page 36.
11 Graham Walker *Varieties of Scottish Protestant Identity* in *Scotland in the Twentieth Century* Eds. TM Devine & RJ Finlay page 254.
12 Graham Walker *Varieties of Scottish Protestant Identity* in *Scotland in the Twentieth Century* Eds. TM Devine and RJ Finlay page 254.
13 Irene Maver *The Catholic Community* in *Scotland in the Twentieth Century* Eds. TM Devine and RJ Finlay page 272.
14 Irene Maver *The Catholic Community* in *Scotland in the Twentieth Century* Eds. TM Devine and RJ Finlay page 276.